Frederick George Lee

Reginald Pole, Cardinal Archbishop of Canterbury

An historical Sketch, with an introductory Prologue and practical Epilogue

Frederick George Lee

Reginald Pole, Cardinal Archbishop of Canterbury
An historical Sketch, with an introductory Prologue and practical Epilogue

ISBN/EAN: 9783743337183

Manufactured in Europe, USA, Canada, Australia, Japa

Cover: Foto ©ninafisch / pixelio.de

Manufactured and distributed by brebook publishing software
(www.brebook.com)

Frederick George Lee

Reginald Pole, Cardinal Archbishop of Canterbury

TABLE OF CONTENTS.

	PAGE
Etched Portrait of Cardinal Pole	ii
Title-page	iii
Dedication	v
Table of Contents	vii
Prologue	ix

Chapter I.
Reginald Pole, his Personal History — 1

Chapter II.
Accession of Queen Mary and her Reign — 35

Chapter III.
Pole's Policy for his Country duly Planned — 79

Chapter IV.
Pole's Policy for his Country duly Effected — 121

Chapter V.
Death of the Queen and the Cardinal-Archbishop our
Nation's Loss — 173

Practical Epilogue — 263

General Index — 305

b

" Meek man — too meek — the brother of the king,
With brow low-bent, and onward-sweeping hand,
Great words, world-famed ' Remember thine account !
The Lord's Apostles are the salt of Earth ;
Let salt not lose its savour !   Flail and fan
Are given thee.   Purge thou well thy threshing-floor !
Repel the tyrant ; hurl the hireling forth ;
That so from thy true priests true hearts may learn
True Faith, true love, and nothing but the Truth.' "

AUBREY DE VERE.

PROLOGUE.

" Although, in an age of doubt and selfishness, it is highly improbable that any man who stands forward to destroy a false tradition, and to repair the breaches of the Past in the things which concern our peace will obtain attention from many ; yet it cannot be denied that the policy of the English Corporate-Reunionists is one in which Faith, Hope and Charity already play their proper part, and the foresight and wisdom of which policy will abundantly commend itself to grateful and generous generations yet unborn."—CARLO DI CONTI (in *Philosophical Annals*).

PROLOGUE.

THE History of the Past is chiefly important, and more specially interesting, as I have elsewhere remarked,[1] because it enables us to learn its due lessons, and to regard its pregnant teaching, in reference to the Present. That "History repeats itself," has become a mere proverbial platitude. Scarcely any study, consequently, can be more practical or more valuable.

Now, in no age of English history did an event ever take place of greater moment to our Nation than that here under consideration. The people of England, by God's favour and through Cardinal

[1] "King Edward the Sixth : Supreme Head," an Historical Sketch. Introduction, p. 1. London : 1886.

Pole's instrumentality, were once again restored to visible communion with the centre of Christian life, acknowledging the due and ancient authority of the Chief Pastor of Christendom; and this with the full assent of the English Monarch and the Estates of the Realm, and amid the sincere rejoicings of every class of the people.

In the text of this volume Cardinal Pole's work in question is duly described. Here, in this Prologue, I take leave to refer to a few historical events subsequent to that great work, which have largely helped to bring about the present grave state of ecclesiastical isolation and political uncertainty in which we live—the practical evils of which demand, both from churchmen and statesmen, the only prompt and efficient remedy at hand. For statesmen who ignore the general power and influence of the Christian Religion, and the special blessings which the Catholic Church has conferred on our nation,[1] appear sadly wanting, even in worldly wisdom.

---

[1] As regards spiritual blessings and Magna Charta, the late Dr. Baron wrote thus: "We owe to the Church of Rome of bygone days an unspeakable debt of gratitude, and much honour, for sending us that treasure of Christianity which, besides all spiritual blessing, has been the key-stone of English freedom and the foundation of English greatness."—*Anglo-Saxon Witness on Four Alleged Requisites for Holy Communion, Fasting, Water, Altar-Lights, and Incense,* by Rev. John Baron, M.A. P. 19. London: Rivingtons, 1869.

At the same time some notes are made of occurrences and events taking place before our eyes, as still further indicating the need of that remedy, and to point the moral of the book.

Mr. Anderdon, a literary layman of high character and good repute, wrote thus of the Great Rebellion and its blessings,—one direct, reasonable, and natural outcome of the Tudor changes:—

"The proposed *jus divinum* of the Presbyterians was a most intolerant form of church government, which soon afterwards filled the land with violence, rapine, and despotism, from one end to the other, until all ranks groaned under the grievous burthen." [1]

And again :—

"The Rebellion, and the death of the King, had entailed upon all classes their own heaviest punishment in a series of national outrages, resulting from the iron bondage of a military despotism. A bold impiety had taken from the people all love of spiritual things ; the Church being overthrown, they were given up alternately to profaneness and hypocrisy, and forced to perjure themselves with successive oaths, engagements, and covenants, under pretext of exalting the Gospel and promoting liberty." [2]

Rebellion, as is thus manifest, however much some may deny or dislike the fact, is found to be the direct outcome of the policy of Protestants and negation-mongers. Rebellion may be either moral or physical, or both in one. Not all rebels, however, are Protestants, nor are all Protestants active

---

[1] "Life of Bishop Ken," by a Layman. Part I. pp. 11, 12. London : 1854.

[2] Ibid. pp. 45, 46.

rebels.   But the principles of Protestantism, both in religion and politics, directly incite to rebellion, as in the long run, and in morals, they unquestionably tend towards, and lead up to, individualism and Atheism.   Protestant jurists and politicians, with painful labour, have again and again appealed from Christian principles and constituted law to brute power and physical force.   In England and Scotland, lawful Christian Authority being repudiated, this was done by Thomas Cromwell, Henry VIII., Rich the lawyer, Knox the preacher, Coverdale the traitor, and others, at the so-called " Reformation." [1]   The same principle, further developed, was applied in England, during the Great Rebellion, and at the Revolution of 1688.   And so effectively have the facts of those three momentous eras been distorted—distorted with intention and success, while the vilest men, with lying lips, strong wills,

[1] Men rejected the chief ecclesiastical Authority in the world, the bishop of bishops, pretending, at the same time, to honour in a special manner that Divine Master Who had sent forth apostles and bishops to guide the Church and teach the world.   Now, however, men, in their blind independence, have come to reject the authority of Christ Himself, and of the Eternal Father. From such negation-mongers only disorganization, disruption, and disorder have followed.   Male and female babblers are consequently found who, at last, deny the very existence of God, and declare that the " Sovereign People are Supreme," the source of all life, authority, and power, maintaining that mankind is God.   As a consequence some fools adopt man in his totality—a somewhat bulky body, still imperfect—as the only proper object of worship.

and powerful battalions, have been made popular heroes—that the falsest and most perverted notions of English history are commonly current and popular. All such examples of rebellion have tended to make Christian principles disregarded and Force worshipped. In modern times, in France, Italy, Greece, Egypt, Ireland, and other States, the same disastrous principle has been adopted and applied—to the weakening of Christian Law and Social Order, and to the danger of individual liberty.

In England the Ancient Faith had been brought hither by St. Augustine, and held by Bede and Lanfranc, Anselm, Edmund of Abingdon, and Wayneflete. The universality of the New Birth, the pure offering everywhere made,[1] were due and

---

[1] The Eucharistic Sacrifice, and the sacred duty of all the baptized to be present at its offering on all Sundays and holidays of obligation, are not likely to be restored until Authority steps in with its advice and monition on the restoration of Corporate Reunion. The Christian Sacrifice, writes an author of great power, " is the great centre of Catholic worship. Every other devotion gathers up into it, as to their common focus. The material church, with its order, ornaments, and furniture, enshrines it. The sacred vestments of the priest, the altar, crucifix, candles, incense, flowers, music, are its sensible expressions. The laws and commandments of Holy Church maintain its paramount dignity. It is the great reservoir of graces; the great act in which heaven and earth unite, and in which the stupendous mystery of the Incarnation is, after a sort, perpetuated in this world of ours. It spans the visible universe by its power, unlocks the purgatorial prison, arrests the howling powers of

daily realities. The old order of things was only cast out, under the Tudors, with art, villainy, and hypocrisy, by a series of base and execrable laws, in the face of the wish and will of all but a fraction of the clergy, and of all good Christian people. The true history of these laws, and what they effected, is becoming somewhat more accurately and better known.

The position of the adherents of the Old Religion at the close of the seventeenth century, is thus described by the late Lord Macaulay. I must, however, remind the reader that the sentiments of this readable writer are tinctured throughout with nauseous Whiggery, one of the most despicable forms of political misbelief and error:—

"The celebration of the Roman Catholic worship had long been prohibited by Act of Parliament. During several generations no Roman Catholic clergyman had dared to exhibit himself in any public place with the badge of his office. Against the regular clergy and against the restless and subtle Jesuits by name had been enacted a succession of rigorous statutes. Every Jesuit who set foot in this country was liable to be hanged, drawn, and quartered. A reward was offered for his detection. He was not allowed to take advantage of the general rule that men are not bound to criminate themselves. Whoever was suspected of being a Jesuit might be interrogated, and, if he refused to answer, might be sent to prison for life."[1]

evil in the midst of their unholy work, and adds fresh light to the aureola of the Saints. Without it there is no altar, no priesthood, no church, no Christian worship."—*Peace through the Truth,* by Rev. T. Harper, S.J., vol. i. pp. 87, 88. London : 1866.

[1] "History of England," by Thomas Babington Macaulay, vol. ii. p. 99. London : 1849.

I do not stay to chronicle that series of historical events—labours, trials, and struggles—which culminated in Roman Catholic Emancipation and the restoration of the Catholic Hierarchy, for which all Christian upholders of Justice and Truth will be heartily thankful; but I quote the following, only, I fear, too accurately describing the state of Canterbury Cathedral—where, as Primate and Legate, Cardinal Pole once ruled—after it had lain practically desolate under Cranmer and his successors for more than two centuries and a half:—

"With my thoughts and feelings thus occupied, I arrived at Canterbury [A.D. 1826], a town filled with venerable remains and awful recollections. I stopped, and, heedless of all things else, almost rushed to view your Cathedral—the place in England where Christ was first effectually announced, where His cross was first erected, where miracles and the virtues of His saints, still more miraculous than their works, first proclaimed that He was God, and that Kent and England were united to His empire.

"But lo! I beheld, in the place I so much longed to see, an empty cloister and a mouldering pile, having the appearance of what was once the 'house of prayer' and the temple of the Most High, but which now might bear upon its porch the inscription which Paul described at Athens, 'To the Unknown God.' It is a wide and spacious waste, cold and untenanted. Its pillars were raised aloft, its arches were seated in strength, its spire sought the heavens—but these were works of former days; it now had no altar, no sacrifice, no priesthood; its aisles were silent as the monuments of the sainted prelates over whom they seemed to bend and weep; and the only remaining symbol of Christianity not yet extinct which I discovered was a chapel in the cloister, where the verger, who accompanied me for hire, observed that 'service was at certain times performed.'

"To detail the thoughts which crowded on my mind—to

convey to paper the emotions which swelled my breast, would not be possible; but I cried out involuntarily, 'My God! and are these the fruits of the Reformation? Is this the ground which Augustine sanctified and Alfred honoured? Is this the metropolitan see of England—the Cathedral of Canterbury—the once renowned seminary of saints and martyrs—the glory of Kent? Where is the Bishop who should here reside, and spread about him benedictions? Where are the canons and the dignitaries, the priests and the altars, the vestments and the ministers, the incense, the lights, the glory which bespeak the Majesty and announce the Presence of Almighty God? But, above all, where is the loud song or the secret canticle of praise, the deep and awful murmur of the crowd, or the silent whisper of retirement and devotion? Are all these fled from Thy temple, and is it no longer Thy delight, O God, to be with the children of men?'

"But I stopped the current of these reflections, and proceeded to inquire as to the state of religion amongst you; and I came to the conclusion that you, O men of Kent, with all those qualities which ennoble you—with an unbounded zeal for the divine honour, a thirst for knowledge not to be assuaged, a disposition to piety too strong to yield to any obstacle—that with a magnanimity proportioned to every sacrifice, and a candour worthy of your ancient fame, you had, like the rest of your countrymen, become the victims of those frauds and violences by which the religion first preached to you, and which saved your sainted forefathers, was taken away, and the desolation exemplified in your cathedral imposed upon you under the fictitious title of 'a reformed faith.'

"Even upon that day, and in the midst of the once-hallowed walls of your cathedral, and upon the stone where the sainted Becket shed his blood, I offered up to God my most humble prayer that He would again look upon you with an eye of mercy, and send down His light and His truth, whereby to dispel the errors and darkness in which you have been so long involved; that He would not remember the iniquities of your former guides and rulers, nor avenge upon you the sins of other men."[1]

---

[1] "Life and Times of Dr. Doyle" (Lord Bishop of Kildare and Leighlin). By W. J. Fitzpatrick. In two vols. Vol. II., pp. 89-90. London: 1861.

There can be little doubt that the restoration of territorial jurisdiction for prelates of the Old Faith, but with an arrangement of perfectly new dioceses, in 1850, was made in the hope that Corporate Reunion might subsequently follow. Such an obvious motive lies on the face of the act.[1] Anyhow, **the** existence of thirteen or fourteen new cathedrals **in** certain modern cities of England was the source **of** great satisfaction to all true Christians ; while **the** services of those cathedrals,—their order, their open doors, the lapsed traditions concerning worship which they make living realities, and the unfailing blessings they impart,—have most efficiently taught members of the Established Church how adequately to use those old cathedrals they themselves still possess. The lesson—God be thanked!—is being duly learnt. Witness, amongst others, St. Paul's,

[1] The ancient Dioceses of England, **even** from a Roman Catholic standing-point, have never been formally suppressed. Theological students of certain Colleges of Rome were described as belonging to the old dioceses so late as 1880. It is true that these dioceses were not filled by the Pope when the English prelates, who dissented from the Tudor changes, Goldwell, White, Watson, and Peyto, or Peto, died. It is equally true that when the R. C. hierarchy was made territorial, the old English sees were not taken. It may be presumed, therefore, that they were certainly known to exist. In the future, when, by God's mercy, Corporate Reunion takes place, the archiepiscopal sees may fittingly be Canterbury, York, Westminster, and Caerleon or Menevia, with the existing Anglican and Roman suffragans territorially apportioned to each.—See "History of the Restoration of the Catholic Hierarchy in England." By Bishop Ullathorne. Pp. 53-62. London : 1871.

Lincoln, Ely, Litchfield, Worcester, and Salisbury.[1] Of course, the more accurately and perfectly this necessary lesson is learnt, and the more faithfully the old traditions are everywhere restored, the better it will be for our beloved country, which in religion appears in such great danger of drifting from its old Christian moorings.

Those who have eyes to see perceive all too clearly, and perceive with sincere regret, that as a teaching body the Established Church—presumed at least to teach the Three Creeds—is slowly but surely renouncing its function. Just as a law which has been purposely made indefinite, carries with it, as to observance and obedience, but slender obligations; so a national communion which fails to teach the Nation (tolerating anything and everything in the way of opinion and sentiment at variance with the Faith), must in the long run forfeit the Nation's confidence and be looked upon first with decreasing interest, and finally with well-merited contempt. The "Church of the Reformation,"[2] as we all know, was created and set up

[1] The future alternative of Corporate Reunion for those sacred buildings will be the comprehensiveness of agnostics and heretics. Under the latter anti-Christian policy, our restored Cathedrals and parish Churches may become lounging-places, lecture-halls, or local-museums—whatsoever, in fact, the votes of their locality may determine.

[2] "Laity and Clergy, learned and unlearned, all ages, sects, and degrees of men, women, and children of whole Christendom (a

because, as the *Homilies* averred, all Christendom had for no less than eight hundred years been sunk in hopeless idolatry.[1] This was at least a positive and incisive dogma, however fantastic in itself and disastrous in its nature and consequences, and was openly taught amongst others by Cranmer, Bale, and Hooper. Now, however, that no existing " school of thought "—neither the Platitudinarian, the Latitudinarian, nor the Attitudinarian—is wild enough to accept this impressive dogma; and the wickednesses, falsehoods, and disasters of the Tudor era have been duly exposed to view, many persons are slowly coming to the rational and wise conclusion that, as the Catholic Religion is certainly the most ancient and venerable, so also it is the most useful; and is likely to be not only the most lasting, but also the only sure check upon, and

horrible and most dreadful thing to think) have been at once drowned in abominable idolatry ; of all other vices most detested of God, and most damnable to man, and that by the space of eight hundred years and more."—*Homilies Appointed to be Read in Churches*, p. 201. Oxford : 1816.

[1] " Our Church is the Church of the Reformation, founded under Edward VI., by Cranmer, and other men of high scriptural attainments."—Rev. J. C. Ryle, now Protestant Bishop of Liverpool. The late Bishop Short, of St. Asaph, however, perhaps more accurately placed its foundation about twenty years earlier : " The existence of the Church of England as a distinct body and her final separation from Rome may be dated from the period of the Divorce."—*History of the Church of England*, by T. V. Short, D.D., Bishop of St. Asaph. P. 44.

triumphant opponent to the gathering forces of heresy, schism, atheism, and chaos combined.

In truth, the only important alternative to Corporate Reunion, the reunion of the nation as a body, such as Pole effected, is an agreement to allow doctrine [1] to lapse—not to abolish one Creed, as Dean Stanley and Archbishop Tait proposed, but all. This policy is rapidly and actually becoming popular, having been adopted by a few men who accurately know their own minds, and are apparently preparing to construct the late Archbishop Tait's too-nebulous institution, " The Church of the Future." [2] They have more followers

[1] " Doctrine can be no foundation for church unity."—From a Sermon by Canon Wilberforce at St. James's Church, Toronto, reported in the " Dominion Churchman "; while, at a meeting in England, Archdeacon Farrar " utterly repudiated the idea of heresy being made the ground of exclusion from the Church."— Congregational Board of London, " Guardian," Dec. 1st, 1886, p. 1790. The Archdeacon seems to have been indebted to Mr. Voysey, who thus wrote :—" The God who loves only a chosen few, is, as far as other men are concerned, simply an enemy. *The God who requires you to procure a ticket from some church before you can enter Heaven, is an object of deserved distrust and dislike.* The God who *can* save all men from their unrighteousness, and yet hereafter *will not* do so, is one with whom to dwell would be everlasting torment. The God who *would* save all but *cannot*, is no Almighty God at all. And the God who would only rescue from ruin at the price of another's suffering, is the worst of all false gods, inasmuch as this is the lowest abasement below the common level of human goodness yet reached."—*The Sling and the Stone*, New Series, by Charles Voysey, B.A. Part X. p. 23. London : Trübner and Co.

[2] Of this " Church of the Future " and its living poet, Arch-

than some of us may be ready to allow. Their aims, apparent enough, need not be characterized.

The hopeless impracticability of so-called "Home Reunion"—*i.e.*, an agreement between the Established Church and the sects to allow all contentious subjects to become open questions, to be accepted or rejected as men please—has been abundantly shown in the following :—

"To begin with, we must not teach that our Saviour Jesus Christ is God and man, to be worshipped and prayed to, and trusted in, for the Unitarians do not believe it. Nor must we

---

deacon Farrar thus spoke in Gower Street at the opening Session of the Browning Society for 1886-87 :—" Moreover, a man could only receive as much as he could hold, and if we could not receive what Browning gave us, the obscurity might be in ourselves and not in the poet. Browning was in the most marked degree a deeply religious poet, and the ' Church of the Future ' would not need to seek her poet. She would find him ready and waiting for her theology to grow up to his poetry. His religion, like his philosophy, was a religion of charity, tolerance, and love, and to him the essence of all religion was to believe in God and to live our lives as in His presence." See also Canon Fremantle's recent Essay in the " Fortnightly Review," which has been simply ignored by Anglican Authority, and " The Kernel and the Husk," an anonymous book, said to be from the pen of a clergyman of the Established Church, recently issued by Macmillan and Co. Of such as these the following too true remarks have recently been made :—" It need hardly be observed that the Socinianism of men like Hoadley or Maltby is far outstripped by the fundamental heterodoxy of many Anglican divines and dignitaries of our own day, whose names will readily occur to the reader, though it might be invidious to specify them."—*Symposium on the Reunion of Christendom*, by Rev. H. N. Oxenham, in " Homiletical Magazine," p. 72, for August, 1887.

say that His Death upon the Cross has made atonement for our sins, because they do not believe that either. These things must be left as open questions that do not matter much to anybody, whether true or not. Then we must leave out Baptism and the Holy Communion, because all Sacraments are rejected by the Quakers; and for the same reason we must have no ministry of any kind. We cannot believe in a visible Church as the Kingdom of God on earth, because while one party says it consists of all the baptized, another says it means only those true Christians whom God knows will be saved at the last. Even if we leave out the Quakers as too few to count for much, we still must give up Infant Baptism to please the Baptists—and Bishops, Priests, and Deacons to please Dissenters generally. We must not tell our children that they belong to the family of God, because many think that this cannot be true till they have been converted. We must not call our Lord the Saviour of the world, because the Calvinists say He only died for a chosen few. Nor must we insist upon the necessity of repentance and amendment of life, because some tell us that all the sinner has to do is to believe that he is already saved. It will hardly do to speak much about duty and good works, because some think that faith does not need these things, and faith itself must not be spoken of, because there are three or four different opinions as to what faith really is." [1]

Obviously, the work of the Oxford Movement of 1835, fifty-two years after its initiation, remains very incomplete; the present standard of Faith and worship, taken as a whole, being possibly considerably lower than that of thirty years ago. [2]

---

[1] "The Dawn of Day," for July, 1886. P. 88.

[2] Several indications of this exist; one of the most notable being the great increase of that offensive innovation—Evening Communion. In the diocese of London, such profane orgies are perpetrated—at the fag-end of an idle day and on a full stomach —in no less than one-sixth of all the churches. At Cambridge, Evening Communion takes place in one-third of the churches of

Where the bishops did not lead, others, without
adequate authority — like Dr. Pusey and Mr.
Keble, Archdeacon Denison and Dr. Mill—were
forced, even against their wills, to become leaders.
Thus private individuals, who were learned and
estimable clergy of the second order—and not the
Established Church in its corporate capacity, and
by its actual episcopate—stood in the forefront and
gave the word of command for action to a militant
ministry of isolated stragglers. Hence so much is
continuously seen to have always depended upon
personal individual labour, and so little upon the
united co-operation of Anglican Authority. For
Anglican Authority was either with the *Homilies* or
conveniently and discreetly dumb. Hence, furthermore, when a particular and active individual died

that town. Seven of the Anglican bishops have directly or indirectly approved of, or sanctioned the profanity—three in their
public Charges. What kind of " custodians of the Eucharist "
can they be who thus act? While, as the late Bishop of Arras
remarked to the late Bishop Wilberforce, " What moral argument
against the value of English Post-Reformation ordinations could
be stronger or more direct?" On the other hand, the Bishop of
Chester, a man very learned in English Church History—who
knows accurately the source and extent of his own authority—
a few years ago, to his honour and credit, put forth the following
indirect Injunction to his clergy :—" He was not disposed to set
forth Injunctions which would not be obeyed, or to make recom-
mendations which would not be adopted, but he would state
definitely that any clergyman of that diocese who hereafter
introduced Evening Communion into his church would do it in
direct opposition to the opinions and wishes of his bishop."—
The Guardian, p. 1591, Oct. 27, 1886.

or dies, his work too often died or dies with him.
Changes involved by such deaths—a setting-up
anew of the Abomination of Desolation, for example
—often try the faith of thousands. Disaster and
Dismay, hand in hand, then stalk through the parish.
Every diocese can supply numerous examples of
this sad fact; while, if any distinctively " Church
work " (as it is termed) needs to be at any time
undertaken, a separate Society, and not the national
Communion itself, is planned and constituted in
order to get it done.

Thus, in all practical matters, the necessity for
restoring Catholic Authority—independent of the
Nation and universal in its action—runs parallel
with the ever-pressing need of visible Corporate
Reunion. With such actual blessings would likewise come a restoration of Canon Law,[1] as much

[1] As has been so acutely and ably observed by a competent
writer, " The whole question as to the possibility of the existence
of Canon Law as a distinct branch of Law turns upon the view
taken of the nature of the Church. For if the Church be not a
visible society, but only what philosophers would call a subjective
association, or the sum total of those who think alike on certain
religious matters (who can, therefore, never be known in this
world), there can be no such thing as Canon Law, and what is so
called is only a subordinate branch of Civil Law, and derives all
its force from the Civil authority. The same result follows if the
Church be considered as necessarily conterminous with the
Nation, after the analogy of the Jewish Nation of old. For a
long time it appears that one or the other of these views largely
prevailed in England. Hence, in a great measure, the neglect of
Canon Law."—*The Elements of Canon Law*, by the Rev. O. J.
Reichel, B.C.L. P. 10. London: 1887.

needed by Roman Catholics as by Anglicans. Its loss has led to a state of confusion amongst ourselves which no words can adequately describe. How a restoration of Authority, Visible Unity, and Canon Law have been neglected and passed over may be seen at a glance. For the snarls and snorts of mere Ritualistic Latitudinarianism are far too frequently heard. But the due consideration of Authority and Reunion can neither be safely postponed nor intentionally ignored. Nought else is of such great importance. Three centuries and a half of division, isolation, and impotence in our beloved country and its Church have been more than the Enemy of Souls—inspiring the original traitors and negation-mongers—should have been permitted to have made use of.

The dull and decorous " Guardian " appears to be sufficiently awake to write of the present situation as follows :—

" Indications are not wanting that what are commonly called ' Church Principles ' are either very loosely held, or are held in combination with opinions and principles that are really inconsistent with them. Is there not a danger of estimating a man's Church principles by the frequency of his services or the flowers in his church ? Yet, in some cases, these things are to be seen along with practices directly opposed to Church order, and with doctrines which might be taken from the Salvation Army. In other words, much of the so-called ' Churchmanship ' of the day is superficial and unsound, and will compare very ill, we will not say with the severe Tractarianism of the last generation, but with the simple loyalty to the Church which marked such families as the Kebles and the Hooks of still earlier days . . . . . Men

who would be injured if the name of ' High Churchmen ' were
denied to them, seem to be misled by an *ignis fatuus* which
deludes them into the belief that the cause of Christian Unity
can be advanced by ignoring the divinely-constituted limits of
the Church.   Such High Churchmanship as this is dearly purchased by surpliced choirs and improved music." [1]

The same writer remarked to the same effect, in
September, 1887, as follows :—

"I agree with you in denouncing the ' school-of-thought
gentry,' and in heartily renouncing them and all their works.
Some of these men, who, under the influence of scientific specu-
lators, having lost their Faith in Christianity, and living solely
for the present, speak of our holy religion as recommending a
short-sighted ' other-worldliness,' deserve the sincerest repre-
hension.   In order intentionally to degrade their office, they
dress like laymen, to show their contempt not alone for the
Catholic priesthood, but for any form of the Christian ministry.
They would be severely reprimanded by the bishops did the
latter but possess half-an-ounce of authority and any courage,
which it is to be feared is not the case; and would be repudiated
by ' High Churchmen,' so-called, did these at heart own a mere
modicum of those principles which, with many shortcomings,
made Hook, of Leeds, respected in a Yorkshire town, and John
Keble a power throughout the whole Church."

The practical influence of such men—distinctively destructive—is, of course, made use of to
weaken the Christian principle.   Everywhere they
work—mutually admiring each other—with this
object in view; and nowhere with greater disaster
than in the case of Education.   In several cases
in the Universities and the Public Schools those

---

[1] "An Ecclesiastical Retrospect," " Guardian," pp. 932, 933.
June 23, 1887.

who disbelieve in Christianity have long ago secured the most advantageous positions for indoctrinating the young, both of the upper and middle classes, with their pestilent negations and anti-Christian " views."

Thirty years ago, one of the Founders of the Association for the Promotion of the Unity of Christendom, who so accurately apprehended the then situation, wrote as follows:—

"There is another evil that, more perhaps than any other, affects society at the present moment, the direct consequence of our religious differences, and which nothing but a reconciliation of Christians can heal; I mean the impossibility, on any other principle, of establishing a sound system of National Education. The legislature, indeed, strives to meet the evil, by aiding all to educate in their respective systems of religious belief. The State is wise in doing so, it is the only way of meeting the circumstances of the case at the present moment; but at the same time it must be acknowledged that such a policy amounts to a profession of practical indifference (on the part of the State) to the distinction between truth and error, and sooner or later the effects of such a policy will be felt in the growth of scepticism in the minds of public men, and in the general weakening of the religious principle. But even this evil, gigantic as it is, would be annihilated by the restoration of religious Unity." [1]

Since this was written the policy of the State has undergone a momentous change, while the Education Act of a political Quaker, framed for a once-Christian nation, has been passed and applied.

[1] "On the Future Unity of Christendom," by Ambrose Lisle Phillipps, Esq. Pp. 61, 62. London : 1857.

And let it be noted that since that day, during the last thirty years, as in Religion, so in Education, our national descent has been rapid. Could Julian the Apostate have anticipated the policy of the School Board, short work, humanly speaking, might have been made of Christianity. Everywhere around us now in this nineteenth century—in cities, towns, and villages—this disastrous system is working untold and possibly irreparable mischief. Bishops and clergy [1] who have not the courage to oppose it, with some adroitness have recently taken to beslaver it with praise. Resistance to its triumphant progress (after noble acts of self-denial) is found to be but labour in vain. The huge Board Schools, morally as well as materially, now overtop and overshadow the old parish churches of London and its suburbs, efficiently nullifying their worship and teaching. Such schools are the powerful and efficient instruments for the practical propagation of Atheism. Moreover, with the aggressively-atheistic publications, some of which are so foul and revolting, both in

---

[1] The working men, whom these so earnestly profess to regard and respect, are never told the truth, and seldom taught their duty. It is not by pandering to the vitiated taste of the populace, however, that the clergy will either gain respect or maintain the Established Church. The cynical maxim, *Populus vult decipi*, is not true: on the contrary, the working man—indifferent rather than unbelieving—is willing to be taught, if only those who are presumed to have authority will exercise it, and teach him.

text and illustration, that no further reference can be made them, but of which nearly 500,000 are said to be issued week by week in London alone; with the sustained attacks on Christian marriage-laws, and with the aid of the filthy Divorce Court, and its consequences, home teaching of religion is rendered more and more difficult or impossible. For the children of the poor forced into the Board Schools are often underfed at home, and always overworked at school. Therein the State, denying parental rights and obligations, has arbitrarily interfered between parent and child. The family idea is thus broken up, and its home-blessings shattered. Philanthropy—of the earth earthy—then fussily steps in, with its pompous cant and vitiating influence; and so education-without-God (formally systematized and legalized because of our unhappy divisions), with all its dire and deadly consequences, is undermining Christian influence, social order, and national religious life.

Let the advice given to the Irish clergy by a high-principled and wise Member of Parliament be taken to heart by all :—

" Let them train their flocks—the young and the old—to know God, and knowing Him they will obey His commandments. Let them instruct them in the dogmas of their religion, and, understanding, they will fulfil them. Let them explain to them over and over again, the precepts of the Moral Law, and, saturated with their divine influences, they will spurn the seductions of the Socialist, the Communist, and the Infidel. Let them impress on the minds and hearts of their people that the Decalogue underlies all ritual, and all church organizations, all civilizations, all politics, all governments, and all laws. It corresponds in theology with natural facts in physical science. Ignore those facts, and the material structure falls—'a house built upon the sand.' Ignore the Moral Law, the Ten Commandments, and every religious system falls, the solidarity of the human race perishes, society dissolves, and humanity itself, losing its spiritual element, ceases to be human." [1]

A knowledge of the present position of the Established Church, its trials and difficulties, on the part of the present Holy Father, and the bearing of Christian Education on the well-being of the State, are apparent in the following impressive and benevolent " Encyclical on Education," addressed, in 1885, to the Roman Catholic Bishops of England :—

"In your country of Great Britain we know that, besides yourselves, very many of your nation are not a little anxious about Religious Education. They do not in all things agree with us; nevertheless they see how important, for the sake both of society and of men individually, is the preservation of that Christian wisdom which your forefathers received through St. Augustine, from our predecessor Gregory the Great, which wisdom the violent tempests that came afterwards have not entirely scattered. There are, as we know, at this day many of an excellent disposition of mind who are diligently striving to retain what they can of the Ancient Faith, and who bring forth many and great fruits of charity. As often as we think of this, so often are we deeply moved, for we love with a paternal charity that island which was not undeservedly called ' the Mother of

---

[1] " The Priest in Politics," by the late P. J. Smyth, M.P. P. 14. Dublin : 1885.

Saints,' and we see in the disposition of mind of which we have spoken the greatest hope, and, as it were, a pledge of the welfare and prosperity of the British people."

Yet, if the Christian Religion is to be preserved in England, some more active action must speedily be taken to secure fair play for those who on principle uphold Christian Education. Amongst Roman Catholics, lapses and losses are numerous. This fact is fully admitted and heartily deplored. Surrounding indifference, fostered by the School Board system, and mixed-marriages are working moral ruin. So it is with members of the Church of England, though many refuse to face the fact. Recent statistics, however, carefully taken in certain representative parishes, tell a tale which is as deplorable as it is saddening to read. Had the rulers of the Established Church, by which I mean the Bishops, in conjunction with the Catholic prelates,[1]

[1] A Catholic friend of mine, a priest, now resting in God, complained most earnestly of the policy of one of his chief prelatial Authorities, which he went so far as to designate Antichristian. "I do not say 'Antichristian' unadvisedly," he wrote, though no one would charge ———— with having written directly *in odium Christi*. . . . . His first act is to open the gate of the citadel, and to let the Enemy have free ingress. He concedes that the Civil State has the right to be the schoolmaster of its subjects. But to concede this right is the denial of the parental right under the first law of Creation, and the right of the Sacerdotal Order to be freely chosen by the parents, as those in whom they have confidence, and of their joint autonomy. Here speaks the [writer] betraying the right of the Christian Society to its own autonomy. From this there is no escape : either it

firmly resisted the passing into law of Mr. Forster's
Antichristian Education Act, and repudiated all
responsibility for its irreligious proposals, it could
never have become law. Weighty blame, consequently, should be awarded to both. Perhaps,
however, in their isolated and independent position,
they were at once unwilling and unable to co-
operate for such a holy purpose. If so, this fact
was a dark disaster for England, and stands out as
one more powerful reason for promoting Corporate
Reunion on the principles adopted by Cardinal Pole.

And here I would set forth the following considerations, to disarm unfriendly criticism. The
monarchical theory of the Church of God, viz.:
that, as it is a Divine kingdom, so it has a Divine
Head, is recognized by many. This Divine Head
is represented on earth, in the parish by its appointed minister, in the diocese by its Chief Pastor,
in the Province by its Archbishop and Metropolitan, in the one earthly Kingdom of Christ by
His Vicar,[1] and this latter, as Bossuet taught, not

is a betrayal of a divine right, or there is no divine right to
betray." In the MS. document from which this remarkable
quotation is taken, it was suggested that the Order of Corporate
Reunion should make a personal appeal to Catholic Authority
upon the grave subject of Christian Education. Such, I believe,
was indirectly done in 1883. The remarkable Encyclical on
the subject, already quoted, was published subsequently.

[1] In reply to Dr. Pusey's *Eirenicon*, and the proposals therein
suggested or made,—proposals which were not over-definite,—
Father Harper wrote thus :—" The conclusion which we deduce

by human contrivance or assent, but by Divine decree. But another theory—that on which the Tudor and other Protestant changes were effected, and upon which modern reforms and confiscations are based—is that Truth is only what man from time to time troweth; moreover, that such truth is frequently changing and can alone be discovered by the lofty principle of counting votes, and then only adequately defined and set forth by the catch-penny assent and united acclamations of the populace. Which of these theories is held by the Church of England nobody exactly knows nor can tell. With our bishops subject to their metropolitans, and with Canada, Capetown, and Australasia admitting appeals to Canterbury, the principle of the first-named theory *appears* to be upheld in principle. With Parish Councils, however, universal and useless chatter, and special lay-co-operation in tedious talk and everlasting change, the last-named theory clearly seems to be at length steadily developing, and now equally current and accepted.

One other point demands notice—touching the honour of Reunionists. It has been asserted more

is this; that all other schemes of Reunion must, from the nature of things, be abortive—cannot possibly succeed—save that of corporate or individual submission of the Greek and Anglican communions to the Catholic and Roman Church."—*Peace through the Truth*, by Rev. T. Harper, S.J. Vol. I. p. lxviii. London: 1866.

than once,—only, however, by jaundiced and one-sided persons,—that any proposal from an English clergyman for Corporate Reunion is at once dishonest and disloyal. Now, if to believe the whole Catholic Faith without negation-mongering or reservation, and to endeavour to restore people to its obedience be dishonesty, it would be interesting to learn how such would define "honesty."

While, as to disloyalty, when a man talks about the duty of "being loyal to the Church of England," analyze his sentences, and it will be seen that he is really and truly not talking sense. Ordinarily speaking loyalty is a virtue rendered personally to a sovereign, not to a "sovereign-people"—a cluster of congregations—to a nation in its bulk or to a nobody. What such a speaker evidently means, though for modesty's sake he dare not exactly venture upon saying it, is that, from his own point of view, it is the distinct duty of his listeners to be "loyal" to him—the individual who is so earnestly orating. What he asks for under the term "loyalty" is active assent or hearty agreement with himself, his sentiments, and what he probably calls his "views."

This *must* be the actual position, for loyalty to the Church of England, just as belief in the same is an impossibility, and is demanded of none. If one is personally "loyal" to Bishop Ryle or to Bishop King, to Canon Liddon or to Canon Fremantle, to Dean Elliot or to Dean Butler, it does not at all follow that such miscalled "loyalty" is anything more than mere personal admiration for several agreeable and accomplished gentlemen— some of whom—respectively admired, because of their defences of portions of the Christian system, or for their attacks upon it, or for their amiable personal characters, or for their great age—deserve such admiration. To be "loyal" to one or two of these might possibly involve "disloyalty" to some of the others ; while no person in authority, either in Church or State, seems authorized officially to declare either that all equally represent the Church of England, or that Canon Fremantle is distinctly "loyal," while Bishop King is expressly "disloyal." Here then—disentangling juggling words from joking exhortations—is another case of a Briton's hearty dislike to objective Truth, and a fresh example of the popular maxim of compromise, "Six of one and half-a-dozen of the other."

I must now prepare to lay down my pen. No person labouring for Corporate Reunion, let it be finally added, desires to see any union with error, superstition, or acknowledged imperfections. What is exclusively wanted is Union in the Truth, *i.e.*, the one true, infallible, and unalterable Faith, divinely-given, divinely-preserved, and alone perfect and incorruptible. A Faith which is not infallible is fallible, and no fallible bundle of religious opinions or agreeable sentiments about religion can satisfy, or be a guide to fallible men. England had this infallible Faith once through ten long centuries. Why should we not have it in all its completeness and perfection once again ?

It may be a sentimental, but at the same time it is a real satisfaction to me to pen these concluding sentences on the thirtieth anniversary of the foundation of the A.P.U.C. That Society, founded thirty years ago on this day in my hired chambers in Westminster, was formed exclusively for daily prayer in common for a common object. It has done, and is doing its work. Other Societies and Orders of more recent date are actively co-operating with it, both by work and prayer. To such prayer for so holy a purpose none can surely object. For such labourers—*Beati pacifici!* How efficacious their united intercessions may prove, when Patience has done its perfect work, let future events—in a near and bright future by God's blessing and the patronage of Our Lady and the Saints—effectively proclaim *urbi et orbi*, both to men and to angels. Amen.

F. G. L.

ALL SAINTS' VICARAGE, YORK ROAD, LAMBETH,
NATIVITY B.V.M., 1887.

CHAPTER I.

REGINALD POLE, HIS PERSONAL HISTORY.

B

CONTENTS OF CHAPTER I.

Reginald Pole, his Personal History.—His Ancient Lineage and Education.—Studies under the Carmelites at Oxford.—Appointed Dean of Wimborne.—Nominated Fellow of C. C. Coll. Oxford.—Settles for study at Padua.—The City and "Studio" of Padua.—Pole's Friends and Contemporaries.—He Returns to England.—Henry VIII. and his proposed Divorce.—Cromwell, Pole, and Fisher.—The Monastery at Sheen.—Pole offered an Archbishopric.—He Retires to Italy.—King Henry's "Spiritual Supremacy."—His Suggestion to Pole.—Pole's Policy Misunderstood.—Created a Cardinal Deacon, and subsequently Cardinal Priest.—A True and Religious Patriot.—Decay of the English Nobility.—Henry VIII.'s Revolution.—His Ecclesiastical Supremacy.—Authority and Liberty Weakened.—Henry's Treatment of St. Thomas.—Pole's Comments on the King.—Policy of Thomas Cromwell.—Pole appointed Legate.—Declared to be a Traitor.—Treatment of the Cardinal's Kinsfolk.—Effect of the Executions.

CHAPTER I.

EGINALD POLE is believed to have been born during the month of March, in the year 1500. The place of his birth is said to have been Stour Castle, in Staffordshire. The exact date—as the Registers of Religious Houses have been lost or destroyed, and Parish Registers did not then exist—remains uncertain.

He was the fourth son of Sir Richard Pole, Knight of the Garter, by Margaret Plantagenet, Countess of Salisbury—whom Henry the Eighth so barbarously murdered—only daughter of George Duke of Clarence, sister and heiress to Edward Earl of Salisbury and Warwick.

This George Duke of Clarence—whose lady was Isabella, eldest daughter and co-heiress of Richard

Nevill, Earl of Westmoreland—brother of King Edward the Fourth, was great-great-grandson of that renowned monarch Edward the Third, King of England and of France, and Lord of Ireland, who was also the Founder of the Noble Order of the Garter.

In the female line Reginald Pole was descended from the Lady Isabella, youngest daughter of Peter, King of Castille and Leon; from the Lady Anne, daughter of Roger Mortimer, Earl of Marche; and from the Lady Cecilia, youngest daughter of Ralph Nevill, Earl of Westmoreland.

A nobler lineage for an Englishman of that period could scarcely be discovered, while his faith was that of the Fishermen of Galilee, which had permeated the Roman Empire—a Faith which St. Austin had brought hither, which Bede with such divine grace and literary skill had set forth to bless and benefit our ancestors; and which for long centuries had made England to become, and to be looked upon throughout whole Christendom as verily an " Island of Saints."

His early education was received at the Carthusian Monastery at Sheen, near Richmond, in Surrey, in close proximity to his mother's residence. At that time most of the religious houses of both sexes provided schools for the various classes and ranks who lived near, and such were generally patronized.

When, in 1512, Pole was twelve years old, he was placed amongst the scholars of the White Friars in Oxford—a school situated within the parish of St. Mary Magdalene of that city—which at the period in question enjoyed a great and well-deserved reputation. The Carmelites had long been amongst the most successful instructors of youth in the University. Efficient teaching, strict discipline, and a careful and systematic practice of the duties of religion were this school's leading features. Here, therefore, no doubt Pole's natural virtues were steadily strengthened, and his enlarging mental powers fortified. For, in after years, he more than once made reference in his letters to literary friends to the benefits which had been conferred upon him by judicious and reasonable discipline both at school and college in Oxford.

He is believed to have entered St. Mary Magdalene College about the same year, having rooms in the President's lodgings. In the archives of that venerable society (at that time the Royal College) there are no early Registers of non-foundationers;[1] but three years afterwards, *i.e.*, in 1515, he was still in residence there, having already supplicated

---

[1] From information given to me by my kind and venerable friend, the Rev. Dr. Bloxam, of Magdalene College, whose painstaking and interesting literary labours have done so much to provide valuable materials for a perfect history of that College.

for the degree of B.A. on the 3rd July, 1513, a grace not then granted. On the 1st May, 1514, however, he again sought for the degree in question, was accepted for the same, disputed on the 5th May, and was admitted thereto on the 26th of June of the same year. Special privileges were granted to him; as for example, free access to the Public Library, *sine habitu*, on the 29th November, with other privileges as a member of the Royal House.

On the 12th of February, 1518, he was appointed Dean of the Minster Church of Wimborne, in Dorsetshire, a magnificent specimen of third-pointed architecture, grand in its conception, and fair in its elevation, a glory to the county in which it stands. On the 10th of February of the following year, 1519, he was made Prebendary of Gatcombe *Secunda* in the cathedral church of Sarum. The unfortunate and irregular custom then too often current of presenting such benefices and dignities to laymen, who obtained clerics to fulfil the official duties, cannot be justified or reasonably defended. Such was an obvious and disastrous abuse.

In the year 1523 Dr. John Claymond, President of Corpus Christi College, Oxford,[1] admitted Pole

---

[1] Extract from the *Register of Admissions* at Corpus Christi College, Oxford, A.D. 1522-1523.

In Dei nomine, Amen. Per hoc pubblicum instrumentum cunctis appareat evidenter et sit notum quod anno domini millesimo quingentesimo vicesimo tertio Indictioni undecima pontifi-

to a Fellowship in that society, a position to which he appears to have been recommended by Richard Cox, the Lord Bishop of Winchester, and founder of that college.

It seems doubtful, however, whether he ever resided there. Soon afterwards the University of Oxford was deeply stirred by the subject of the Queen's divorce and the sacrament of matrimony. Wise, foreseeing men, who respected the old order of things, marked the storms brewing.

In certain cases tokens of coming disorder were

catus in Christo patris ac domini nostri domini Adriani hujus nominis sexti anno primo mensis vero ffebruarii die quarto decimo. In aula Collegii Corporis Christi in Universitate Oxoniensis. In mei notarii pubblici et testium inferius nominatorum præsentia per peregregium virum magistrum Joannem Claymond dicti collegii praesidem ac etiam authoritate reverendi in Christo patris ac domini domini Ricardi ffox Wintoniensis episcopi illius collegii fundatoris admitti erant in veros socios [dominus *Reginaldus Polli*. These words seem to have been erased, and then written in again. About three or four words succeeding have been erased, and *not* written in again. In the margin is, in another hand, *Reginaldus Pooli;* also in a third hand, Dˢ Reginaldus Polli, Dˢ Joannes Fox Socii assumpti] Dominus etiam Joannes ffox Londinensis diœcesis [another erasure, f'tro, or these words irrecoverable like the former one] non obstantibus statutis de probationi nec ullo alio acta sunt hæc omnia et singula prout super scribuntur et recitantur sub anno domini indictioni pontificatus mense die et prædictis præsentibus tunc ibidem discretis [or dissertis] viris Roberto Morwent et Galfrido Ley artium magistris Wigorn et Dunelmens testibus ad prœmissa requisitis. The attestation is by Henricus Williams, "publicus authoritate [apostolica erased] notarius." The word "apostolica" is usually erased in the Register, but sometimes so partially as to be recoverable, but not in this case.

distinctly seen. In some particulars Society was sick at heart and sad. Intellectual languor prevailed. If learning was venerated at Oxford, Religion by a small minority was too often tabooed and morality scoffed at. The number of students gathered near the banks of the Isis was found to be less than heretofore. Many of these were distinctly influenced by the Pagan renaissance.

At that time the " Studio " of Padua, as it was termed, was the most renowned university of Europe. It had been the city of Livy, of Petrarch and Giotto. Aspiring students flocked to it from all parts of Christendom, and learned to love it for its teaching and memories. Most striking is this ancient place, rife with rich and venerable traditions. Pole must have known well the Palazzo della Ragione, with its Gothic loggia and armorial shields, its vast Hall (from the design of Father Giovanni, an Austin Friar), and splendid paintings ; the solemn church of Padua's patron, St. Anthony, with its seven Oriental domes and three minarets, its awe-inspiring interior, adorned with an overwhelming mass of mystic enrichment and decoration, and its twin lamps of purest gold in the dim and distant sanctuary. Nor was the Chapel of Our Lady of the Annunciation then wanting in engrossing interest. The groups of the blessed, pictured by Giotto, expressively-wrought scenes from the life of the Blessed Virgin and of our

Divine Lord; sacred allegorical mysteries dimly depicted, ancient tombs, and rich imagery were found in abundance on all sides—tokens that Christian faith had made a deep and lasting impression on Paduan art. As a city it had experienced numerous changes and reverses of fortune since the fall of ancient Rome and the days of Attila; peace and war, sunshine and shadow having constantly alternated there. On no less than eight occasions its form of government had been altered. In one century the sovereigns of Lombardy had been its benevolent patrons: in subsequent years, after conquest by strangers had been effected and crowned, and further changes sealed, the triumphant Venetians, early in the fifteenth century, added Padua, with its rich and fertile plains, to their adjacent flourishing dominions on the Adriatic shores.

In the sixteenth century its masters and teachers were the most thorough and successful instructors in the ancient learned languages. The rich and prolific traditions of antiquity had been handed down from time immemorial almost unbroken; so that living teachers kept their lamps burning, in the Halls of Theology, polite Literature, Art, Philosophy, and Laws, with singular ability and success and with deserved and world-wide approbation. The great treatises of Aristotle, the valued records of Livy, the deep philosophy and theology of St. Thomas Aquinas, the acute works of Duns Scotus were there attentively studied and held in high regard. Moreover, some of the most valuable tractates of Christian learning—philosophical, political, theological—were there likewise planned and completed. Gaspar Contarini, Lazarus Bonamico, Bembo, and Sadolet, amongst many others, were names had in renown; while the printed works of Pole's literary contemporaries, teachers, and learners, would of themselves even now form a most considerable and valuable library.

To this city of general learning,[1] gathered youths of rank and nobility from every European country. Here Reginald Pole is found, with a suitable and sufficient income provided by his family and the king of England, surrounded by the cultured and refined; having for his special friends and companions a young Englishman named Thomas Lupsett, Aloysius Priuli, a noble Venetian, and Christopher Longolius, a native of Flanders. With such as these, and their teachers and masters, all that was good and righteous, noble and true amongst the writings of the ancients served but to strengthen the foundations of the Christian Faith. Originally it seems quite certain

---

[1] Its four faculties of theology, laws, humanity and medicine were all renowned. Each faculty has a Director, a Dean, and a Rector, who together form the Senate; while the number of students still averages two thousand every year.

that Monetheism was the religion of ancient Rome.[1] There, in its chief city's earliest age, Order was upheld, Law respected, Justice maintained and administered, and Virtue extolled. Of course all these beneficent gifts have their roots in man's original belief in One Supreme Being,—a bright recollection of Paradise. The like may surely have been the case with Padua in the days of its founder Antenor. Hence, upon the sure and solid foundation in question, by natural growth, rose a knowledge of the sacred Scriptures, the Greek and Latin fathers, the councils with their canons and decrees, together with the varied and beautiful traditions of every kind which had found their origin in Bethlehem and Calvary, the Upper Chamber and Patmos ; and subsequently in the Mamertine Prison and the Cœlian Hill,—each tradition converging in the Son of Mary, the Saviour of mankind, the central Object of the World's disentangled History.

In 1526 Pole returned to England to find the subject of the King's proposed divorce from his queen Katherine uppermost in the public mind, and everywhere the subject of discussion. It was the burning question of the day. From the outset— though on one occasion misunderstood—Pole had

---

[1] " Monotheism, the Primitive Religion of the City of Rome," by the Rev. Henry Formby, M.A., London, 1877: a closely-reasoned and masterly book by a powerful Christian writer.

studiously refrained from showing the slightest sympathy with the proposal. His words to the King had invariably been dutiful and respectful, but ever clear and firm. The Christian law of marriage was well understood; and he had no temptation to swerve from plainly setting it forth, if asked to do so. He had always maintained the Christian principle therein embodied, and deprecated the King's suggestion, or any of the proposals regarding it. At the same time, he had invariably and consistently maintained the authority and jurisdiction of the Holy See as final in the determination of every such question.

A fruitless endeavour had been made to refer the subject in dispute to the consideration of four spiritual and four temporal peers, whose judgment, to avoid further discussion, it was proposed should be final. But Queen Katherine, on being waited upon by certain friends of her royal husband, distinctly declined even to entertain the proposal. Secure in her position of right, and trusting implicitly to the justice of the Head of the Visible Church, she stood firm; unwavering and full of confidence that justice would be done to her, and that in the end right would prevail.

"God give the King a quiet conscience," she replied with dignity and feeling, "but this must be your answer. I am his wife, lawfully married to him by authority of Holy Church, and so will

I remain unless the Court of Rome, privy to all from the beginning, shall have made an end thereof."

The King soon afterwards, by the same messenger, ordered her to leave the Palace of Windsor, to which, never swerving from her point and position,—she replied, "Go where I may, I shall still be his lawful wife." Soon afterwards, in sorrow, but in faith and hope, she left for Ampthill in Bedfordshire. There at least she was away from a spot where she could not but witness, or hear of, the unfeeling indecency of her rival, and the heartless cruelty of her husband.

During the year 1528, Pole had retired to the Carthusian Monastery at Sheen. With this pleasantly-situated house he was well acquainted, for here he had received a part of his earliest education. Although some few public men had followed Thomas Cromwell in his unprecedented proposal to the King, yet, as regards Religion, the vast number of courtiers and statesmen evidently hesitated to put themselves in opposition to the great body of English divines and ecclesiastics— with Bishop Fisher at their head. Pole, no doubt, felt that neither his age and position nor his learning would warrant him in presuming to forestall the character of the decree, which sooner or later Rome might be expected to promulgate ; and, though his opinion was even then distinct and definite enough, in favour of the validity of Queen Katherine's marriage, he obviously thought silence to be at once more prudent and more respectful to Authority.

Within the precincts of the Sheen Monastery, John Colet, sometime Dean of St. Paul's, had by arrangement built a house for himself—a kind of retreat for his old age, when weighted by years and unable to execute his official duties, he might properly retire to a quiet home, where, in the silence of the Library, with its tomes of manuscript, and choice volumes of black-letter from Venice, Flanders and Westminster, and in the society of sympathizing friends, he could solace himself with the companionship of those holy religious whom he respected and loved.

After residing in this house at Sheen for about two years, Pole signified to the King his desire and intention of going to the University of Paris, with the aim of continuing his studies. Henry VIII. at once acceded to this suggestion; and as Bellay, —Bishop of Bayonne, French Ambassador at the English Court, in a Letter dated the 4th Oct., 1529 —informed the High Steward of the French monarch, that Pole, " this young nobleman, was nearly related to the King, and was one of the most learned personages of the age: that his intention was to see France, and continue his studies; that Henry, moreover, had commanded him to pay his respects to the King; and that his family, who were persons of great merit and of high rank, desired that he might be particularly recommended to him." Pole travelled as became his position, and lived in France in a due state of dignity.

At this time the subject of the proposed divorce had been formally before the Holy See.

There can be little doubt that, on its vacancy, the Archbishopric of York had been offered to Pole *with conditions*, and that these were most probably of a nature which no honourable Christian man could have accepted. It is possible that those dexterous partizans who had desired to entangle him with the King by promises, and indirectly secure his aid for their Machiavellian policy, were both disappointed and vexed at his dignified and righteous attitude. It is not given to many to say, *Nolo episcopari*. But Pole had not studied Cromwell's character in vain. His royal Master he had already read through and through. The light of faith had enabled Pole to apprehend without shadow or fleck or mistake what was approaching. To such a policy as that of the King —evidently inspired from beneath—he could in his conscience be neither a party nor a partizan. No wonder, therefore, that the vexation of the Erastian monarch-worshippers was at once bitter and keen, or that the paroxysms of anger in which

Henry was found should have appeared to bystanders little less than demoniacal.

At this time Pole, glad to be far away from a scene of controversy and strife, returned to Italy, where he devoted himself entirely to religion and literature.

Here, however, he received from Henry a royal mandate to consider at once two important details then under consideration in the case of the Queen's divorce, and to answer two distinct and definite questions in regard to certain opinions concerning the same. Pole was in no haste to reply. But, on learning that the death of Anne Boleyn had taken place, he wrote boldly and unambiguously, in a manner and by a method entirely worthy of him: first, that the divorce of Katherine was distinctly unlawful; and, secondly, that the recent assumption of supremacy in things spiritual was destructive of unity, and altogether contrary to the fundamental principles of the Christian faith. A trusty messenger bore this remarkable treatise to the King—the distinct consequence of a royal command. Whether it was acceptable or not, it was at all events given in answer to a plain request. And, let it be noted, neither of the replies was ambiguous.[1]

---

[1] In this case of the divorce of Henry VIII. from Katherine, Pole was no partizan, but a nobleman desirous of doing justice to the Queen, and of never forgetting his personal responsibility

But Pole did not stop here. He felt bound to point out the King's enormities, publicly criticized throughout Christendom. That monarch had married, or pretended to marry, a second wife during the lifetime of the first, and had dared to disregard Christian authority in reference to this Sacrament. He had thus laid the foundation of dangerous and fatal schemes, by which all authority might in the long run be weakened. He had caused to be martyred Sir Thomas More, Bishop Fisher, and the Carthusian brothers, because of their bold and needful repudiation of his pretended supremacy in the Church of God; and, on the other hand, had taken an active part in the examination and condemnation of heretics. Thus had he made himself and his name the bye-word and execration of Christendom.

His so-called "spiritual supremacy," no less its jest than its scandal, was notoriously set up by the secular power alone; in spite of, and in direct opposition to the clergy, by divine appointment its spiritual overseers and acknowledged rulers.

as a Christian. He was obviously bound to the King by several acts of kindness, yet because of these he never allowed himself to forget his duty to God. Pole's letters from Paris—when that University was considering the formal legal questions submitted to it by Henry's agents—were always cautious and clear, courteous and considerate. But he never swerves from impartiality, and never violates truth. Least of all is he at all designing and double-faced, as a recent random writer endeavours to make out.

Thus the whole scheme of Church government, as set up by Christ Himself, was deliberately overturned. The secular judge invaded the sanctuary. Persons like Thomas Cromwell, altogether unqualified by their state even for the lowest ecclesiastical preferments, were raised to the most exalted dignities in the Church; so that those whose duty it was to submit themselves obediently to the appointed rulers of the same, were actually made the spiritual directors of their own ecclesiastical guides.

In reply to Pole, the King—at Cromwell's dexterous suggestion—took the greatest care to evince not even the appearance of irritation at the rebuke referred to, but answered his critic in the mildest phraseology, and with the most honeyed words. Let them, he suggested, calmly discuss these complex religious questions either with the other, in private and in peace, to their own mutual satisfaction and common benefit. And to bring this about as soon as possible, let Reginald Pole return to England at once, and begin the desired consultation.

But the net, though carefully spread, was spread in vain. It needed no second thoughts to point out Pole's danger to himself with directness and force. The bloody exhibitions of malignant injustice; scaffolds red with the blood of holy and innocent men; the Tybourne timbers splattered with gore; the eyeless heads of innocent victims smeared with pitch, with a batch of mutilated limbs of martyrs on lances set up over the gates of the City of London, were in themselves an impressive exhibition and a powerful warning.

The charge against Pole that he was artfully stirring up strife and war, in order, as a member of the Royal House of York, to set aside Henry and craftily obtain the English crown for himself, when his own confidential and official letters are studied, is seen to be entirely baseless. That he was in full sympathy with the ancient nobility, faithful clergy, and noble yeomen of the North in their dislike for the religious revolution; and that he was ready to aid them both by moral and material means in their resistance, is not only perfectly true and accurate—any other attitude in so truly noble and Christian a personage would have been utterly unworthy of him—but displays his commendable courage and righteous zeal in a light in which all Christian people can distinctly behold and admire the same.

This being so, no surprise need exist, either that Cromwell should have expressed a resolution to " make him eat out his heart with vexation," [1] or

---

[1] " I herde you say wons that you wold make hym to ete hys owne hartt, which you have now, I trow, brought to passe; for he must nedes now ette hys owne hartt, and becum as hartlesse as he is gracelesse."— *Wright's Letters on the Suppression of the Monasteries Latimer to Thomas Cromwell*, p. 150.

that the King should have then and thenceforth regarded him with deadly dislike and an almost diabolical hatred.

Early in 1537, Pole was created Cardinal Deacon of the Basilica of SS. Nereus and Achilleus [1] on the Appian Way—a church, founded A.D. 759, of singular interest and renown. There, behind the high altar, still stands the actual episcopal throne from which our English benefactor and saintly patron, St. Gregory the Great, had read his twenty-eighth Homily; and in this sacred Basilica had been held the actual Council presided over by that Pope in person. In it still remain the two very ancient *ambones* with an artfully-wrought marble Pascal taper-stand: while, up above, mosaic work of hoar antiquity, but dulled with age, sets forth a representation of the Annunciation, Our Blessed Lady with Her Divine Child, and, on the face of the arch over the sanctuary, the Transfiguration of our adorable Lord. Beneath are preserved the relics of its Patron-Saints, and of St Domitilla; while the subsequent restorer of the Church, Cardinal Baronius, has left a sculptured warning in marble against any destruction of its renowned

---

[1] "1537. Feb. 7. Creavit legatum de latere R^{mum} D. Rainaldum Polum, Sanctorum Nerei et Achillei diaconum Cardinalem, Anglum, cum facultate prout in literis, et eum destinavit ad res Angliae componendas."—*Acts of the Consistory (from the Original at Rome).*

antiquities.   **Here** Pole was solemnly enthroned—taking formal possession of his church—according to rule and custom; while **his** official connection with this basilica, so dear to Englishmen, must have given rise to feelings of gratitude for **the** past and—though probably flecked with **sadness** —of earnest hope for the future.

Subsequently, when he was created a **Cardinal** Priest, his title was changed to that of St. **Mary in** Cosmedin. This church, built by St. Dionysius in the third century, was restored by Pope Adrian the First, A.D. 782. It had **been** visited by Siricius, previously Bishop of Ramsbury (to which he was consecrated **by** St. Dunstan), and subsequently appointed Archbishop of Canterbury, who went to Rome to do homage to the Holy Father in the year 990, when his translation **to the** chief archiepiscopal See of England had been completed. Here again, then, Pole **was** reminded of **the** Christian life and ecclesiastical glories of his native land, and of **its** long-enjoyed **spiritual** connection **with** the Apostolic See.

On March 8th, 1538, Cardinal Pole was created and confirmed Warden of the English Hospital at Rome, Thomas Goldwell, **the** exiled Bishop **of** St. Asaph, being Chamberlain of the **same.** Subsequently His Grace **became** in **turn** Protector thereof, with Goldwell as Warden. Afterwards William Peto, Bishop of Salisbury, received the office of Warden. This bold and devout dignitary had long previously rebuked[1] Henry VIII. for his wickedness, and had been threatened with death. But he prudently escaped to the Continent and did a good work for Christianity abroad.

At Rome, Pole was ever watchful on behalf of his beloved country. He respected its glorious traditions, honoured its righteous laws, loved its true religion, and therefore daily remembered its growing necessities at the altar before God. He constantly asked the intercession of the saints on high, on behalf of his countrymen, who were being then so sorely tried and treated by those who had obtained, and grasped so tightly, the whip-handle of usurped power. Cardinal Wolsey—a true states-man, one who had accurately read the signs of the times—it is to be feared, however, had short-sightedly done something to open the flood-gates of change, and to create precedents for further inno-vations; but it was reserved for that cardinal's low-born servitor, Thomas Cromwell, to suggest to the King the disastrous and wicked breach of unity which was being so artfully and successfully accom-plished.

Upstarts, like Rich and this Putney armourer's son—men of iron wills, and singular craft and skill—became leaders in a new policy, and destroyers

---

[1] See, for details of this rebuke, my "Historical Sketches of the Reformation," p. 291. London : 1879.

of true religion, under both Henry and his son
Edward.   And this to the general detriment of
the kingdom, and to the special loss of the poor.

It is sad to note how, under these Tudors—
Queen Mary excepted[1]—the ancient nobility, as a
body, had ceased to exercise their former beneficial
influence, having in many cases become extinct.
Several old English families having grown poorer
by degrees—their manors alienated, their lands
sold—in some instances became actually needy.
Those members of the same which still existed had
often squandered their remaining wealth in folly,
ostentation, and frivolity.   In other cases, having
plucked up courage to oppose the monarch's arbi-
trary will, and often unjust commands, bills of
attainder and legalized murders of powerful noblemen who had dared to resist the King, had not failed
to exercise a direct and deterrent influence upon
those who remained; more especially on the new
and pushing adventurers, and crouching slaves,
ready and willing by nature and low natural cunning for any despicable suggestion of the monarch,
and who, born amongst the lowest plebeians, had
recently secured for themselves much-coveted
honours, dignities, and wealth.[2]

[1] The advisers of this Queen, it will be noticed, were mainly
persons of blood and rank.   She evidently mistrusted the new
men, so many of whom were bent on mere self-seeking in every
form and phase.

[2] Here is Cardinal Pole's testimony:—" Sic nobiles semper

Alas! I know the despicable and saddening story in its bare baldness all too well. Going to ancient records and legal instruments, to original private letters and ambassadors' confidential reports, new facts are discovered, and old partizan romances (which some style "History") are found to be wholly misleading and in themselves so mischievously false. Some persons, living in the light of faith, cannot even now nerve themselves to read a true record, and let its cruel and revolting details sink into their minds; it being too distressing to contemplate, either in its first initiation or in all its miserable consequences. Here are its outlines: Henry the Eighth, for the unhappy people under him, renounced the authority of United Christendom in order to overthrow the rights of women, to degrade matrimony and to practise concubinage; while, on the other hand, rather than alter by one iota that divine policy which had dignified matrimony as a Sacrament, the Holy See was obliged to behold, with sorrow and suffering, one of its fairest provinces torn from Catholic Unity. The spiritual jurisdiction of the old English Church—exercised

tractavisti, ut nullius principatu minore in honore fuerint: in quos, si quid leviter deliquissent, acerbissimus fuisti; nihil unquam cuiquam condonasti; omnes despicatui habuisti; nullum apud te honoris aut gratiæ locum obtinere passus es: eum interea semper alienissimos homines ex infima plebe assumptos circum te habueris, quibus summa omnia deferres."—*Epistola Poli*, p. 83.

in due subordination to that of corporate Christendom, represented by its visible head—was thus directly and effectually transferred to the King.[1] Convocation had openly promised to make no new enactments for the government of the Church, either in faith, morals, or any other particular, without the monarch's express sanction. Hitherto a pall, the ancient symbol of jurisdiction, had been graciously

---

[1] By virtue of this supremacy ecclesiastical the King's Majesty is made the ultimate judge of heresy and the determinator of what is agreeable or repugnant to God's law. And all his subjects are obliged to receive, observe, and submit unto the godly instructions and determinations set forth by his Majesty. And if any spiritual person or persons shall preach or teach contrary to the determinations which are or shall be set forth by his Majesty, that then every such offender offending the third time shall be deemed and judged a heretic, and shall suffer pains of death by burning.—*Act for the Advancement of True Religion,* 37 *Hen. VIII.,* **cap.** 17.

On this point, here are the weighty words of B. Cardinal Fisher:—" I think, indeed, and always have thought, and doe now lastly affirme that His Grace cannot justly claime any such supremacie over the Churche of God, as he nowe takyth uppon him : neither hathe it ever been seene or hearde of that anie temporale prince before his daies hathe presumed to that dignitie. Wherefore if the King will now adventure himself in proceeding in this strange and unwouted case, no doubt but he shall deeply incur the grievous displeasure of Almighty God, to the great damage of his own sowle and manie others, and to the utter ruine of this royalme committed to his charge, whereof will ensue some sharpe punishment at his hand. Wherfore I praye God His Grace may remember himself in time, and harken to good counsaile for the preservation of himself and his royalme, and the quiettance of all Christendom."—*Speech of John Fisher, after condemnation,* **from an ancient** *Sixteenth Century MS. Notebook.*

sent from Rome and dutifully received. Rome-scot had been at once a reality and a sign of active union between mother and daughter. The successors of St. Augustine of Canterbury had invariably appealed for protection and patronage to the successors of St. Gregory the Great, a long line of Fathers of the faithful (guardians of the Faith and protectors of the Church's liberties); henceforth the oppressed in England had no appeal against change, oppression, tyranny, and wrong. A lay Vicar-General, who himself appointed lay-deputies in various dioceses, administered the usurped office of the monarch, binding the obsequious clergy with strong Erastian bands, and scourging them, as it were, with scorpions. Authority and Liberty fell prone at one stroke, and have ever since been both prostrate and sorely and seriously crippled. The property of the Church and the poor soon found its way into the King's treasure-house; while, after endless controversies and vain contentions, " truth " eventually came to be looked upon as merely and only " what each man himself troweth." The pretended sweeping and garnishing of the House, as in the Gospel narrative, have served only to bring in seven other devils. But from generals to a particular.

The sacrilegious iniquities perpetrated by order of Henry VIII. in destroying the Shrine, and in burning and scattering the ashes of the relics of

St. Thomas of Canterbury, duly reported and considered at Rome,[1] gave Pole an opportunity of setting forth a scathing indictment of the English Nero.

For what was the true state of the case? Here was that of a martyred Prelate, who had been held in veneration for three hundred years as a most zealous and favoured servant of God, who with inflexible determination had laid down his life in defence of the Catholic Faith and Church freedom, and was regarded by all Christendom as a most potent patron and intercessor for England before the Throne of God.[2] His shrine in Canterbury Cathedral, gorgeous in itself and most rich in the costly offerings around and about it, originally erected with every effort of art and magnificence, to be worthy of its treasure, was first violently

[1] 1538, Oct. 18. "S. D. N. significavit novam saevitiam et impietatem Regis Angliae, qui corpus Beati Thomæ Cantuarien. comburi jusserat, et cineres spargi et dari vento, expilata arca et vasis aureis et lapidibus pretiosis, quorum magnus numerus in ea arca inerat. Quapropter S^{tas} sua deputavit R^{mos} D.D. Cardinales Campegium, Ghinuccium, Contarenum et S^{ti} Sixti, qui de his rebus inter se consultarent et S^{ti} suae referent."— *Consistorial Acts (from the Original at Rome).*

[2] "If the cause in which this Prelate suffered and died has appeared equivocal to the low estimates of worldly prudence, it has pleased the wisdom of the Almighty to declare in its favour by miracles which were so frequent and so well-attested by the unanimous consent of authors of those days, that without questioning whatsoever History may have transmitted to us, these certainly cannot be contested."—*History of the Variations,* etc., by J. B. Bossuet ; vol. i. book vii. sec. 114.

rifled, by Henry's command, and then utterly destroyed. Worse than this, the impious Monarch in question, at Thomas Cromwell's suggestion, issued a Proclamation,[1] in which he maintained that, having carefully weighed anew the merits of the original cause, he had discovered that Thomas à Becket had been killed in a riot when endeavouring to obstruct the execution of his Monarch's lawful orders; and, therefore, instead of being a Martyr as all the World fondly believed, was only a Rebel.[2]

Pole, therefore, aptly and forcibly contrasted Henry's impious conduct with that of the Mahometan Turks. These triumphant conquerors, having successfully taken the Island of Rhodes, and being saturated with superstition, yet behaved with decency and humanity in their triumph. They scrupulously regarded the feelings of the conquered, and specially respected the monuments of Saints—even permitting the Christians to remove their remains, so precious and venerated, to places of safety and security. Cromwell's policy,

---

[1] See Dr. Thomas Stapleton's interesting account of St. Thomas, in which the Latin Proclamation in question is set forth. It will be found in his book *Tres Thomae, seu De S. Thomæ Apostoli rebus gestis, De S. Thomæ Archiepisco Cantuar, et Martyre, D. Thomae Mori Angliæ quondam Cancellarii Vitæ. Authore Thoma Stapletono Anglo.*—Duaci, Ex officina Ioannis Bogardi : 1588. (Lambeth Library.)

[2] Wilkins's " Concilia," vol. iii. pp. 835, 836, 841.

of which all this was but a detail, thus adopted by the King, was ingenious and consistent throughout. Its iniquity and injustice were sufficiently marked, while its unity and completeness secured for it an eventual triumph.

The insurrection in the North of England was a sure indication of the excessive dislike with which the religious changes, suggested by the King's Minister, were regarded. At this period of the "Reformation" this unscrupulous politician appears to have given scarcely a moment's consideration to the minor details of the contemplated change. On such he looked with mere pitiful contempt. He had no regard for doctrinal phrase-mongering, and such at that time with the noisy and notorious was exceedingly popular in the work of change and destruction. The points at issue were—Is the Church of God one and universal, or is it composed of diverse and conflicting local nationalities? Is it governed in its final determinations by monarchs or by pontiffs—by laymen or by ecclesiastics? But Cromwell noted all this, and had taken in the exact situation at a glance. The King's supremacy in ecclesiastical and religious matters, instead of the Pope's, could, being decreed by one single stroke, alone destroy the old order of things in its very foundation. Once get this change effected and the great work of demolition was done. Here, then, was the crucial change. This was the key of the citadel. Such deliberately given up, there was little else to contend about or to struggle for.

No one saw this amongst the ecclesiastics more distinctly than Bishop John Fisher and Reginald Pole. The subsequent conduct of each—their roads were slightly different, but their aims were identical—abundantly proves the point.

At Rome, the Northern Rising in favour of the Ancient Faith, and in opposition to Cromwell's plans, would, it was believed and hoped, exercise a great influence on King Henry: and no stone was left unturned, consequently, to alter his policy. Pole, who had not yet openly broken with him, was appointed Legate beyond the Alps; and, with sufficient instructions, set out for France to serve the holy cause of Religion and Truth. No sooner had he set foot on the French soil, however, than the English Ambassador, in virtue of a secret treaty between the two Crowns, asked that he should be given up as King Henry's avowed enemy, and sent a prisoner to England. The French king, by a private messenger, discreetly urged Pole to continue his journey with no delay, to seek no interview with his Majesty, and so to avoid greater complications.

On this Pole promptly progressed on his journey, and soon reached Cambray. The Court of Brussels, however, at Cromwell's instigation, had been at once threatened and terrified; so much so, indeed, that the queen-regnant, to the astonishment of many of her subjects, withheld permission for him to enter her territories. In England, Henry, at the same time (maddened by the plain home-truths which the Cardinal had told him,—a careful consideration of which at leisure had caused His Grace intense irritability), declared his kinsman to be a deeply-dyed traitor, offering fifty thousand crowns for his decapitated head; while, in return for his body delivered up alive, the King volunteered a force of four thousand soldiers, duly armed and equipped, during the war with France.

From Cambray, therefore, Pole, with due prudence, speedily went on to Liége, and then, later in the year, returned safely to Rome.

In the meantime, momentous events were taking place in England. A dark moral shadow hung over the land. Men's hearts, as of old, were failing them for fear. Might roughly putting aside Right was beheld in all its potency. Justice was being banished of purpose. Tyranny was in the ascendant, and triumphed.

The Cardinal, whether in France or elsewhere, had been received with every consideration; for his judgment of Henry's policy and doings in England was in harmony with the opinion of the most influential authorities abroad. When this reception was from time to time reported at

Greenwich or Windsor, the King, dwelling upo
it, became furious. But Pole, secure in hi
position abroad, might defy the malignity of th
monarch, though his unfortunate mother, brother
and relations in England could not.

Henry resolved, with no delay, therefore, t
compass the destruction of Henry Courteney
Marquis of Exeter, and arranged that certai
court officials should be sent into the West o
England to collect matter for accusation agains
that nobleman.[1]

Soon afterwards, Sir Geoffrey Pole, one of th
Cardinal's brothers, was arrested, brought before
the Council and committed to prison. This wa
followed by similar treatment for the Lord
Montagu, for their venerable mother, the Countess
of Salisbury, for the Marquis and Marchioness o
Exeter, and for Sir Edward Nevill, younger
brother of Lord Abergavenny. All these belonged to families which had been adherents o
the White Rose; so that, during the Northern
insurrection, had their loyalty not been very deep
and firm, they might in judicious combination
have efficiently aided the down-trodden in repudiating by force of arms the authority, dominion,
and tyrannical rule of Henry the King.

The Lords Courteney and Montagu were
arraigned before their peers late in the month

[1] "Archæologia," vol. xxii. p. 24.

of December, 1538, while early in 1539 the accused commoners were called before common juries, on vague and ill-defined charges of having endeavoured to advance one Reginald Pole, sometime Dean of Exeter, to the crown, and to deprive the reigning monarch of his title, state and dignity. Sir Geoffrey Pole was practically acquitted, but all the other persons charged were found guilty of treason, and condemned to death by decapitation. Sir Nicholas Carew was also beheaded for no other offence than having acted as Counsel to Lord Courteney.

The effect of these executions, both at home and abroad, was to create a deep-seated and universal horror amongst all classes, and to intensify the dislike of many to the King.

CHAPTER II.

ACCESSION OF QUEEN MARY, AND HER REIGN.

CONTENTS OF CHAPTER II.

Accession of Queen Mary and her Reign.—Desire for religious truth.—Thomas Cromwell's Policy condemned.—General increase of Poverty.—Loose Morality popular.—Disastrous influence of Calvinism.—Birth and Baptism of Queen Mary.—Work of the new Nobility.—Their unprincipled Policy.—Bishop Nicholas Ridley.—His treasonable Discourse.—The populace loyal to Mary, and send her military aid.—Enthusiasm of the London Citizens.—Certain Prisoners pardoned.—Protestant Plots defeated.—The true position of Queen Mary.—All Classes tainted with Errors.—Force in Government.—Fanaticism and Cant disregarded.—Loyalty of the Citizens of London.—Coronation of Queen Mary.—Enthusiasm of the People.—Lenient treatment of Cranmer.—His heresy and profanity.—Latimer's seditious demeanour.—Execution of influential Traitors.—The Emperor's advice to Queen Mary.—Lady Jane Grey.—Queen Mary's wishes and hopes.—She counsels prudence and caution.—Sir Thomas Wyat's rebellion.—Opposed by the Duke of Norfolk.—Plunder of Winchester House.—Death of Jane Grey and her husband.—Further Execution of Rebels.—Lenity and kindness of the Queen.—Deprivation of intruded Bishops.—Foreign Innovators ordered Abroad.—Cranmer and others sent to Oxford, and condemned for heresy.—Cranmer appeals to Heaven.

CHAPTER II.

THE fearful details of Henry's death—at which event he apparently believed chiefly in himself and his own works of reform,[1] rather than in his Creator—had left a deep impression upon the onlookers and those to whom the truth concerning that occurrence had been told in all its nakedness and simplicity. "All is lost!" was an awful sentence of self-condemnation with which to depart this mortal life. The disregard of this King's wishes expressed in his last Will and Testament, had astonished those acquainted with the persons to whom he had en-

[1] "The King continued yet his rigour to those that disputed either his authority or Articles; insomuch that both the Reformers and maintainers of the Pope's authority suffered so frequently that his enemies said, while he admitted neither side, he seemed to be of no religion. Howbeit, this was but calumny, for he stood firmly to his own Reformation."—*Life and Raigne of Henry the Eighth.* By Edward, Lord Herbert of Cherbury, p. 463. London, 1649.

trusted the fulfilment of his dying injunctions, and had still more astonished others unknown at the Court. The portent of dogs licking up his blood at the desolate monastery of Sion House in 1547, when a fissure had been found in his coffin on its way to Windsor—by which the well-remembered prediction of William Peto in his warning homily at Greenwich, on Easter Day, 1532, had been literally fulfilled—likewise left an impression upon the minds of the people, not easily effaced.

In consequence of all this, and the presence and pressure of practical evils, many more Englishmen than heretofore openly expressed their desire for an immediate return in religious and ecclesiastical affairs to the old order of things. Their eyes and their hearts naturally turned to the Father of the faithful. They longed for Corporate Reunion. This was so at Edward the Sixth's accession : but, six years afterwards, upon his death—after further ruin had been sealed and greater disorder made still more rampant—the feeling and desire had not only steadily deepened, but found public expression in very plain and pertinent language. However sharply some men were punished for their plain words, others were found to speak out bravely and boldly. There were many to follow in the right path, if only the leaders had led. The old regard for law and order, the ancient religious solemnities, the consolation which a True Faith and godly obedience had bestowed upon so many persons of every class and rank, were realized more and more with the advancing years.

The consequences of change and disorder at the same time were everywhere apparent. For instance, the citation of St. Thomas of Canterbury, to appear and answer ridiculous charges made at the King's suggestion,[1] had tended to bring the Courts of Law into contempt. Thomas Cromwell's policy, when adequately realized, was condemned and repudiated: first by the old nobility, who were the people's natural leaders, then by the common people themselves. Again, the monarch taking upon himself to sift divine truth from human error,[2] to judge and burn heretics, was not cal-

---

[1] The empty absurdity and acted nonsense, set forth, in deed as well as in word, by this histrionic travesty of common sense and ordinary decency, shocked Christendom when it was reported. Friends of Cardinal Pole in England took care that it *was* reported and known abroad. In Padua and in Paris it was sarcastically commented on, to the annoyance of some of the King's foreign agents. One " Richard Croke," a Buckinghamshire man, " much misliked it," as he told his relative, a person engaged in the reforming business at home.

[2] The King " did sit openly in the Hall, and presided at the disputation, process and judgment of a miserable heretic sacramentary who was burned on the twentieth of November. It was a wonder to see how princely, with how excellent gravity, and inestimable majesty, His Highness exercised there the very office of Supreme Head of the Church of England . . . . . I wish the princes and potentates of Christendom to have had a meet place to have seen it."—*Letter of Cromwell to Sir Thomas Wyat*, dated 28 Nov., 1538, preserved in the Harleian MSS., quoted in vol. iv. of Collier's " History," p. 428. London : 1845.

culated to impress favourably his Catholic subjects. In the general religious disputes and ecclesiastical disorganization, the whole nation directly suffered. The people were thus being taught by a bitter experience that God could not be insulted, robbed, and disregarded with impunity. Cardinal Pole's *Letters* show how completely he realized all this. Everywhere, therefore, poverty increased, " pauperism,"—as it was then first so expressively termed—became a living and lasting canker in the body-politic. It vexed both rulers and ruled. The enclosures of waste lands, which the upstart owners of the old monastic manors [1] and estates had proceeded to make, together with rack-renting, everywhere so cruelly enforced, had driven the yeomen and husbandmen from their old grange and cottage homes,—the meads and commons, the gentle slopes and sheltering woods around which had been so familiar to them all from generation to generation. Such men, ruined both in body and estate—for they had been treated with the greatest harshness—flocked to the chief towns and cities in the hope of keeping body and soul together; while those of the lowest and poorest class, who had so often been relieved at the gate of the adjacent monastery, went about in gangs,

---

[1] Fifty-four larger monasteries had been dissolved in London alone under Edward VI.—a fact carefully verified by me from the State Papers and the works of Sir William Dugdale.

disappointed and vexed at heart, to ask an alms of barley bread and small beer from the gentles and yeomen of the various depopulated shires, who, themselves being correspondingly overburdened with taxes and charges, and having been more than once distinctly and directly robbed by the authoritative issue of base coins,[1] were unable to aid with any effect these miserable and starving wretches who implored their assistance.

As for the morals of the people, these had notoriously become looser and most depraved. Even the "reforming preachers," and the "superintendents" of Edward the Sixth's reign admitted this to be the case. Whatever detail be considered, the same law of retribution is found to be actively and incessantly at work. It was seen to be impossible for the nation to have swallowed moral poison and to remain unaffected by its consequences. Even the designing impostors from abroad—the Bible-quoting bankrupts from Geneva, the effeminate idlers from Flanders, the unpunished convicts from Berne, Antwerp, and

---

[1] The depreciation in the value of the coinage under Edward VI. had been excessive. Such was nothing less than robbery by authority. See the printed *Proclamations* for effecting this in the Library of the Society of Antiquaries. Also Ruding's "Annals of the Coinage," vol. ii. p. 107; and the "Wardmote Book of Faversham in Kent," from which it is clear that certain property then recently valued at £120, on account of such depreciation, only realized £60—just one-half. See likewise Harl. MSS. Brit. Museum, No. 353, folio 107.

Strasburg—whom Cranmer had imported to enable him to complete the revolution, were compelled, for the sake of appearances and in order to satisfy their hearers, to moan and mourn over the immoral atrocities everywhere so current and common. Thus lying became a controversial necessity: hypocrisy a very virtue in the new preachers. The rich consequently—when they listened to picturesque word-juggling and pious self-laudation—became indifferent and callous to the wants and sufferings of the poor. Frauds of the most artfully-designed kind were perpetrated by the aid of adventurous scriveners, apostate religious, and shark - like lawyers of the lowest type. Sanctimonious usurers, who had been smitten with admiration for John Calvin's new and blasphemous gospel, became active, designing, and most iniquitous in their all-too-successful policy. For whatever such persons may have done in direct contradiction to the moral law, they believed that their own eternal salvation in the life to come was both absolutely predestinated and amply secured. Juries, at the same time, were secretly bribed, and judges often efficiently corrupted. Too often the sacrament of marriage was despised and perverted:[1] prosti-

---

[1] "The xxiiij day of November dyd ryd in a cart Cheken parsun of Sant Necolas Coldabbay [round] about London, for he sold y' wyff to a bowcher."—*Machyn's Diary, sub anno* 1553. Brit. Museum, Cotton MSS. Vitellius F. v. (damaged by fire).

tution and viler crimes were winked at, adultery
was condoned.   The old restraints upon such
notorious sins, having been deliberately removed,
it was found that the ecclesiastical courts, from
those of the Archbishops' down to the lowest local
official, having lost their divine authority—having
been cut off from the source of valid spiritual
jurisdiction—first became enervated, then para-
lyzed as regards the enunciation of truth, right,
and justice, and eventually utterly corrupt.   Subsequently, these courts were mainly maintained
and farmed for the personal benefit of their hungry
officials, who, upon the rich suitor, with his well-
filled purse, and upon the influential seeker-after-
licences in favour at Court, bestowed by vellum
instruments, drawn up in Scriptural phraseology,
full liberty for licentiousness; thus removing the
ancient and lawful restraints upon crime, and this
in return for liberal benevolences and the payment
of newly-extended fees.

Mary was born at the Palace of Greenwich on
Monday, February the 18th, 1515-16, and baptized
on the 21st of the same month in the grand church
of the Grey Friars adjacent to the Palace.   The
Princess Katherine Plantagenet and the Duchess
of Norfolk were her sponsors, Thomas Cardinal
Wolsey being her godfather.   This Sacrament,
administered in a silver font preserved at Canterbury Cathedral, was celebrated with great splen-

dour and dignity. The gifts bestowed upon the infant princess were of much value—the Duchess of Norfolk providing a richly-illuminated " Book of Hours," with highly-finished drawings of saints, and rich borders of archaic marygold-flowers, strawberries, and marguerites.

The early part of Mary's life—save as serving to illustrate her character as a monarch—is intentionally passed over, as beyond the immediate scope of this volume; it being the great principle of Corporate Reunion, sanctioned by her as Queen, and eventually carried out by Cardinal Pole, which is herein under particular consideration.

A few of the special events of the early period of the Queen's reign, however, need detailed notice. Those only, nevertheless, that bear directly upon the subject of this volume—a mere historical sketch—need be dealt with at any length. But such, in certain cases, may be found to demand careful amplification, so that the full importance of the leading subject referred to may, in all its bearings, be adequately realized.

And here let one of the darkest features of the period, mainly the work of the newly set-up nobility and their creatures, often men of low birth, but of great capacity and cunning, be duly remarked.

The endeavour of the Duke of Northumberland to exclude Mary from the throne was certainly and at once artful, well-designed, and bold. The innovating party to a man, knowing their own rickety position, were in favour of it. Edward VI. had been induced in his last Will and Testament to leave each of his sisters £1,000; while the supposed claims of Lady Jane Grey were being everywhere pressed forward, upon the death of Edward, which had taken place on the 6th of July, 1553. It was believed by some—and the rumour gained strength and coherence during its passage from lip to lip and from place to place—that Northumberland had hastened the death of the Duke of Somerset.[1] Anyhow the stakes for which the former had played were heavy, and his method in playing for them was adroit and vigorous.

This nobleman, both from accurately gauging public utterances and from private information, mistrusted the adherence of the citizens of London. Nevertheless (as he thought he was able to forecast) Bigotry, duly sustained by Falsehood and Cant, might exercise a certain practical influence; so he formally exhorted the "licensed preachers" of the Boy-King to become more noisy and active on his behalf, and to continue the work they had always done of stirring up the perverted and detestable sentiments of all the rabble-audiences which flocked together to be amused, flattered, and cajoled.

Nicholas Ridley, validly but irregularly conse-

---

[1] Harl. MSS. Brit. Museum, No. 353, folio 121.

crated,[1] who in 1547 had been intruded into the diocese of London without election or confirmation, but merely by that most unprecedented method, the issue of Letters Patent, had shown himself an earnest and determined innovator. His innovations commenced with his rejection of the Ancient Faith in its completeness and integrity, these were continued in the mode of episcopal consecration he was ready to receive, wanting due and ancient spiritual authority; and were crowned in the unworthy and dangerous work he had been so willing, at Northumberland's suggestion, to undertake.

On the following Sunday, therefore, this Nicholas Ridley appeared in the stone pulpit at St. Paul's Cross, to address the Lord Mayor, the sheriffs, several of the aldermen, and a goodly concourse of citizens. It was a fair day in July. The sunshine fell upon the stately cathedral in warmth and splendour. Its lofty spire and carved pinnacles, with the light and beautiful flying-buttresses,

---

[1] " The practice uniformly pursued by the Catholic Church," remarks a clear and lucid writer on the subject, " was to acknowledge the validity of the orders conferred during schism, provided they were conferred according to the Catholic rite and preserved the form and intention of the Church, but to deny and ignore the jurisdiction of bishops who were consecrated without the licence, and in contempt of the authority, of the Pope [Ridley's case exactly], and to deny the validity of all the orders or consecrations which were performed according to the Protestant Ritual."—*The Episcopal Succession*, vol. iii. p. 18. By W. Maziere Brady. Rome : 1877.

clustering round tower and transepts,[1] stood out against the deep blue sky. Below, the external galleries of its northern transept, facing the out-door pulpit, were filled by a gathering of notables; while the populace in general, citizens, apprentices, and artizans, stood in closely-packed groups around its canopied structure, anticipating a lively dialectical performance. They were not disappointed. The preacher maintained by a queer kind of logic that both the daughters of Henry VIII. were illegitimate. That Elizabeth Boleyne was in this state few then doubted. But as regards Mary, the Queen, his assertion was distinctly and directly false—so false indeed that no homiletical rhetoric, however artfully phrased, could make it even seem to be true. The preacher was remarkably free with his remarks on the " two competitors for the throne," as he termed them. The Lady Jane, in his judgment, was pious, orthodox, and gentle; Mary was haughty, Papistical, and bigoted. Such a judgment from such a person was at once untrue, impertinent, and unjust, while his previous assertions were distinctly treasonable.

But Mary, who had been kept well informed of the course of events, was at Hunsdon when the fact of her brother's death was communicated to her. Thither had gone true and confidential

---

[1] See an oil painting of this cathedral in the apartments of the Society of Antiquaries, Burlington House.

friends. She thus soon learnt of the proclamation of Lady Jane Grey, which Northumberland had enjoined to be made. In conjunction with her trustiest advisers and truest friends, therefore, Mary took every lawful and proper means to disabuse the people of misrepresentations actively circulated,[1] and to defend her obvious rights. A few friends—tried and trusty—who acted together with determination, zeal and prompt vigour, were worth some hundreds of mere word-splitters and boasting brawlers, as events proved.

Within a week no less than thirty thousand men, from all parts of the kingdom, devoted to her person and cause,[2] gathered together, refusing any pay for their services.

[1] The following is copied from an original printed impression of the Queen's Proclamation:—

"Marie the Quene,—

"Knowe ye all the good subjects of this Realme, that yor most noble Prince yor Souraigne Lord & King, Edward the VIth is upon thursday last dep'ted this world to God's marcie. And that now the most excellent Princes, his sister Marie, by the grace of God ye Quene of E. & Y. and verie owner of the Crowne, Government and tytle of E. & Y. and all things thereunto belonging, to God's glory, the honor of the royalme of England, and all yor comfortes. And her Highness is not fledd thys royalme, ne intendeth to do, as ye most contraly surmysed."

[2] The following sets forth the opinion then held in Lincolnshire:—"And so tolde me that the Lady Jane was p'claymed at London, as a frend of his told hyme at Grantham, wiche was newe come from London, and hard hir p'claimed. And I said God forbyde y^t shulde be so, for she hade no right to the Crowne; and the Quenes majestie was here-apparent to the Crowne of Englond, & that hir grace shuld have hir right, or else there wold be the bloddyest day for hir grace that ever was in

" In the East of England the Earl of Essex, Lord Thomas Howard, with the Pastons, Bedingfields, and Jerninghams of those parts had risen in behalf of their lawful sovereign. The Earls of Bath and Sussex had loyally done the same some days previously. From Oxfordshire and Buckinghamshire Sir Edward Peckham, Sir John Williams, and Sir Robert Drury had levied, and co-operated in equipping, nearly ten thousand men, who were assembled at Lord Paget's suggestion near West Drayton. From Thame nearly a hundred sturdy yeomen and others marched thither under the command of Captain William Lee, prepared to dare and do on behalf of their rightful Queen." [1]

The enthusiasm was everywhere great. On the 19th of July, consequently, she was proclaimed Queen,[2] and on the 3rd of August, as lawful

England.   .   .   .   And I told hyme that Quene Mary shulde be p'claimed Quene of Englonde, and shuld Raigne Quene over us as long as pleased God, or els I and an hundred thowsande such as I would p'rish for her grece's sake."—From *A Petition of Richard Troughton to the Privy Council*, Harl. MSS., Nos. 6,215-6,232.

[1] " History of the Prebendal Church of Thame," folio, p. 71. London : 1883.

[2] This was done [*i.e.*, Mary proclaimed Queen] "at the Crosse in Chepe, and from that plasse they whent unto Powlls and ther was *Te Deum Laudamus*, with song, and the organes playhyng, and all the belles ryngyng through London, and bone fyrres, & tabuls in evere strett, & wyne and bere and all, and evere strett full of bonefyres, and ther was money cast away."—*Diary of Machyn*, Cotton MSS. Vitellius, F. v. *sub anno* 1553.

monarch, made her triumphal entry into the City of London. Ten thousand of the flower of the upper classes accompanied her on horseback in costly and picturesque habiliments, the old nobility ever conspicuous; while the sympathy and applause of the population in general, cheering the Queen to the echo, were at once hearty and general.

The home-made heretics, like moles and bats, withdrew from the sunshine into shadow.[1] The foreign importations, whose new Gospel was not on that occasion in very great request or favour, raging at Fate, gnashed their teeth with disappointment and fury.

It was a marvellous sight, thus described by a contemporary:—

"Greate was the triumph hear at London; for my tyme I never saw the lyke, & by the reporte of otheres the lyke was never seen. The nomber of cappes that were throwne uppe at y* Proclemation wear not to be tould. The Earle of Pembroche threwe awaye his cape full of aigelletes. I saw myselfe money was throwne out at windowes for joye. The bonfires weare withoute

---

[1] In certain of the foreign cities to which they had hoped to resort, and from which their own reforming allies had been originally imported by Cranmer, the municipal authorities refused them permission to settle, on the reasonable ground that the moral and political principles they advocated were calculated to disturb law and order, and to promote unrest, dissatisfaction, and sedition.

nomber, & what withe showting and cryinge of the people & rynginge of belles, theare could noe one man heare almost what an other sayde, besides bankettinge & supping in the strete for joye."[1]

At the Tower of London a touching incident occurred. On the approach of the Queen, near to the little churchyard of St. Peter, the State prisoners, who had been confined by the mere wills or decrees of Henry VIII. and his son, were found humbly kneeling upon the green. Edward Courteney, a prisoner even from his youth, heir to the Earl of Devon, supported the aged Duke of Norfolk, under sentence of death, as the latter bent his feeble knees. Side by side with these knelt the Duchess of Somerset, who first greeted Her Majesty, while those irregularly-deprived bishops, Stephen Gardiner and Cuthbert Tonstall, addressed her with congratulations and supplication.

For a few moments, glancing at each, and soon recognizing all, and bursting into tears, she most kindly and charitably raised them up one by one, exclaiming, " Ye are my prisoners now, good friends and cozens." Then kissing them each on the forehead, and extending her right hand to be kissed in turn by all, she at once gave them their liberty. The officers of the Tower soon made known what had taken place. From the throng at

---

[1] See also Cotton MSS., Vitellius, F. v. folio 19, and Harl. MSS. No. 353, folio 139.

the Tower-gates shouts of wildest acclamation were heard.

All the details of this day, with its outburst of joy and satisfaction, were duly reported to Cardinal Pole at Rome. Friends and relatives seem to have vied with each other in obtaining true reports, and in transmitting them to that Prince of the Church without change or exaggeration. Thus high and noble hopes were born at Rome—some of which were soon realized, and others in the end dashed to the ground and destroyed.

Thus, the detestable plot of the chief advisers of the deceased Boy-King, and certain of the new aristocracy, to exclude the rightful heiress to the throne, was utterly brought to nought, as Justice determined; and this by the almost unanimous voice of the people; who, though for half a century they had been both demoralized and degraded by the public policy of Henry VIII. and his son, were anxious that the old order of things, both in religion and social order, in Church and State, should be at once restored. Mary, the Queen, therefore, by God's favour, came out from the deep shadow of persecution, neglect, and bitter suffering,[1] into

---

[1] The following forcible and noble sentence, from the pen of the late Sir Frederick Madden, F.S.A., deserves to be here reproduced : " The deeply-rooted principles of the Princess, which had enabled her, when she had scarcely attained the age of womanhood, to resist the menaces of a tyrant father and his myrmidons, ought to have convinced the counsellors of the new monarch

the full sunshine of a people's favour, a nation's welcome, and the benediction of Providence. In time, however, the shadows gathered anew and became deeper and darker. To many the change at her accession seemed a distinct divine blessing: to a few it appeared like a very miracle.[1]

Her position as Queen, however—when the actual circumstances were truly faced—was full of the gravest practical difficulties. When she assumed the sceptre and first wore the crown, the people were found to have become both demoralized and degraded[2] by the revolution in religion which had

[Edward VI.] how vain would be the attempt to force her conscience, or, by the whining of a boy and the mandates of an upstart nobleman, to subdue the spirit which had for so many years learned how to endure oppression."—*Privy Purse Expenses of the Princess Mary*, p. cv.   London: 1831.

[1] Thus far John Foxe wrote: "God so turned the hearts of the people to her, and against the Council, that she overcame them without bloodshed, notwithstanding there was made great expedition against her both by sea and land." See also Lansdowne MSS., Brit. Museum, No. 840, A, folio 155, in which Michele, the Venetian Ambassador, beautifully and earnestly records his similar convictions.

Dr. Nicholas Sander—his words are translated—is identical in his historical record: "After a schism which had lasted twenty years God vouchsafed the victory in a wonderful manner to Mary, the Catholic princess, over almost all the nobles of the kingdom; and this was effected without shedding one drop of blood. Here, then, was an obvious miracle in favour of the Catholic Faith, wrought before the whole world."—*D. V. Nicholai Sanderi, De Origine et Progressu Schismatis Anglicani, Liber.* Lib. iii. 1.   Coloniae Agrippinae, A.D. 1585.

[2] Queen Mary writes from St. James's, Jan. 22, 1553, to Sir Hugh Pollard and others of Devonshire.   Evil-disposed persons

been so artfully effected. Such had touched and tainted every class. Such had besmeared politics [1] with its false principles; and tinctured social order and family life with its practical and pernicious evils. Mary, however, clinging firmly to the faith of her forefathers—to that which St. Augustine had brought hither nine hundred years before, and in which St. Thomas, and More, and Fisher, and her own saintly mother in the flesh had so recently died—found herself in the hands of those advisers who, as they believed, for the safety of the State,

thereabouts are reported to be endeavouring to hinder the Catholic religion being practised, and divine service as of old restored. A little later, that is, on Feb. 4, 1553, Sir John St. Leger writes to the Council that Devonshire is now well-affected to the Queen, and that divine service is every-where attended. Similar information is also intimated to Mr. Secretary Petre.—*State Papers*, Public Record Office, *sub anno* 1553. In the same year an Order in Council, held at Hampton Court, was formally made to find out whether John Barnarde and John Walshe carried about with them the bones of one Pigott, executed, representing them to be relics, and enjoining the people to resist the reimposition of the ancient faith.—Harl. MSS., No. 643, folio 45 b.

[1] "The political side of the movement (of Luther) was in some respects the most important, for it transferred from one class to another not far short of one-third of the whole landed interest of the Empire. It was indeed a bitter day to the very poor, for they lost many a kind friend, many a comfortable night's lodging, and many a hearty meal at old abbey gates ; but spendthrift nobles and rollicking citizens became rich again, and vied with each other in establishing petty princedoms and here-ditary honours which shone with the glamour of almost sacred traditions."—*Centenary Studies*, by Edwin de Lisle, p. 78. London : 1884.

were ready to apply the same strong measures to
their opponents as their opponents, when they had
had the opportunity, had applied to them. Herein
Reginald Pole, the exile, duly surveying the situation, was somewhat at variance with those personally near the Queen, counselling caution, prudence,
and care. There is, of course, much to be said for
vigour of method in governing. If mild measures
and mere nominal punishments avail not for the
malignant and the incurably-malicious, stronger
and more disagreeable methods often have to be
adopted. Such methods are universal. Without
Force there can be no actual government. The
English laws against the disorderly—traitors, sub-
verters of the constitution, obstinate heretics,
schismatics, murderers, and blasphemers — were
certainly strong, and perhaps not at all too strong.
It was those iniquitious personal enactments of
Henry VIII. and Edward VI., however, formulated
by their own mere malignant motions, or at the
suggestion of their favourite advisers, and put into
operation because of the efficacy of Tudor privy-
seal and sign-manual only, which so tended to
elevate cruelty to an art, and brought direct discredit upon all the mere official instruments by
whom such disagreeable enactments had to be
actually and painfully enforced.[1]

---

[1] Persecution of all who ventured to hold opinions contrary to
those favoured by authority was a general rule of policy with

Though Northumberland, for his own personal convenience, had kept the officers and servants of the Crown three years in arrears of their salaries, the Queen at once issued two Proclamations, which were everywhere received with unfeigned thankfulness. Through the first Proclamation, the base money issued by her brother's advisers was called in, and a new coinage, of great and singular purity, and of fair artistic character, was issued. The loss involved was borne by the Treasury. Through the second Proclamation, she remitted to her subjects, as some acknowledgment of their devotion, certain hard and pressing taxes, the removal of which was everywhere greatly appreciated.

The fanaticism of the men who preached the new religion had been such that robes and dresses suitable to the rank and dignity of the upper classes, as well as all innocent and rational amusement, had been everywhere condemned.[1] Gloominess in garb and feature had gone hand in hand with Cant, while Hypocrisy stood by with upturned eyes and deep sepulchral utterances. Such,

every communion in the sixteenth century ; and this fact accounts for, though it cannot justify, the conduct of the Queen of England and the contemporary King of France, as well as that of Cranmer and Calvin."—*Annals of England*, p. 325. London : 1876.

[1] This subject is dealt with at length in a letter dated " from Richmond, near London," in August, 1552, sent from James Haddon (sometime Prebendary of Westminster) to Henry Bullinger.

however, was all altered at Court. England became "Merry England" again for a few years —a change cordially welcomed in every class; though a few gloomy and melancholy fanatics like Aylmer were found to condemn it.

So early as the 12th of September the citizens of London began to adorn their official and private houses for the coronation. The houses were hung with standards, Turkey carpets, rich tapestry, cloths of gold and silver, and heraldric devices. The Genoese merchants bore the charges of one of the most elaborate displays in the City, where music was heard without intermission, ballads recited—"the goodlyest playing with all maner of musyssoners" (as is on record)—continuing all day long. Pageants were duly prepared with great elaboration in Fenchurch Street and Gracechurch Street, in Cornhill, Cheapside, St. Paul's Church-yard, Ludgate, and Fleet Street. These attracted crowds. Everywhere the old religious ideas were now found in the forefront.

On the 30th of the same month the accustomed Royal Procession made its way from the Tower to Westminster—the populace greeting the Queen with a cordiality and heartiness which deeply im-pressed the foreign ambassadors and greatly dis-comfited the new men.

At the Queen's coronation in Westminster Abbey, on the 1st of October, all the ancient customs were restored, with the Catholic rite, carefully rendered by Bishop Gardiner, of Winchester. "It was done royally," wrote Fabyan, "and such a multitude of people resorted out of all parties of the realm to see the same, that the like had not been seen tofore." Every important detail in the stately ceremony of anointing and coronation[1] was performed with scrupulous care. Scarcely a single high officer of the State was absent. These and all witnessed a rite of remarkable splendour and rife with such an outpouring of divine grace.

The Mass of the Holy Ghost was said with every due and proper act and ceremony. No respected precedent nor ancient custom was disregarded. The *Gloria in excelsis* and *Credo*, with the special *Offertorium*, were chanted by two clustering bands of choristers and singing-men in rochets, over scarlet cassocks embroidered with gold; and this after the ancient mode. Round the lighted altar, under the very shadow of St. Edward's shrine, where seven newly-kindled lamps burned, were gathered, in cope and mitre, prelates true to the Faith and priests loyal to the Father of the faithful. When the thick incense-cloud was scattered by the

---

[1] In the sanctuary Elizabeth Boleyne, who appeared as a Catholic, carried the crown. She is said to have whispered to M. Noailles, "It is mightily heavy." He promptly replied, "Be patient, madam; it will seem much lighter when you find it on your own head."

sunshine, the duly anointed Queen was seen prostrate at her faldstool before receiving the Bread of Life at the hands of Gardiner, and pledged herself anew to respect the freedom and independence of the Church, and to restore the ancient Faith.

Even an opponent paints the picture with perfect accuracy and considerable colour. Not in London alone, but elsewhere, in other cities, the joy was evidently sincere, and the longing for ecclesiastical peace and oneness hearty :—

" The Papists, who had been always longing for this most-wished-for day, dig out, as it were, from their graves their vestments, chalices, portasses (*i.e.*, breviaries), and begin Mass with all speed. In these things our Oxford folk lead the van. . . . . At the Proclamation of Mary—even before she was proclaimed at London, and when the event was still doubtful—they gave such demonstrations of joy as to spare nothing. They first of all made so much noise all the day long with clapping their hands that it seems still to linger in my ears. They then, even the poorest of them, made voluntary subscriptions, and mutually exhorted each other to maintain the cause of Mary. Lastly, at night, they had a public festival, and threatened flames, hanging, the gallows, and drowning to all the Gospellers." [1]

---

[1] Dated from Strasburg, 20th Nov., 1553, and written by

After Elizabeth's apparent return to the Catholic Faith—a mere pretence, as subsequent events served to prove,—the various innovators had not unreasonably looked to Thomas Cranmer for his personal and practical aid in their gathering difficulties.   As yet, Queen Mary's advisers had given no cause of complaint for very harsh treatment of the Archbishop at all.   On the contrary, he had been more than leniently dealt with.   Himself the artful and astute author of the late Queen Katherine's divorce, the actual decreer of Queen Mary's so-called " bastardy," the foremost clerical conspirator under Northumberland against his lawful Sovereign; while, from the outset of his archiepiscopal career, he had craftily perjured himself in St. Stephen's Chapel at Westminster, on the day of his irregular consecration, in several respects a dangerous and evil-principled man,—he certainly deserved a far heavier punishment than at first he received.

For he was merely directed to confine himself within the precincts of Lambeth House—no great hardship, and no particular inconvenience.

There, it is stated that he grew moody, as, upon due reflection, well he might, considering the almost inconceivable mischief he had wrought both to Church and State.   There he began to

Julius Terentianus, who had just come from England, and probably from Oxford, to John ab Ulmis.

learn and note that his hopes for working further mischief were apparently dashed to the ground; and that the Calvinistic and Zuinglian orgies which for several recent years had degraded and defiled the ancient Catholic cathedrals and churches of his country, were evidently to come to an end.

Within a week of his confinement, news was privately brought to him by some of his foreign friends that the ancient Christian rites had with pomp and dignity been restored at Canterbury; and, as certain dwellers in that city averred, at his own official instigation and desire. It was furthermore added that he himself had been reported as anxious to say Mass in the presence of his Sovereign, and to reverse at once and openly, by present action, his past innovations and heretical teaching.

To this report—at hearing which he became furious—he gave a prompt, violent and bitter denial; reiterating his profane and shocking assertion that Holy Mass "was a device and invention of the Devil, the father of lies," and declaring that he was most anxious to show the people, as well as the Queen, that it involved "horrid blasphemies." [1]

He also undertook to prove that the Calvinistic and Zuinglian orgies referred to, were almost

[1] "Archæologia," vol. xviii. p. 175.

absolutely identical with the rites and doctrines current everywhere during the first ages of Christianity. The document itself, in which these random assertions were set forth, printed and circulated, was, from any point of view, a despicable production. As a theological statement, however, it was plainly absurd and misleading; while its publication, as a matter of State policy, was at once seditious, dangerous, and, for the sake of the misguided multitude—ever delighting in wordy contentions, popular disputations, and artful hair-splitting—thoroughly deserving of prompt condemnation.

This, without delay, it received. For the Council, having requested the attendance of Cranmer, relaxed the benevolence already mistakenly shown, and committed him to the Tower.

Hugh Latimer, another of the same destructive gang, equally heretical, bitterly persecuting[1] and much more violent in his words and predictions, because of his "seditious demeanour," often so ostentatiously and abundantly made manifest, was very properly sent to the same place.

---

[1] The indelicacy and indecency of the pulpit under these persons was notable. Take for instance Hugh Latimer's persecuting discourse before Edward VI. :—"There lacketh a fourth to make up the mess, which so God help me, if I were judge, should be *Hangum tuum*, a Tybourne typpet, to take with him; if it were the Judge of the King's Bench, the Lord Chief Justice of England; yea, if it be my Lord Chancellor himself."

The Duke of Northumberland and his son, the Earl of Warwick, were tried for treason before the Duke of Norfolk, Lord High Steward, and their peers. They pleaded guilty on the 18th of August, 1553, no other plea, when the facts are known and noted, being open to them.

Sir John Gates, Sir Henry Gates, Sir Andrew Dudley, and Sir Thomas Palmer,—Northumberland's most active allies—were, on the following day, tried upon a similar charge, and, the facts being patent and undisputed, these pleaded guilty likewise.

Of the above, only the Duke of Northumberland, Sir Thomas Palmer, and Sir John Gates, were beheaded on the 22nd of the same month. Face to face with death, these unhappy men all openly professed the ancient Faith, warning the onlookers in terms evidently coming from their hearts, against sedition and irreligion.[1] Such sentiments, at such an end, were good and edifying.

[1] John Banks, one of the Duke's servants, gives a somewhat different account in regard to his master, as follows :—" Certain wicked wretches endeavoured to draw him away, while in prison, from the faith and confession of the true Christ. But they were in no wise able to move him, for he confessed the Lord Christ even to his latest breath. And at the same time he was led to execution, though the Papists brought forth one of the Council, a swine out of the herd, who defended the Catholic Church (!) the mass, the fathers, and customs established by length of time,. yet he would not acknowledge any other atonement than that which was perfected by the death of Christ."—*Letter from John Banks to Henry Bullinger, " from London,"* March 15, 1554.

On the following day, Stephen Gardiner, Bishop of Winchester—who, with other prisoners, had been released from the Tower on the 3rd of August, and reinstated in his See—was formally made Lord High Chancellor. He was likewise elected Chancellor of the University of Cambridge, and there did a good work.[1]

Nothing, it may here be remarked, could have been wiser nor kinder than the advice which the Emperor Charles V. tendered to Mary with regard to the Duke of Northumberland and his co-conspirators. The Emperor evidently took in at a glance the wide field of political and ecclesiastical controversy, and its baneful influence upon Christian states. Upon such a view he acted both with charity and wisdom. Of all those in England who were engaged in that nefarious plot of robbing the rightful heiress of her crown, and the people of a pious and benevolent monarch, only seven, as has been shown, were selected for prompt and im-mediate trial. All these had notoriously been in close alliance, in order to compass their base and unworthy object. Existing laws, perfectly righteous and just, they disregarded. They had

---

[1] The Queen, from Richmond Palace, August 20, 1553, writes to Bishop Gardiner, Chancellor of the University of Cambridge, and others, commanding that the ancient statutes, foundations and ordinances of the University be inviolably kept and observed. —*State Papers, Record Office.*

stuck at nothing in the details of their scheme. In its initiation, falsehood, chicanery, bribery, perjury, had one and all been enlisted to aid the conspirators in their dangerous undertaking. Their dupes were numerous and in earnest. They saw unerringly how much depended upon their personal success, and what would be irretrievably lost if they failed. Never, therefore, were such conspirators against the Monarch more deserving of prompt and righteous punishment. The Emperor would have had Lady Jane Grey included in their number. For though her youth was attractive and her person fair and noble, yet her shallow and sentimental cant—though she may have acted according to her light—was distasteful to many, while her religious principles were false and dangerous. But Mary—though it was pointed out to her that if this advice were short-sightedly neglected, she could never reign in security—could not, as she asserted, find in her heart and conscience to send her unfortunate cousin to the block. For such must be the issue of her trial. Lady Jane, as the Queen so truly and charitably averred, had been rather a puppet than an accomplice. Dangers arising from her pretensions to the crown, as Mary hoped and trusted, were but imaginary and fantastic. Such need not be seriously contemplated.

Pope Julius III. appointed Cardinal Reginald Pole his Legate to Her Majesty, but His Eminence, being exceedingly anxious to find out exactly how public events and feeling stood,[1] suggested to Dandino, the accomplished Papal Legate at Brussels, to send over some trusted and confidential ally to England with this object in view, and to make inquiries on various points. Gianfrancisco Commendone, the person selected, —and an excellent selection it seems to have been —at once started from Gravelines for London, where, accidentally meeting one of the Royal Household, William Lee, obtained through him a private audience with the Queen. Her Majesty at once frankly stated her wishes, asserting that no desire lay nearer her heart or was more sincere, than that England should be corporately restored to visible communion with the Holy See. But no one knew the obstacles more accurately than herself, nor apprehended more exactly the difficulties, both proximate and remote, which stood in the way of success. The innovators had both bribed the upper and middle classes with Church plunder, and demoralized the lower classes by proclaiming vicious principles and immoral enactments. Prejudice was deep, and the Court of Rome by many mistrusted.

---

[1] All this, and more, may be gathered from a study of Cardinal Pole's *Letters*. How thoroughly he was informed of English affairs, and how accurately he judged of his nation's need, may be abundantly and distinctly gathered from the same.

Her Majesty, however, further assured Commendone that she meant to set about procuring the repeal of all such laws as trenched on the True Christian Faith, or upon the ancient and desirable discipline of the Catholic Church, and this without any needless delay.

At the same time she earnestly expressed a hope that no difficulties might be raised at Rome; and that the Sacred Pontiff himself might do all in his power to smooth the path of progress for such necessary negotiations, and both by art and charity advance the sacred cause of Reunion. She furthermore added that if the project were to succeed, it would be essential for all concerned to act with the greatest prudence, the most equable temper, and the utmost caution; to take into consideration recent changes and disturbing events, the attitude of conflicting parties and interests, the existing state of disorder in religion, and the obvious prejudices, both political and ecclesiastical, of many of her subjects. At the same time no trace of any private communications with the Holy See, or with Cardinal Pole, should, as she advised, be permitted to be discovered or made public. Here were true wisdom and real charity.

In the Parliament which had been dissolved at the close of 1553, a distinct and perhaps uncalled-for expression of dislike at the Queen's contemplated marriage with Philip of Spain, son of the

Emperor Charles V., was heard. To this objection the Queen replied with perfect truth and admirable dignity:—" For their loyal wishes, and their desire that her issue might succeed her, she thanked them; but, inasmuch as they essayed to limit her in the choice of a husband, she thanked them not. For the marriages of her predecessors had been perfectly free, nor would she surrender a privilege that concerned her more than it did her Commons."

Sir Thomas Wyat,[1] of Allington Castle, in Kent, a youth of twenty-three, son of Sir Thomas, the poet, in conjunction with Sir James Croft, Sir Nicholas Throckmorton, Sir William Pickering, and Sir Nicholas Arnold, had already combined to hinder the same. To these were subsequently joined, in the Midland counties, The Duke of Suffolk, his brother Thomas, Lord Grey and his sons, who, towards the close of January in the following year, had vainly endeavoured to raise troops at Leicester. Sir Peter Carew, a violent and bitter Calvinist, in Cornwall, with a like

[1] This Sir Thomas Wyat was nephew, by marriage, of Sir Anthony Lee, of Quarrendon, co. Bucks, Knt., the first lady of the last-named having been Margaret, daughter of Sir Henry Wyat, and sister of Sir Thomas, the Poet, of Allington Castle, co. Kent; and it is said by Browne Willis, of Whaddon Hall, that there remained some very interesting letters and papers at Quarrendon, Bucks, in regard to this Rebellion until about the year 1712, when the family of Lee moved to their Oxfordshire mansion.

object, had equally failed, upon which he fled to France; and the same was the case with Croft in Wales. Wyat himself was at first more successful. He had gathered no less than 2,000 men at Rochester, the Castle and bridge of which city were promptly and efficiently fortified.

The old Duke of Norfolk, a great general, was sent against Wyat, and had a certain Captain Brett and five hundred of the City trainbands under his command. Brett, however, was secretly in harmony with Wyat, to whom he openly revolted at Rochester. On seeing that so large a part of his force refused to fight against Wyat, the Duke was obliged to retire, and flee for his life.

Sir Thomas Wyat, who thus by treachery was enabled to reach Deptford on the 1st of February, maintained, in answer to a herald from the Queen, that Her Majesty should change her advisers, give up the Tower of London to him, and take up her abode there under his custody. He was but the tool of the irreligious innovators, and was evidently in his random arrogance, actively inspired by them. At the same time, on the other hand, the promptest action was being taken in the cities of London and Westminster; and this with vigour and effect. The spirit of the true-hearted Queen, sustained and strengthened by her faith, never either flagged or fell. In direct response, loyalty was everywhere apparent. At the same time, Mary was constant at her devotions, committing her cause to God and the Saints. On the morning of Candlemass, at daybreak, Dr. Weston said Mass in Whitehall Chapel with a coat-of-mail under his cassock and chasuble. Lord William Howard was made Lieutenant of the City of London, and the Earl of Pembroke General of the Queen's armies in the field. Later in the day the Queen went to the Guildhall, animating her supporters by her presence and bearing.

In Kent Wyat's forces advanced up to Southwark, where they broke into and plundered the Palace of the Bishop of Winchester. The fanatical destruction here wrought was appalling. Pictures, works of religious art, literary treasures, were all destroyed. Most of Wyat's leading supporters were fanatical " new-men."   " They left not a lock on a door," as Stowe the chronicler declared, " or a book in his gallery uncut or rent into pieces; so that men might have gone up to the knees in leaves of books cut and thrown under foot." They were, however, unable to force the southern gates of London Bridge. On marking the guns of the Tower pointed against his forces, Wyat on the 6th of February prudently marched on to Kingston-upon-Thames, hoping by a round-about and unanticipated, but certainly bold, course to surprise the Queen in her palace at Whitehall. He advanced from Kingston so far as the Knightsbridge fields, where it was found that the royal forces had been efficiently posted. These, with the main part of his followers, he seems to have avoided by a feint; but received a direct and vigorous attack from Sir John Gage a little to the west of the village of Charing. At Ludgate, Lord William Howard was so successful in defending that point of the City, that Wyat, perceiving his efforts were fruitless, and his rebellion was then in vain, surrendered himself to Sir Maurice Berkeley, and was soon afterwards conveyed to the Tower.

There can be little doubt that all these varied insurrections had been secretly planned in conjunction with the heads of the so-called " Reforming-party," and this with the direct intention of hindering the restoration of the old order of things and Corporate Reunion. The bitterness and malignancy of the innovators were deep, while the loose principles regarding authority adopted by them, was soon seen to be a direct and actual danger to the State. For without authority obedience dwindled and died out.

As a consequence of this rebellion, Lady Jane Grey and her husband, Lord Guilford Dudley, suffered death. Much sympathy has been reasonably enough given to their sad memories and suffering, because of their youth and good looks, and because they had evidently been used as useful puppets by daring adventurers and able schemers for supreme power—to whom their misfortunes and deaths were directly due. It was believed, and not altogether wrongly it is to be feared, that their friends and allies had secretly approved and fostered the rising. Hitherto their confinement in the Tower had been anything but rigorous.[1] By an Order in Council, dated so far back as December 17th, 1553, because " that divers be and have been ill at ease in their bodies for want of air," Lady Jane herself, the Dudleys, and Thomas Cranmer were permitted to have " the liberty of the walks within the gardens of the Tower."

The Duke of Suffolk, Lady Jane's father, was tried by his peers and convicted on February the 17th; her uncle, Sir Thomas Grey, pleaded guilty on March the 9th, and was executed on April the 27th. Sir Thomas Wyat pleaded guilty on March the 15th, and suffered death upon April the 11th. Sir Nicholas Throckmorton and Sir James Croft were tried on April the 17th: the former was acquitted; the latter, on a second trial, convicted and then pardoned.

[1] The same had been the case on a previous occasion :—" At Richmonde the x day of Sept., aº 1553—a letter to the Lieutenant of the Towere whereby he is willed to permitte these Ladyes following to have accesse unto their Husbandes, and there to tarry with them so long and at such tymes as by him shalbe thought convenyente. That is to say the Lord Ambrose's wife, the Lord Robarte's wife, Sir Francis Jobsoue's wife, Sir Henry Gattes his wife, and Sir Richard Corbett's wife."—*Harleian MSS.*, *Brit. Museum*, No 643, folio 8.

The Queen displayed remarkable lenity in dealing with the insurgents in general. Utterly unlike her father and brother, and contrary to advice tendered by certain persons, she showed great mercy and much kindness. Of the hundreds of prisoners, who were either taken in arms or war, or who subsequently surrendered themselves in the hope of pardon, not a tenth received any punishment at all. They were looked upon as the dupes — sometimes fanatical, occasionally passive—of their leaders, and were graciously forgiven.

On February the 20th, no less than four hundred rebel soldiers had been taken in pairs before the Queen in the Tilt-yard at Westminster with halters round their necks; and then, on promise of future good behaviour, were generously set at liberty.[1]

About the same time, in order that no delay should occur in the restoration of the Old Religion, formal Injunctions were issued to the bishops to restore the ancient laws as they had been in force under Henry the Eighth—the Oath of Supremacy *in spiritualibus* being abandoned; and Proclamations were sent to the different shires to restore without further delay religious oneness of worship and faith.[2]

---

[1] Machyn's *Diary, sub anno* 1553. Cott. MSS., Brit. Museum, Vitellius, F. v.

[2] For evidence on this point, may be consulted the " Proclamation by the Queen for avoiding the inconvenience and

The married clergy—some of whom were disreputable in their methods, having allied themselves to women of the lowest class [1] and loosest characters—were either expelled from their benefices, or separated from their wives. The scandals created by many of them were deep and dark. From early times, it had been held that a priest was already married to the Church; and, consequently, if he took a wife, he was as much looked upon as a bigamist as a layman would be now regarded who might secure to himself two wives at the same time. On Sunday, the 4th of November, 1554, three married priests, and two laymen, both of whom had actually married two wives each, did public penance at St. Paul's Cross. [2]

About this period, other desirable personal changes were made without delay. Robert Holgate, who occupied the See of York, Paul Bushe, of Bristol, John Bird of Chester, Robert Ferrar of Gloucester, John Harley of Hereford, and John Taylor of Lincoln, were one and all deprived of their Sees. Judged by the ancient laws of

dangers which have arisen in times past through the diversity of opinions in questions of religion." Dated Aug. 18, 1553.—*State Papers, Record Office*

[1] One " Checken parson of St. Nicholas Cole Abbey," sold his wife to a butcher, as Machyn, in his *Diary* puts on record; giving elsewhere other cases of scandal caused by the clergy in connection with this relaxation of discipline.

[2] Machyn's *Diary, sub anno* 1554.

England, and those of the Church of God, these men were traitorous, heretical, irregular, and intruders.   William Barlow of Bath and Wells—the very curse of the various Sees he had held—wisely and at once resigned; while John Scory of Chichester, promptly abandoning his wife, and submitting to the needful penance, avoided resignation or expulsion : though he was soon afterwards promptly turned out, when his numerous moral delinquencies had been adequately established.

On the 17th of February, 1554—the work of true reform thus progressing—the congregations of foreign innovators were authoritatively ordered to quit the realm. While such were considering their action under this laudable and most necessary order, Coxe, Grindal, Horne and other preachers and writers of the same opinions—who had either secretly or openly combined with them—discreetly retired to Germany.   These fanatical and self-seeking foreigners, with words as smooth as oil, yet having war in their hearts, were one and all stirrers-up of strife and sedition, and preachers of heresy, and self-pleasing, of schism and immorality. Their firmly-held principles, like those of Wickliffe, Luther, and Calvin, were inherently dangerous to the State, and to all good order and peace.[1]

---

[1] See *Centenary Studies*, by Edwin de Lisle, M.P. (dealing with Wickliffe's and Luther's heresies).   London, 1884.

Wherever such persons settled in England, further dissatisfaction and confusion, as a matter of course, at once arose, and often broke out into disorder. They undermined the faith of the poor, caricatured their worship,[1] befouled their minds, perverted the good old principles of justice generally current amongst commercial men,—the armourers, wool-dealers, and yarn-spinners of the country,—and everywhere laboured to subvert and cripple the divine and beneficent influence of the Church of God and true religion.

On March the 13th, 1554, Cranmer, Ridley, and Latimer, who, as has been recorded, had each been committed to the Tower for treason,[2] were

[1] For example :—A cat with a shaven crown (in disparagement of the clergy and the Faith), and dressed in an alb and chasuble, had been hung up, with an imitation Eucharistic wafer fastened between its paws, on a sign-board in Cheapside. See Machyn's *Diary, sub anno* 1554 ; Stowe's *Chronicle*, p. 623 ; and the " Acts and Monuments of Foxe," vol. iii. p. 99. Soon afterwards a Proclamation was issued, offering a reward of twenty marks to the person who should discover the offender.

[2] Cranmer having been arraigned at Guildhall, in conjunction with Lady Jane Grey, Lord Guilford Dudley, and two others, they were all condemned to suffer death as traitors. Lady Jane Grey had pleaded guilty, and received sentence of death. " At the Starre Chamber, the viij of Sep., aº 1553. This presente daye Thomas, Archbishoppe of Canterbury appeared before the Lordes (as he was the day before appoynted) after longe and serious debatynge of his offence by the whole boarde, it was thought convenyente that as well for the Treason committed by him againste the Queenes Matie as for the aggravatynge of the same his offence by spreading abouto seditious Billes moving

conveyed to Oxford.[1] In the middle of the following month, a tedious and useless disputation on
the doctrine of the Eucharist, lasting three days,
was held in that University. Of the old faith,
held both East and West, there could be no doubt;
while the modern misbelief and irreverence, which
had wrought such practical mischief in Germany,
Geneva, and England, was defended and upheld
by the innovators with a certain amount of dialectical skill. At heart and in essence, as several of
their arguments show, the new men were obviously
rationalists. These propounded negations with
some coarse satire and great malice. But they
were answered quite calmly by brilliant logic and
incisive replies. The worthless disputation in due
course came to an end; and when, upon April
the 28th, the innovators were enjoined in vain to
conform to the Faith of the Church, they were
very properly pronounced by lawful authority to
be " obstinate hereticks."

Hereupon Cranmer, the most notable and influen-

tumults to the disquietnes of the presente State, he should be
com'itted to the Towere, there to remayne and be referred to
justyce or furthere ordered as shall stand with the Queen's pleasure."—Harl. MSS., No. 643, folio 9.

[1] " The viij day of Marche cam owt of the Towre of London
the Archbysshope of Canterbere Crenmer, and bysshope of
London was Rydley, and master Lattemere condam [i.e. quondam,] and so to Brenfford, and ther Ser John William reseyved
them and so to Oxfford."—Machyn's *Diary*, *sub anno* 1553.
Cott. MSS., Brit. Museum, Vitellius, F. v.

tial of the three, exclaimed, "From this, your judgment and sentence, I appeal to the just judgment of Almighty God, trusting to be present with Him in heaven, for Whose presence on the altar I am thus condemned."

CHAPTER III.

POLE'S POLICY FOR HIS COUNTRY DULY PLANNED.

CONTENTS OF CHAPTER III.

Pole's Policy for his Country duly planned.—The Spanish Marriage.—Policy of the French King.—Elizabeth Boleyne sent to the Tower, having plotted against the Queen.—Tries to justify herself.—Concerning the Rule of a Female.—Inconsistency of the Queen's Opponents.—The Undoubted Law of England.—Details of the Marriage Treaty.—Arrival of Prince Philip.—Solemnization of the Marriage.—The Cathedral Church of Winchester.—Made desolate under Poynet.—Splendour of the Marriage Rite.—The Solemn Nuptial Mass.—Bishop Gardiner's Wise Policy.—Various Restorations Effected.—Opponents of such Restorations.—Cardinal Pole's Policy.—New Parliamentary Measures.—Such Unanimously Passed.—Cranmer's Innovations Set Aside.—Various Episcopal Visitations.—Their Beneficent Results.—Jealousy of the Cardinal.—He Addresses King Philip.—Return to the Ancient Faith.—The Cardinal's Presence Desirable. — His Chief Object in coming. — His Attainder Reverted.—Messengers despatched to him.—Pole's Statesmanlike Plans.—He sets out for England.—His Arrival at Dover.—Is Restored to his Honours.—Comes by River to London.—His Jurisdiction Authorized.—Welcomed by King Philip.

CHAPTER III.

CARDINAL POLE, in communication both with the authorities at Rome and with Queen Mary,[1] still waited abroad to see that no indiscreet haste on his part should mar the design of Corporate Reunion, so distinctly desired by each. To the devout and far-sighted Christian, who believed in the unity and visibility of the Kingdom of God, no other policy was open or possible. The nation, as a nation, lapsed from its perfect Faith: as a nation, therefore, it needed to cast out all heretical *virus*,

---

[1] The Cardinal's correspondence with Mary and others, when carefully studied, conclusively shows how lofty and noble his truly Christian principles were, and what a discreet and successful ecclesiastical statesman he proved himself to be.—*Guirini*, vol. iv. p. 122.

and to be restored to visible unity by national corporate action, and this by lawful authority. Nothing less could overcome existing difficulties, whether ecclesiastical, political, or social. This Pole distinctly saw and admitted.

The Cardinal had left Brussels for Paris, from which place it is said that a private letter was sent from one of his suite to the Queen, dissuading her, in gentle but firm terms, from the marriage with Philip:—a letter which the Emperor at all events believed to have been either actually written or suggested by Pole himself. Some authorities maintain that the deep feeling which existed amongst the leading English nobility had been confidentially communicated to the Cardinal, and that his own opinion had been strengthened by the fact and consequences of Wyat's rebellion. Anyhow, the Emperor Charles is reported to have henceforth treated Cardinal Pole with something very like indifference. Subsequently the Cardinal returned to Brussels.

In Parliament the delicate and momentous subject of the Spanish marriage had been closely discussed and considered. From many and various points of view, both its direct and remote influences were dwelt upon. Many objected to it for various reasons. The relations of England with Scotland, France, and the Netherlands had often been complex and sometimes disorganized.

Continental combinations were occasionally dangerous. It is clear that the French King and his ambassador at the English Court were doing all in their power to avert the marriage, which they disliked and dreaded; and even became active co-operators with the disorderly and rebellious subjects of Mary. His Majesty not only furnished asylums for the rebels who had fled from justice; but went so far as to encourage them to become pirates, and to prey on the ships of the Emperor. With the Protestant faction in England, for his own advantage, using them as convenient tools, he was in active alliance. By his ambassador (who certainly misused his official opportunities and position in a very scandalous manner), he endeavoured to browbeat and threaten the Queen herself. Hinting that, by King Edward's death, all existing treaties had come to an end, that official compelled Mary at a certain interview bravely and nobly to remark, in reply, that, if this were so, she must take prompt measures to secure her own and the nation's rights.

While preparations were being made in England for the marriage, the French ambassador took upon himself to collect all the wildest tales, and the most insolent comments and tittle-tattle of the Reforming party, everywhere against the match, and to send them off to his master. Sometimes— as when in his despatches he remarks that the

Queen is about to reside at York, because York is near to Bristol, at which the Prince intends to land—he is somewhat bungling in his story-telling and exaggerated in his gossiping reports.   Sarcasm seasoned with buffoonery, and wit often damaged by coarseness and vulgarity, however, were rife among these " new-men," and were duly chronicled and reported.   The Queen is described by him as " an old woman longing for the advent of her young bridegroom," with other personal comments, as unseemly as they were out of place and indelicate.

At the same time, other events then taking place need a brief notice.   Some of them will be seen to be of singular importance.

On the 18th of March, 1554, the Princess Elizabeth Boleyne was sent to the Tower.   There can be no doubt that she had been privy to Wyat's insurrection, and in actual communication with those who at heart had wished it success.[1]   An officer of Elizabeth's household had mentioned that a so-called " French pastor "—one of the foreign mischief-makers and preachers of sedition, righteously enough banished from their own country— had visited her; and, as it was also asserted that he was in active alliance with some of Wyat's

---

[1] See " State Trials," by Howell, vol. i. p. 863; " Memorials of the Reformation," by Strype, vol. iii. p. 83; the MSS. of Renard, vol. iii. folios 287-289.

allies, and this became noised abroad, Lord Paget, of Beaudesert, sent a special messenger to admonish Elizabeth of her duty to the Queen. She had gone to Ashridge. Two private letters to her from Wyat had been intercepted by the authorities. These, though somewhat ambiguous in their terms, go far to show what her actual policy was. That she knew what was being attempted is perfectly clear; because, at his trial, Sir Thomas Wyatt himself acknowledged the genuineness of the private communication in question.

The charge against Elizabeth and Lord Courteney, of having plotted against the Queen, though not absolutely proven, appears exceedingly well-founded. This seems to have been believed to have been the case at the period referred to. Elizabeth, therefore, had been summoned to the Court. But she pleaded illness and indisposition —probably the latter was a sound plea—and declined to go. The Council, however, very properly resolved to enforce their order, not made without adequate consideration, and the Queen herself— well aware of the situation—wrote her a very kind letter of invitation. She arrived in London after considerable delay, having come by short stages with Lord William Howard and two others, who had been specially despatched to bring and escort her, but only at the end of a fortnight. She looked wretchedly ill as she was borne on a litter or chariot through the streets of London, suffering evidently from mental anxiety; and was soon duly lodged in a safe and secure part of the palace.[1] Soon afterwards, however, an order was made out for her committal to the Tower, for the Queen much misliked being her gaoler. Fresh evidence, distinctly damaging, had been discovered, and this precautionary act, consequently, was distinctly justified.

"To this present hower," she wrote, "I protest afore God (who shal juge my truethe, whatsoever Malice shal devise) that I never practised, conciled, nor consented to any thinge that might be prejudicial to your parson any waye, or dangerous to the State by any mene. As for the traitor Wyat, he might paraventur writ me a lettar; but, on my faithe I never received any from him; and as for the copie of my lettar sent to the French Kinge, I pray God confound me eternally, if ever I sent him word, message or token by any menes, and to this my trueth I wil stand in to my dethe."

There can be no doubt, throughout all the proceedings immediately following this incident,

---

[1] "The same tyme and day betwyne iiij . . . . . cloke at nyght my lade Elssabeth grace c[ame] to London thrught Smythfeld unto West[minster] with a C welvett cottes afor her grace. A[nd her] Grace rod in a charett opyn of boyth sides . . . . . . and so thrught Fletstret unto the Cowrt thrught the qu[een's] garden, her grace behyng syke."—*Cotton MS., Vitellius*, F. v., *sub anno* 1553.

growing directly out of the Kentish insurrection, that Bishop Gardiner preserved Elizabeth from very serious dangers.[1]   Renard, the imperial ambassador, more than once urged her immediate trial.   There was much to be said for such a course, considering her origin, position, and secret tactics.   She had plotted and was still plotting.   The evidence in hand, Renard felt confident must lead her to the scaffold.

In Parliament everything was reasonably done, both by statement and argument, to fortify the Queen's position.

When the plot for placing Lady Jane Grey on the throne was being hatched, none of the preachers, "new-men," and reformers had the smallest objection to the rule of a female sovereign.   For example, Taylor, Hooper, and Harley, all Edwardian "superintendents," were known to be devoted to this particular lady; and, of course, beheld grave personal dangers threatening them if she were not successful.   But, when the nefarious plot in which they had secretly taken a part failed, they suddenly and most conveniently discovered

---

[1] Renard remarked in the presence of Queen Mary and Gardiner, that the latter had admitted to him in conversation that " So long as Elizabeth was alive there was no hope that the kingdom could be tranquil."   At the same time it is quite evident that, whether the above fell from Gardiner's lips or not, he was always acting so as to shield her from danger, and did the same to the end of his life.   Of written evidence to the contrary there is not a shred known.

the great and heinous wickedness of suffering any woman to reign over them. A full chorus of jubilation gave place to a low wail of woe. The Old Testament was quoted in their own favour—according to custom—as were also certain Statutes of the Realm. The arguments from Holy Scripture were as involved, tedious, and irrelevant as they were in some cases coarse and profane. Kings alone, as they declared, possessed the Royal prerogative—not queens. A king taken from the midst of his brethren, as in David's case, distinctly excluded all women from the choice of the children of Israel. The situation in which they found themselves under Mary made the language of these shifty logicians very severe ; while their rhetoric became inflammable. It was no wonder, therefore, that, for peace and quietness' sake, authoritative steps had been taken for duly stopping their mouths. The Queen's Commission,[1] addressed to Gardiner, the Chancellor, to Tunstall, Bonner, Day, Wharton, and Kitchen, authorizing them to deal efficiently with such dangerous firebrands, was not issued a day too soon.

[1] " Mary, by the grace of God, &c., to the righte reverende fathers in God, our right trustie and righte welbelovid counsellors, Stephine bussoppe of Winchester, our chauncellor of England, Cuthbert bussoppe of Duresme, Edmund bussoppe of London, Robert bussoppe of St. Asaphe, George bussoppe of Chichester oure almoner, and Anthonye bussoppe of Landaffe, gretinge.

" Whereas John Taylor, doctor of derenitie, namynge hymselff

But Parliament — separating rhetorical chaff from wheat—answered all such unreal contentions promptly and most decidedly. No dissentient either amongst the Lords or Commons was found to deny that by the ancient and undoubted law of England, whatsoever person, male or female, is duly and properly invested with the kingly

bussoppe of Lincoln, John Hoper, namynge hymselffe bussoppe of Worcester and Gloucester, John Harley, busshoppe of Hereforde, havinge there said several pretensed bushoprickes geven to them by the letters patentes of our late derist brother, kyng Edwarde the Sixte, To have and to hold the same duringe theire good behaviors, with this expresse clause, *Quamdiù se benè gesserint*, have sythens, as hathe byn crediblie broughte to oure knowledge bothe by prechinge, teachinge, and settinge forthe of erronious doctrine, and also by inordinate lief and conversation, contrarie bothe to the lawes of Almightie God and use of the universall christen churche, declared themselfes verie unworthie of that vocation and dignitie in the churche.

"We, mindinge to have these several cases dulie hard and considerid, and there uppon suche ordre taken withe theme as maye stande withe justice and the lawes, have, for the speciall trust we have conceivid of youre wisdomes, leruinge, and intrigritie of liefe, appointed you fouere, thre, or twoo of you to be oure commissioners in this behalfe : gevinge unto you fouere, thre, or twoo of you, full powere and authoritie to call before you, if you shall thinke so good, the said John Taylor, John Hoper, and John Harley, and every of them, and therupou, eithere by ordre of ecclesiastical laws, or of the laws of oure realme, or of bothe, procede to the declaringe of the saide bushoprickes to be voide, as theye be alredie in dede voide, to the intent sume suche othere mere personages may be elected thereunto, as, for there godlie lief lerninge and sobriety, may be thought worthie the places. In witnes whereof, &c. Teste Reginâ, apud Westmonasterium, decimo quinto die Martii."—Rymer's *Fœdera*, xv. p. 370.

office, he or she should own power, and exercise fully and completely all pre-eminence, jurisdiction, and authority belonging of right to the Crown.[1]

As regards the proposed marriage, it was further abundantly shown that, considering the contemplated relations between the Royal Families of France and Scotland—for the Dauphin was about to marry Mary of Scotland—and the danger in which England might stand, a due and proper counterpoise would thus be at once found in the marriage of Philip and Mary. Even if the issue of Mary Queen of Scots and the Dauphin inherited the crowns of France and Scotland, the issue of Philip and Mary might inherit those of England and the Netherlands.

It was further shown, from the very terms of the marriage-treaty itself—a document evidencing wit, wisdom, skill, and foresight — that every security which patriotism and ingenuity could have devised had been distinctly obtained. By its terms foreigners were excluded from office; while the honour, the rights, the due positions and dignities of all Englishmen were placed beyond the danger of contention or controversy. This position was seen and admitted by many who, for

[1] See " MS. Collections of Sir W. H. Nares," p. 22, some time in the hands of John Anstiss (Garter), subsequently in the Library of Sir Thomas Phillipps, of Cheltenham, Bart., collections full of legal and historical interest.

a while, had owned doubts as to the wisdom of the alliance. During the discussion of the question cobwebs had been swept away and many insincere and far-fetched arguments overthrown.

An Act was therefore at once agreed upon formally confirming the treaty of marriage, for which the Queen, amid remarkable acclamations again and again repeated, thanked her Peers and Commons, and then dissolved the Parliament. Prior to this the two Houses had dutifully assured her Majesty that Philip of Spain would receive a thoroughly hearty welcome from her obedient and affectionate subjects.

This turned out exactly as had been anticipated. Nothing could have been more cordial or dignified than the reception of the Prince. From the beginning to the end of his voyage and journey to Winchester he was greeted with respectful cordiality.

Philip sailed from Corunna, in great state, as became a prince, and within a week, escorted by the combined fleets of England, Spain, and the Netherlands, reached Southampton.

The Lords of the English Council, with numerous attendants and officers of the Queen's household, went to meet the Prince, who, having already signed the marriage-treaty, further took an oath to observe the laws, liberties, and customs of England. On reaching the shore, he was at once formally invested with the Order of the Garter, the special and official ceremonies being omitted by authority of a Royal warrant, and was received with cordial acclamations. His dignified manner, gracious words, and handsome face and bearing attracted those who had come to welcome him. In a well-delivered Latin speech, terse and much to the point—indirectly correcting popular misconceptions which the followers of Wyat had circulated—he declared that it was neither want of men nor of money which had drawn him to England, but regard for a most virtuous Sovereign, whom he had come to wed. Consequently, he desired, henceforth, to be regarded, not as a foreigner, but as an Englishman; and then, amid applause, drank to his adopted country in a silver tankard of ale.

His fleet at once returned to Flanders; but not before he had sent to Queen Mary a basket of very magnificent Spanish and Flemish jewels, valued at no less a sum than one hundred thousand crowns.

On the Feast of St. James, the Patron Saint of Spain, the marriage of Philip and Mary took place with remarkable magnificence. The Cathedral of SS. Peter and Paul and St. Swithun at Winchester is a pile of great antiquity and beauty and of singular interest. It had taken the place of one still more ancient, the Church of the Holy Saviour, which the prelates Fugatius and Duvian, in a century long past, had consecrated, and from the seat of which Bishop Devotus had piously ruled. Kinegils, the first Saxon King, had been baptized there; Birinus, Hedda, and Frithstan had ruled there; Bishops Swithun, Walklin, De Lucy, and Wayneflete—the last so devoted a client of Mary—had blessed and benefited the city by Christian graces and the Cathedral Church by their pious munificence. No less than thirty altars—in addition to the chief altar and that in the Lady Chapel —had been set up and used as occasion demanded, in transept and nave, in chapel and chantry. Numbers of illustrious persons, from time to time, had been hearty benefactors of the Cathedral Church: saintly bodies of such therein once rested. Some mortuary chests, their contents in a state of utter disorder, still remain. While, from time to time, when men had faith, notable miracles there wrought proved that the hand of God was not shortened nor His condescending mercy withdrawn.[1] In Queen Mary's days this Cathedral was a magnificent building. Ravaged and robbed it had been under Edward VI., with the connivance and approval of Poynet, its scandalous superintendent, now so properly expelled and degraded; but still some of its ancient and glorious treasures in marble and alabaster remained. Relics of the saints and

[1] The following inscription still remains :—

Corpora sanctorum sunt hic in pace sepulta,
Et meritis quorum fulgeri miracula multa.

images of Our Divine Redeemer and His Blessed Mother had been removed, trodden under foot, and cast out by men of impious and flagitious lives.[1] The abomination of desolation had been set up under Poynet; Sacraments were disused and neglected, the old services had been abolished, and the beautiful songs of praise silenced. Altars had been hewn down and the lamp of the Sacred Presence put out ; yet telling of God and the Saints, still the Cathedral, upon which the sunshine fell, rose magnificently on that happy St. James's Day in a pleasant southern valley well watered by the Itchen. Its low Norman tower and transepts, its stately nave, magnificent choir and beautiful Lady Chapel were as yet untouched by the destroyer's hand.

On the occasion of the royal marriage the Church

---

[1] " The untimely death of King Edward," wrote Bishop Gilbert Burnet, " was looked on by all people, as a just judgment of God upon those who pretended to love and promote a Reformation, but whose impious and flagitious lives were a reproach to it. The open lewdness in which many lived without shame or remorse gave great occasion to our adversaries to say they were in the right to assert justification without works, since they were as to every good, reprobate. Their gross and insatiable scrambling after the goods and wealth that had been dedicated with good designs, though to superstitious uses, without applying part of it to the promoting the gospel, the instructing of youth and relieving the poor, made all people conclude that it was for Robbery, not for Reformation, that their zeal made them so active."—*History of the Reformation*, by Burnet, vol. iii. p. 216.

was adorned as of old. Cloths of Bruges and
Oriental carpets, tapestries interwoven with incidents of Sacred History, and banners of triumph
appeared on all sides. The rood-light was re-
kindled, and silver lamps had been hung adown the
choir. Every chantry had been lighted with
tapers. In the Lady Chapel everything had been
prepared for the marriage rite and solemn nuptial
mass.[1]

An old *Manuale* of the Church of Sarum, in use
for four hundred years, had been brought hither
for the occasion. Service books, containing the
Catholic rites, the *Missale, Ceremoniale Episcoporum*,
and *Graduale*, were taken out of their hiding-
places for prelate, clerk, and chorister ; while the
whole ceremony was carried out with the utmost
dignity and splendour.

Crowds of foreign noblemen were present in
their gorgeous and picturesque garb, while the
gathering of English nobility and gentry was
enormous. When Figueroa, an Imperial Councillor
formally despatched, presented to Bishop Gardiner,
in a set speech, two legal instruments by which
the Crown of Naples and the Duchy of Milan
had by his royal master been duly bestowed upon

---

[1] For several of the above details the Author is indebted to
the graphic account by Rosso of the ceremony, which is set
forth with power, conciseness, and effect. The " Continuation "
of Fabyan's " Chronicle " also contains certain details of interest.

and conveyed to Prince Philip—so that the dignity of the bridegroom should not be less than that of the bride—the English nobles were filled with admiration and satisfaction.

Then followed the actual marriage and the mass: At the elevation of the Host, amid the ringing of silver bells, the scarlet-clad minstrels, in a gallery, played soft music, and then the choir sang the praises of God-manifest-in-the-flesh—a glad and welcome strain taken up in chorus by crowds which thronged the nave. The faldstool used by the Queen is still preserved at Winchester—the only memorial of an event which certainly bore a two-fold character. Though there may be something of sadness in recollections of the days in question,—for this marriage had much to do with a second and more lasting breach with the Father of the faithful,—yet the personal piety and sincere devotion of the Queen, her beautiful character and remarkable patience, the noble deeds of charity and self-denial done by her; her thoroughly grand and noble policy as regards religion and Corporate Reunion, render her memory marvellously fragrant, and add a deep interest to the Cathedral Church of Winchester and its beautiful, but now desolate, Lady Chapel, where the marriage-rite took place.

At the close of the service—in which every detail had been rendered with the greatest care and precision—the King and Queen, surrounded by the high officers of State, and with a canopy of cloth-of-gold borne over them, walked from the Church to the Episcopal palace, with all the *insignia* of royalty carried before them. The swords of Justice and of Mercy were unsheathed. At the head of the moving throng—clerks and dignitaries and state officers—was upborne the Bishop's processional crucifix, flanked by taper-bearers with lights; while the incense arose on high, as the choir chanted *Laudate Dominum*. The Bishop of Winchester was everywhere greeted with acclamations. He had lived to behold a change indeed, and several times during the service his eyes were seen to have been filled with tears of happiness. It was an impressive spectacle, while the joy of the populace seemed sincere and universal.

The vigour which had been shown by the Chancellor, Bishop Gardiner, in the question of this important marriage, and the manner in which it had been carried out,—notwithstanding the traitorous words of heretical foreigners (then ordered to leave the country),[1] and of their English allies—

---

[1] "The Queen's Proclamation for the driving out of the realm strangers and foreigners" may be seen in "Acts and Monuments," Foxe, vi. p. 429. "The queen our sovereign lady, understanding that a multitude of evil-disposed persons, being born out of her highness's dominions, in other sundry nations, flying from the obeisance of the princes and rulers under whom they be born, some for heresy; some for murder, treason,

proved abundantly how much the failure of the various insurrections had tended to strengthen the power of the Sovereign and her advisers; and how thoroughly the people had already accepted the partially-completed return of the nation in its corporate capacity to the Ancient Faith. Hence, further restorations to the old order of things were resolved on. What had been already done had been well done, and thoroughly welcomed. The statute abolishing the disastrous revolutions of Henry and Edward had been at once put into force with scarcely any opposition. The Canon law had been actually restored. The bishopric of Durham, suppressed under Edward, had been set up again. The unoccupied sees, with the tacit consent of the Father of the faithful, had been filled by prelates duly consecrated by Bishop Gardiner. The ancient rites had been almost everywhere adopted anew, and welcomed by the dazed and distracted people; who execrated in their inmost hearts, as so many testified by deed as well as word, both the innovators and their innovations. In too many cases

robbery; and some for other horrible crimes, be resorted into this her majesty's realm, and hence have made their demurrer, and yet be commorant and lingering, partly to eschew such condign punishment as their said horrible crimes deserve, and partly to dilate, plant, and sow the seeds of their malicious doctrine and lewd conversation among the good subjects of this her said realm, on purpose to infect her good subjects with the like. Insomuch as besides innumerable heresies which divers of the same, being heretics, have preached and taught," &c.

the nobility, and specially the low-born, ignoble churls who had received knighthood or been elevated to the peerage in order to aid the Protestant cause, stood aside to see what was about to happen. Such were ready for any and every change if they themselves could only benefit by the same. Their old religious convictions had been destroyed or weakened; opinion took the place of Faith; contentions had become common, and wild and vain controversies almost interminable. Such people found it wise, therefore, to adopt only flexible and easily-held opinions. And with these persons, often daring, aggressive, and desperate, Gardiner had to reckon. Another class, likewise, as he so clearly saw, might exercise considerable power in thwarting all good and righteous measures, unless they themselves were dealt with with great prudence and discretion. This class had its active representative in almost every influential family throughout the realm. When kings and prelates, forgetting their solemn trusts and sacred duties, had so recently robbed God and His Church—by securing, for greedy adventurers and grasping heretics, church manors, sites of religious houses and their granges, the rents of chantry-lands and other charges; besides duly clearing out—wherever such was possible and practical—every article of value by which the old sanctuaries had been so well furnished, it was obvious to the least acute that such purloiners were not very likely to welcome with any special favour the restoration of an authority—consistently applying the unchangeable laws of right and wrong, of justice and equity—which might call them to account for their deeds of robbery and sacrilege; unless it were made clear that their supposed legal rights of possession would not be invaded nor overborne. Hence, Gardiner and the trusted allies beside him were bound to act with consummate tact and care. He and Cardinal Pole, with the other great men who were preparing for the completion of the work of Corporate Reunion, were, it must be admitted, not exactly at-one in the initiation of the scheme. Pole looked for the faithful restoration of all that had been illegally taken. Others, however, on the spot in England, better and more accurately appreciated the grave difficulties which existed in carrying out such a policy. It was desirable, therefore, still further to consider the subject in all its bearings before any practical action was taken, so that such action might be unanimous, prompt, and effective.

Here a brief record of what had already been done may be set forth, in order that the importance of carefully noting the exact situation in all its complex bearings and grave issues, and of duly crowning the good work, may be adequately realized.

In 1553, two Bills, both dexterously drawn and showing sound statesmanship, had been introduced in Parliament, the first confirming the marriage of King Henry and Queen Katherine; and the second having reference to Public Worship. Both these are known to have been suggested by Cardinal Pole, or possibly even by a higher authority.

As regards the first, it was shown abundantly that after King Henry and his Queen had lived together in lawful matrimony for twenty years, the so-called " divorce " had been only brought about through threats, intrigues, and bribery by scheming and interested persons; and that the perjured prelate, Thomas Cranmer, against every principle and rule both of equity and justice, had wickedly taken upon himself, of his own motion, without lawful church authority, and in the Queen's absence, to pronounce sentence and to issue a decree of divorce; and, consequently, that such acts, and every one of them, were altogether null and void, and all such statutes as confirmed the said divorce were thus and then absolutely repealed. At the same time it was formally asserted and decreed that the marriage in question, perfectly good and valid by the law of God, was adjudged both true and lawful. So ably was this Act drawn under Gardiner's direction, and so powerful were the arguments used in both Houses of Parliament in behalf of at once passing it, that no single voice was raised against it in either House of Parliament. As the Queen wrote to Pole, it had become law *sine scrupulo aut difficultate.*

As regards the second, while avoiding certain questions that might have been prematurely raised, and distinctly passing by the alienations of church lands, tithes, and goods, it did not curtail nor alter the so-called " ecclesiastical supremacy of the Crown." This was a subject to be dealt with subsequently by another and higher authority. However, it distinctly and directly repealed no less than nine most mischievous and disastrous Acts, passed by the intrigues of an artful and dangerous faction during the previous reign. There were some comments made and exceptions taken against the proposal in the House of Commons, to which adequate and most satisfactory replies were immediately forthcoming. But, though a considerable minority of the members of that house, cherishing laxity of morals, or upholding the new tenets of the Zuinglians and Calvinists, were believed to dislike the proposition, the Bill happily passed even without a division.[1]

The enthusiasm of so many for a prompt return to the old order of things went onward without any apparent check; for, amid difficulties which were not small and dangers that at one time looked

[1] " Statutes at Large," 1 Mary, Session II., chaps. 1, 2.

very threatening, the Bill was both so fashioned
and guided by those in authority, that the "new-
men" became prudently passive, and subsequently
stood aside.

By this enactment the blundering and destructive handiwork of Henry's Erastians and the
Edwardian innovators was toppled over and shattered.   All the artful devices of Cranmer and his
home and foreign tools were exposed, and their
labours for a time brought to nought.   Both the
" Books of Common Prayer " of Edward VI.—the
First, which, perhaps, with far too little reason,
was boldly asserted to have been compiled under
the direct inspiration of God's Holy Spirit, and
the Second, with which the foreign importations
had had so much to do—were so accurately and
truly declared to be " a new thing, imagined and
devised by a few of singular opinions."   The Acts
of Edward VI., utterly ignoring the spiritualty,
and respectively authorizing the use of these two
" Books of Common Prayer," the bald, bare, and
new-fangled (if not barren and disastrous) Ordinal,
the administration of the sacrament of the altar in
both kinds, the marriage of the clergy, the abolition of ancient fasts and feasts, the dismal Calvinistic "superintendents," created by Letters Patent,
and their Erastian exercise of so-called "jurisdiction," were one and all repealed and done away
with ; while the old forms of worship, rites, cere-

monies, discipline, ecclesiastical duties and obligations,[1] as existing under King Henry VIII. were formally and legally restored.

The joy of the people, both noble and common, on learning this knew no bounds. Some of the foreign ambassadors notice this in their letters and comments. The sons and daughters of those Englishmen who in Lincolnshire, Yorkshire, and the west country had been slaughtered in batches merely because they rose in defence of their Faith and the ancient sanctuaries of God in the land, were overcome with gladness at this happy change; believing that the intercession of the saints of old and the prayers of recent sufferers for their Faith, behind the veil, and waiting for the dews of grace, had been heard in Heaven, and thus mercifully answered.

At this time, the month of July, 1554, the Bishops made various visitations to enforce obedience to the ecclesiastical changes already effected. Some visited in person, others by deputy. In all cases the state of the fabrics of the churches seems to have been carefully investigated. A time of moral and religious confusion is generally rather a

---

[1] On June 28, 1554, the Chancellor and University of Oxford, in a Latin letter, testify their gratitude to the Queen for the benefits conferred upon them by the restoration of the ancient discipline, and have intrusted this address to Dr. Tresham.— *State Papers, sub anno* 1554.

time of *de*struction than of *con*struction. This period was no exception to that rule. In many cases destruction and robbery had distinctly triumphed. The old service-books had been purloined or destroyed, the sacred vessels stolen, the official sacerdotal vestments taken away. In many cases the roofs of chantry-chapels, and often of choirs, had been stripped of their lead, and the belfries of their bells; while the licentious and dissolute lives [1] of the miscalled "Reformers" had demoralized every parish in which their maleficent influence had been felt.

In many places such Visitations produced practical advantages, and brought abundant blessings.[2] Those who had acted for the bishops, as well as the bishops themselves, appear to have done so

---

[1] The Reformers' "irregular and immoral lives gave their enemies great advantages to say they run away from confession, penance, fasting, and prayers, only that they might be under no restraint, but indulge themselves in a licentious and dissolute life . . . . . The People grew to look on all the Changes that had been made as designs to enrich some vicious courtiers, and to let in an inundation of vice and wickedness upon the nation."—*History of the Reformation*, by Burnet, vol. iii. p. 217.

[2] The author has made notes of no less than twenty-nine cases in which this Visitation of 1554 was duly held in the dioceses of Lincoln, Norwich, Oxford, and Winchester, and where such Visitation was recorded, in some form or another, in the still-existing Churchwardens' Account Books:—in charges for the "Somner," or Summoner; "hys charges for the bishop's man;" "for ryngyng when my lorde ye bushoppe cum;" "in bredd and ale at the visitacion;" and, in some cases, "for wyne & spyce for ye lorde suffregen." In several instances Accounts for the

with the greatest prudence, patience, and charity; and, as a consequence, church after church—though partially unfurnished, and not so rich in service-books and sacred vessels as in times past—soon came to be duly repaired and used as heretofore. Mattins and Mass, Evensong and Rosary were said as of old; while on Sundays and the great festivals, in many parishes, the complex atrocities of the Edwardian innovators, with all their preachments, pratings,[1] and practices most happily came to be well-nigh forgotten. In exceedingly few of the churches had these ever been welcomed. In many the dislike for them had invariably been hearty, sincere, and openly expressed.

In the autumn of 1554, difficulties which the Cardinal had already accurately enough noted seemed likely to increase. Both abroad and at home —at Rome, Venice, Brussels, and Paris—malice, jealousy, and misrepresentation were evidently in league against him. His motives and aims, as well as certain of his words and deeds, were often misunderstood.   The Protestants, seeing this,

following year, 1555, show the immediate consequences of these Visitations, in the due reparation and restoration of the fabrics, vessels, and vestments. Many roods appear to have been set up in the spring of 1556.

[1] The discussions which had been encouraged were most mischievous in their consequences. Such often took place in church, where the fanatical and speculative were invited to prate with the parish priest or perambulating gospeller, to the demoralization of listeners and onlookers.

made the most of it for their own purposes. Any delay, therefore, was welcome, and no method for creating and continuing delay was left unadopted or unemployed. Self-seeking was found to be more easily practised with success, when contentions and disorders were rife. On the spot, in England, moreover, small matters appeared large to the onlookers, and important matters comparatively of no moment; so that some persons would altogether have ceased labouring for the great consummation which Pole so earnestly desired: while he, on the other hand,—with a firm grasp of principle, and seeing that nothing less than Corporate Reunion would remove the numerous existing difficulties,—declined to swerve, even in the smallest degree, from the straight path he had so wisely taken.

In September of the same year, the Cardinal addressed King Philip by letter, pointing out how he himself had personally suffered for the Catholic cause. The loss of his home and friends, his saintly mother's cruel death, a banishment for no less than twenty years from the land of his birth, had all been endured in faith and patience for the sake of his well-loved country; but it was as a public character, as a Prince of the Church, a discreet protector of the religious interests of England, and one so heartily anxious for the nation's corporate return to peace and oneness, that he desired prompt and efficient action to be taken. Delay was dangerous, and might become directly sinful. Unless, therefore, the King and Queen at once used all the means and influence at their disposal for accomplishing this good work at the earliest moment, the guilt of procrastination might become deep and dark.

It was at the same time urged upon the Queen that the restoration of the Faith by Corporate Reunion, through Pole's instrumentality, was the pressing need of the hour. How imperfectly the Edwardian " Book of Common Prayer" set forth the Sacramental system was accurately known to him. He had studied its pages from a copy sent to him in 1549 by the Duke of Somerset.[1] Even the Cardinal's personal aid in the work of religious restoration might be lost, if it were not then at once undertaken. The authorities at Rome, on several occasions, had given abundant indications of the exact method and manner of which they could approve in action. Pole, on this point, was well informed. Such was nothing less than a complete return to the ancient Faith. Moreover, as Mary's ambassador to the Court of Brussels pointed out in a letter, unless the work were at once commenced,

[1] On June 4, 1549, the Duke of Somerset wrote to Cardinal Pole, urging him to take advantage of the Boy-King's mercy, and to return to England; and at the same time sent him a copy of the new " Book of Common Prayer." This copy is still to be seen in the Vatican Library.

Pole, vexed by the indecision and delay of others, might appear to himself obliged to return to Rome. Thus—to paraphrase the actual words of the letter —the realm of England would lose a friend, who, for his wisdom, learning, and eminent virtues, was sought and honoured by every person who had secured the honour of his acquaintance. His conversation was known to be far above that of ordinary men, and adorned with the highest qualities; so much so, indeed, that all persons of influence with whom he had personally come into contact were impressed in their official dealings with him, in the highest degree.

These and other needful representations to the Queen appeared to have their due and immediate effect. It was seen that the Cardinal's return to England was essential. Better and more effectually than any other, he could attempt and complete the necessary work in contemplation. His qualities, his position, and his rank all led up to this earnest and reasonable conviction. Of his high birth and rank all knew; of his loyalty there could be no doubt; while, as regards religion, the scheme by which the nation as a nation—through the public voice and openly-expressed will of its representatives—should corporately return to communion with the Holy See, and regain its place in the orbit of Christendom, could be better and more safely applied by Cardinal Pole than by any other living

mortal.   As regards what had been done under
Edward VI. in the way of destruction, scarcely a
point of importance, whether ecclesiastical, political, or moral, had escaped Pole's notice.   Though
himself absent, yet tried and trusted friends had
informed him of the steady progress downwards,
both ecclesiastically and morally, which had been
taken by way of legislation.   And this had been
done not by the gossip of temporary sojourners in
Rome, not by uncertain rumour, or the utterance
of half-truths by mere babblers; but by a careful
and exact study of the various unhappy steps
towards the plane of negation-mongers and the
dull realm of misbelief which the country had
been duped into taking.   He would arrive at
home not to further destroy or uproot, not to mar
and break up, but to mend.   The first step to be
taken on England's part, therefore, was to reverse
the attainder on the statute-book.   On the 17th
of November, consequently, a Bill to this effect
brought into the House of Lords, was passed
in two days, and at once sent down to the House
of Commons.   Here it was thrice read in one day,
and at once, by act of King and Queen, Lords and
Commons, became law.

This Act of Parliament truly set forth that the
sole and only reason for the attainder of Reginald
Pole was his distinct refusal to consent to the
divorce of the Queen's father and mother, Henry

and Katherine; and that their present Majesties, Philip and Mary, by and with the consent of both Houses of Parliament, in consideration of Pole's lofty and conscientious behaviour in this matter, and in regard of his many excellent qualities, deliberately and of purpose repealed his attainder and restored him to all and every the rights which his deep faith and strict integrity alone had caused him to forfeit.[1]

An impression of the Great Seal, to add dignity and distinction to this important Act of Parliament, was taken off, not as customary in sealing-wax, but in solid gold.

No time was now to be lost in sending special messengers of suitable rank and dignity, to Brussels to invite the Cardinal to return at once to his native country. Two noble Privy Councillors, Lord Paget of Beaudesert and Lord Hastings, Master of the Horse, with a train of forty gentlemen, therefore, were at once despatched thither. Lord Hastings having married Katherine, daughter

---

[1] The Author has carefully gone through several documents in the Record Office, and others in private hands, bearing both directly and indirectly on the passing of this notable Act of Parliament. Many of these show how thoroughly sound at heart the great body of the people of England were in their attachment to their old and holy religion. Throughout the country—in Devon, Oxon, Yorkshire, Essex, Middlesex, and Cornwall—the votes on behalf of the Act, both of peers and commoners, were carefully anticipated and heartily commended.

of the Cardinal's eldest brother, Lord Montagu, who had been legally murdered under Henry VIII., would be thoroughly welcomed by his lady's uncle, while Lord Paget—whose prompt action in favour of Queen Mary when her rights to the throne were set aside temporarily—was a nobleman of high principles, and sincerely attached to the ancient Faith.

These personages, in a despatch, dated November the 13th, 1554, at once inform Queen Mary how delighted the Emperor was at their mission; with what joy the Cardinal himself had received them; and how admirably he had expressed his respect for, and gratitude to, the Queen. His virtues, they go on to declare, cannot be sufficiently admired, while in particular his moderation of language, his wisdom, and the perfect self-command he at all times evidences shine forth abundantly. In the interests of Peace and Unity he is prepared, they aver, to lay aside the character of Legate with which he has been duly invested, and to come to England as a mere private member of the Sacred College and as an ambassador to the Queen. He is ready to assent to all such measures as her lawful advisers on the spot, in their wisdom, discretion, and foresight, have assisted in devising or passing for the good of the country and the honour of God; being the more hopeful that all such in their degree have wisely paved the way for his own great scheme of Corporate Reunion.[1] The idea of reconciling here and there a single influential individual, however pious or useful, or even a family or local clique, never seems to have entered his head. Such could not have satisfied this Prince of the Church. He owned higher and nobler, but not less effective notions, and bolder and more statesmanlike plans. His Eminence trusted, moreover, that the subject of the lands of the religious houses and of the Church, which had caused some dissension, though Queen Mary's luminous speech to her Peers had the true ring about it,[2] should be so duly adjusted as that, while

[1] All the interesting details here set forth are directly gathered either from Pole's own Letters, or from State papers at Rome or in London. Such have served in several particulars to correct accepted convictions.

[2] The speech of the Queen to the Peers on this important subject is so beautiful in itself, so frankly and accurately reveals her true religious character, and is generally marked by such great ability and true wisdom, that it is here put on record as deserving the reader's special attention :—" You are here of Our council," said she, " and We have willed you to be called unto Us, to the intent you might hear of me my conscience, and the resolution of my mind, concerning the lands and possessions as well of monasteries, as of other churches whatsoever, being now presently in my possession. First, I do consider, that the said lands were taken away from the churches aforesaid, in time of schism ; and that by unlawful means, such as are contrary both to the law of God, and of the Church : for the which cause, my conscience doth not suffer me to detain them ; and therefore, I here expressly refuse, either to claim, or to retain the said lands for mine ; but, with all my heart, freely and willingly, without all paction or condition, here, and before God, I do surrender,

Right and Justice should be duly respected, ordinary contentment might happily follow. They end by intimating that, as the Cardinal's bodily health is so weak, he is unable to take long stages in his journey homewards. Moreover in these, the dignity of his person had to be considered and their own duty efficiently done. He would, therefore, make his public progress to the English Court slowly, stage by stage. On the morrow they would lie at Dendermond, then at Ghent, afterwards at Bruges, subsequently at Nieuport, after that at Dunkirk, and so eventually at Calais.

and relinquish the said lands and possessions, or inheritances whatsoever ; and do renounce the same, with this mind and purpose, that [such] order and disposition thereof may be taken, as shall seem best liking to our most holy Lord, the Pope, or else his legate, the Lord Cardinal, to the honour of God, and wealth of this our realm. And albeit you may object to me again that, considering the state of my kingdom, and the dignity thereof, my crown imperial cannot be honourably maintained and furnished without the possessions aforesaid, yet notwithstanding I set more by the salvation of my soul, than by ten kingdoms ; and, therefore, the said possessions I utterly refuse here to hold after that sort and title ; and give most hearty thanks to Almighty God, which hath given me an husband likewise minded, with no less good affections in this behalf, than I am myself. Wherefore, I charge and command that my councillor (with whom I have conferred my mind in this matter before), and you four, to-morrow together do resort to the most reverend lord legate, and do signify to him the premises, in my name, and give your attendance upon him, for the more full declaration of the state of my kingdom, and of the aforesaid possessions, accordingly as you yourselves do understand the matter, and can inform him in the same."

Several of his old Paduan friends accompanied him on his journey hither—amongst whom were Priuli, Floribellus (his Latin secretary), and an aged ally, Stella. But the latter died on the road. The Cardinal and his retinue were attended by a company of no less than a hundred and twenty horsemen.

At Calais a magnificently-appointed vessel was in readiness to receive His Eminence and convey him to England, and six men-of-war accompanied it. For some days the weather had been so lowering and stormy, and the winds so wild, that the safe sailing of his fleet across straits where two strong currents meet seemed an impossibility. However, on Pole's arrival, upon the 21st of November, the clouds all at once suddenly broke, the winds were lulled, and the waves fell; so that, under sunshine and a ruddy sky, with the sea as calm as a lake—which many reasonably looked upon as visible tokens of the favour of Heaven— with the Cross of St. George of England triumphantly floating at the mainmast of every stately ship, the Cardinal safely reached the port of Dover.

He was received here by Lord Montagu, the Bishop of Ely, several of the nobility, and many of his own personal friends and kinsmen. His advent became the one topic of conversation. At Norwich and Oxford, at Lincoln, Winchester, and Sandwich,

he would receive a most cordial welcome, as
Legate;[1] for, as old letters from these places point
out, the people of all ranks had grown thoroughly
sick of the disorders of sad times, and were anxious
to urge upon the Court the only reasonable and
right method of cure. In this reception at Dover
Pole was treated as one of the royal family; though
his special ecclesiastical dignity was at the same
time officially recognized. At Gravesend, amid
the pealing of the church bells and the acclamations of the multitude, he was welcomed by a
great crowd. The Bishop of Durham and the
Earl of Shrewsbury—this last one of the most
influential noblemen of England—duly welcomed
the Cardinal on behalf of the King and Queen;
formally presenting him with the Act of Parliament, which had only received the royal sign-manual
on the previous day. In and by that Act under
which he had been banished, he was restored to
blood, the attainder was duly reversed, and he was
formally and fully reinstated in all his civil rights
and honours. One of the onlookers from Italy,
in the Cardinal's train, remarked that the joy depicted on the faces of the crowd, who there
received his lordship, was so evidently sincere that,
if the rest of the people of the land were as earnest

---

[1] MS. Miscellaneous Letters and Documents, original and
transcribed, in the Author's possession. State Papers, *sub anno*
1554. "Original Letters on the Reformation:" Cambridge, 1846.

in desiring a religious restoration, and a return of the ancient Faith, as those whose cheers had greeted them from Dover to Gravesend, the success of the scheme for restoring unity and peace was already secured.

By the southern bank of the Thames, in sight of the picturesque tower[1] of the Parish Church of St. George, at Gravesend, lay a royal barge, its hulk and sides painted with gold and vermilion. The rowers were in the Queen's livery, with their ancient badges ; a rich awning of blue taffety, adorned and fringed with silver, had been stretched over its broad deck. At the head was placed on high a processional cross of silver gilt, while an English ensign of silken embroidery had also found its due place of honour. Twenty other barges of various kinds followed in attendance. Musicians, from time to time, filled the air with their strains ; and the old *Litany of the Saints* was chanted as the Cardinal passed Greenwich.

Letters Patent, duly signed and sealed,[2] were here presented to the Cardinal, authorizing him to exercise his due jurisdiction as a Legate, and were first read by the Bishop of Durham. In this instru-

---

[1] The old church of Gravesend was pulled down many years ago, and a more recent building, in the Hanoverian style, put up in its place.

[2] These, copied from the original document, are found duly entered in the Register Book of the Cardinal, preserved in the Lambeth Palace Library. They may be seen on folio 66.

ment the King and Queen declare that whereas it has pleased the Sacred Pontiff, Julius III., to send their dear cousin, Reginald Pole, with certain authorities, graces, and jurisdictions, to be exercised on behalf of the subjects of England, the said Legate had for the best of purposes accepted the commission, and such exercise of the same was highly beneficial to the realm. Furthermore that, on this account, his arrival in that character was most acceptable to them, and it was their royal will and pleasure that, in its fullest extent, he should exercise such jurisdiction, and they were well pleased that their loving subjects should have recourse to him according to the nature and quality of such grace as they stood in need of, and as they might have done in the twentieth year of the late King Henry.

In due course, passing the Tower of London, the stately spire of St. Paul's Cathedral, with sixty other picturesque towers and spires rising heavenward from the City around, and the great church of Southwark, with its massive tower on the south, the royal barge from Gravesend,[1] with numerous

---

[1] " The same day Cardinal Pole came from Gravesend by water, with the Earl of Shrewsbury, the Lord Montagu, the Bishops of Durham and Ely, the Lord Paget, Sir Edward Hastings, the Lord Cobham, and diverse knyghts and gentyllmen in barges, and they all [did shoot the] bryge betwyn xij and on of the cloke and against the stellard [steel-yard] of Temes, my Lord Chanseler mett [them in his] barge and my Lord of Shrowsbury

attendant barges, duly arrived at Whitehall Stairs. The Cardinal, in his scarlet robes of office, had been everywhere greeted with respect; he had been met by the Lord High Chancellor ; the citizens, collected in groups all up the river, from Wapping to Westminster—with an unusual throng upon London Bridge, where, in the overhanging houses, every window was filled with happy faces —and these citizens had welcomed him with ringing cheers: while the sailors of English ships, as well as those of various other nationalities, had dressed their vessels, anchored near each strand of the river, with gay, cross-marked streamers, and had invoked the blessing of Heaven, and the favour of Our Lady of Pity—Was not England of old looked upon as the " Dowry of Mary?"—upon the Legate's mission and work.

The Cardinal was met and embraced at the Court Gate by King Philip himself.

had his barge with the talbot, all his men in bluw cotes, red-hosse skarlett capes and white fethers, and so to ye Cort gatt, and ther the Kyng grace met him, and imbrased hym and so lad y^m thrugh the King Hall, and he had borne a-for hym a sylver cross, and he was arrayed in a skarlet gowne and a sqware skarlet cap."—*Cotton MSS. Brit. Museum*, Vitellius, F. v. (the parts in brackets damaged by fire).

CHAPTER IV.

POLE'S POLICY FOR HIS COUNTRY DULY EFFECTED.

CONTENTS OF CHAPTER IV.

Pole's policy for his country duly effected.—Lambeth House. —Its chapel and apartments.—Pole occupies Lambeth House.— Its chapel restored and used.—King Philip visits the Legate.— The Legate in the House of Lords.—His speech on the situation. —Advocates a Wise Policy.—Its impression and effect.—Consequent action taken.—Prayers for its success.—Proceedings in the House of Lords.—Petition to the Legate.—Its prayer granted. —Ancient Faith of the Nation.—Motives of the Revolt.—The Queen providentially protected.—Civil and Ecclesiastical powers. —Absolution of the Nation.—Thanksgiving for the same.—Inducements for Reunion.—Set forth in detail.—Effected with success.—The Legate in the City.—Welcome of the London citizens.—Bishop Gardiner's Sermon.—Effect on the hearers.— Convocation absolved.—Laity and the Abbey Lands.—Petition on the subject.—The Legate's Concessions.—New Collegiate Foundations.—Trinity College, Oxford.—St. John's College, Oxford.—New National Canons.—Action of Convocation.— Restoration of Law and Order.—The Bishops in Synod.—Descent to Immorality and disorder.—Exhortation to the clergy.— Specially to the Bishops.—The Clerical Tonsure and Habit.— Rules concerning ordination.—Churches and their furniture.— Catholic customs re-introduced. — Restoration of the Holy Eucharist.—Further wise reforms.—The Council of Trent.

CHAPTER IV.

ARDINAL POLE, after having been formally received by the Queen, to whose presence he was conducted by the King himself, and by whom he was most cordially received, had a long and earnest conference with Bishop Gardiner, the Lord High Chancellor. The Legate's credentials and papers were formally presented, examined as to their exact nature and character; and then—it having been found that every anticipated form and ancient custom had been properly followed—for order, law, and regularity of action were essential on such a solemn and important occasion—their Majesties' other advisers, with some of the more important officers of the Court, were presented to His Eminence.

After this, the Lord Chancellor conducted the

Cardinal to Lambeth House, the chief official residence of the Primates of all England. In this place Archbishop Cranmer had resided until, accused of high treason and condemned, he had been first imprisoned in the Tower of London, and afterwards removed to Oxford.

At that time Lambeth House was a picturesque though somewhat straggling building, in pointed domestic architecture of various styles, erected partly in timber and brick, and partly in stone; with clusters of large red-brick chimneys in various parts, high gables of irregular pitch, dormer windows, a guard-room, a hall, refectory and book-room, a broad and spacious court-yard, a noble entrance tower, and here and there, amid the gables, several smaller turrets and spires.[1] Many of the rooms, roofed, floored, and panelled in oak, were low in height, lighted by small mullioned windows, and hung with arras and tapestry. The

[1] In 1321, Archbishop Reynolds repaired Lambeth House, when there appear to have been existing "My Lord's chamber," the Hall, the Chancellor's chamber, the great Chapel, and two chambers of the Wardrobe. In the third year of Henry VI. (Lambeth MSS. No. 1193) these were "Magna Aula," "Camera armigerorum," "Claustrum Magnum et Parvum," the Steward's Chamber, the Registry, the Registrar's Chamber, and others. Cardinal Morton erected the Gateway (Morton's "Register," folio 378), and Cardinal Pole himself added on the Long Gallery. The latter also gave some choice pictures, that of Archbishop Warham, now in the Library, a portrait of Erasmus, by Holbein, and the well-known picture of the four Latin Doctors.

furniture—consisting mainly of stools, benches, tressels, and court-cupboards—is said to have been entirely suitable to the residence; and mainly to have belonged to the See. The Chapel, with long lancet windows of Early English work, deeply-splayed, not large but effectively proportioned, was well suited for its purpose; while its ante-chapel and the adjoining chambers at its west end were of singular interest, and even then of some antiquity. Certain rooms in the upper storey of this portion of the building were from time to time set apart for the retention and safe-keeping of rude and refractory persons, judged deserving of im-prisonment by the calm and dignified officials of the Archbishop's provincial Court. Some of those persons who have been imprisoned there have left rude carvings,—their names, initials, devices of the monograms of Jesus and Mary, and various prayers and mottoes on the wood-work and stone walls. These rooms are in what is quite accurately termed "The Lollards' Tower," [1] named, no doubt,

[1] Some persons, thinking that the " Lollards' Tower," adjoining old St. Paul's Cathedral, would have been sufficient to have received all the condemned agitators and heretics of the kingdom, now deny the traditional title to the well-known " Lollards' Tower" at Lambeth. Such persons are entirely mistaken. That at St. Paul's concerned the diocese of London: this at Lambeth the diocese, and, in case of appeal, the whole province of Canterbury. There were, at several periods of riot and rebellion, condemned Lollards enough to have filled both; and most obstinate and mischievous persons, as well politically as eccle-

from the number of persons there confined who had adopted, and had been actively propagating the pernicious and dangerous principles of Wickliffe.

Lambeth, in Cardinal Pole's time, was but a small village, with its chief street running parallel to the river Thames, and its well-furnished parish church, adjoining Lambeth House; and with fields and swift-flowing water-courses, and long rows of willow-trees; farm-houses and commons stretching southwards beyond. The Bishop's Ferry and Boat-House (where all the Archiepiscopal barges were kept) were mediæval wooden structures, picturesque enough, with a stately set of landing-stairs, canopied with high-pitched shingle-roofs, on the river's Surrey strand.

Here, by the Queen's special order, who had furnished portions of the house anew, the Cardinal took up his abode. Cranmer, its recent occupant, was away, lying under sentence of death for treason. He had forfeited his position and place. To the Legate the Queen had also appointed a household, and an income with which to keep up his dignity and rank with all proper state.

The Chapel of Lambeth House had been, in a measure and temporarily, restored to its old aspect;

siastically, they appear to have been. No southern diocese, from the days of Wickliffe to the Tudor era, seems to have been free from their pestilent influence.

and was furnished afresh for the ancient rites. Over the stall of the Cardinal hung a crimson velvet canopy, with his personal arms under a prelate's hat embroidered in colours and gold. The old altar had been flanked anew with rich curtains of cloth-of-silver, powdered with pomegranates, and the rose and the sheaf of arrows;[1] while three Venetian lamps of silver were burning in the sanctuary, and other lights before the restored representation in alabaster of Our Blessed Lady and of St. Gregory the Great on either side the altar. Over the northern door, leading into the Archiepiscopal Sacristy, hung a picture of the Four Great Latin Doctors, with another of the Passion of Our Saviour, and the sacred instruments of the Passion, on the wall adjoining the minstrels' gallery, upon the immediate south side of the sanctuary. The abomination of desolation had thus been efficiently cast out, and Mass was then said daily as of old.

Three days after his grace's arrival at Lambeth, on going to Court at Whitehall, the Cardinal received from the hands of the King himself a packet of letters and instruments which had arrived by special messengers from Rome. These documents, anxiously looked for and heartily welcomed, gave His Eminence the amplest powers

---

[1] These were the heraldic badges of the Queen.

with which to effect the anticipated reconciliation and to complete the desired work of Corporate Reunion. All that was then practically needed was the good-will and assent of the general body of the people, and a blessing from the Most High. Several remarkable, if not directly supernatural, incidents which then took place—and with which their Majesties, the Lord Legate, and the Lord Chancellor by trusty report seem to have become acquainted—were very properly regarded as distinct tokens of the Divine favour, and as Christian omens of an immediate religious triumph. A sound of unearthly song within the Chapel of St. Edward, at Westminster, heard by several persons one midnight in October ; and rays of light appearing suddenly, and seeming to enwrap the figure of St. Thomas of Canterbury in its niche on the northern side of the Lollards' Tower, were not lost upon those who had respectively heard and seen the same. The gross darkness which had covered so many of the people seemed, by God's mercy, to be about to be effectively dissipated.

On the next day King Philip formally visited the Legate, and, in conjunction with others to whom the legal and official preparations had been entrusted, settled all details for completing the great and momentous work in hand. Many persons prayed openly, "May God bless it, and may the powerful saints of our land intercede for its success!" Throughout the country the interest of the mentally-jaded and frequently demoralized multitude was centred in the Houses of Parliament, where, as was generally known, such momentous efforts on behalf of Divine Truth were to be made at once.

On the 28th of November, 1554, the Legate attended the House of Lords in State. His procession and that of the King and Queen arrived in due order and with every accustomed ceremony. All the bishops were there in rochet and cope, with mitre and pastoral staff. The high officers of State were stationed near the canopied throne; while the members of the Cardinal's household, with all his officials—cross-bearer, chamberlains, chaplains and secretaries—with their formal *insignia*, stood around his chair of state at the Queen's right hand. Robed in *cappa magna* of scarlet, with tippet of ermine, the Lord Legate heard that great prelate, the Chancellor, announce, by their Majesties' command, that His Eminence, having already intimated to the King and Queen the object of his coming, was now desirous of making a like public and frank declaration to both Lords and Commons—the nation's due and lawful representatives. At this, amid the profoundest and most striking silence, the Cardinal arose from his faldstool.

His speech, delivered in clear tones, with singular earnestness and vast self-command, was regarded as a marvel of prudence and wisdom. For many years, as at the outset he reminded his attentive and anxious hearers, he had been not only excluded from that assembly, but also from his home and native land, by laws specially and personally enacted against himself. For having recently repealed those laws he returned his best acknowledgments in person both to Lords and Commons, both to King and Queen. These had thus most generously manifested their good-will to him, and nothing better tended to render such both acceptable and welcome than the opportunity of paying back the kindness of them all in a matter of the greatest moment and importance. He had been formally restored to the land of his birth and to the ranks of a nobility which, as nobles, could only boast of an earthly origin; but he was come by high commission and in divine charity to secure for them, as of old, a far nobler dignity, even a true heavenly citizenship; and to reinstate them all in the unity of the One Fold and in the grace and favour of the One God and Saviour. The Almighty had bound and bonded together every Christian of every country into one Divine family, and in the unity and obedience of the Father—and all such, by God's mercy and their own expressed will, might soon be the nation's lot once again. The Lord Cardinal then went on to enumerate and dwell upon the various evils—ecclesiastical, political and social—which they had all endured since the defection of so many, by the action of those who ruled, from the Centre of Unity. On these dark features, and upon the obvious consequences of the same, he dwelt with much force and power. He always spoke in great charity, but also with much vigour. No words were lost; none missed their mark. He then proceeded to insist upon the greatness of the spiritual benefit which was then placed before them, and to the singular favour which the Holy See had invariably shown to England. Without fear or favour, in terms which none might misunderstand, he eloquently reminded them of their past errors, and exhorted them to a true and hearty repentance. They had shown their willingness and readiness to change their minds by their recent action towards himself ; while he, as a Legate of the Father of the Faithful, was, by a sensible and holy joy, most anxious, with no delay, to complete his country's desired reconciliation. His powers, he informed them, were more than sufficient to restore them to perfect union with the faithful throughout the world, and to heal the miserable divisions of the last disturbed and gloomy years. In order, therefore, that the full blessing of God's abounding favour might descend and dwell upon them all, it only remained that, in perfect good faith, with one heart and one mind, they should at once proceed by unanimous action to repeal all those laws by which, whether knowingly or unwittingly, they had visibly cut themselves off from the Centre of Unity and the true source of spiritual jurisdiction. With these words, somewhat amplified it may have been, he ended.

It was at once evident that a deep impression had been made by the Legate's closely-reasoned, comprehensive, and most effective address. No one saw this more accurately than Bishop Gardiner, who, both by experience and quickness of judgment, knew the temper of both Houses of Parliament exactly. To have so impressed bodies—the Peers were a somewhat mixed multitude, while many of the Commons were ruder in race and stamp than heretofore—in both of which conflicting interests were silently at work, and where religious faith was certainly not so strong and uniform as it had been of old, was the work of a wise diplomatist and a great statesman.

Parliament met again on the morrow, when the great subject before the Peers and Commons was again duly considered. No real opposition was offered to a carefully-drawn-up proposition that the whole nation should at once seek to return to outward and visible communion with the Apostolic See. Those who had been entrusted with promoting this measure saw clearly enough, from the tempers of men at the outset, that it was being received on all sides with general approbation. And such indeed turned out to be the case. Faith, hope, and charity, evidently dominated many. Both Houses, by a joint and formal petition—accepted independently by each—were there and then prepared, on the part of the nation, to follow the advice which their own English Cardinal had just before so earnestly and eloquently recommended to them. The Petition was accepted by acclamation. And so—amid many congratulations either for other, both by Peers and Commoners—each House adjourned.

The next day was the popular Feast of St. Andrew. This festival was ushered in both in London and Westminster by the ringing of bells and the rejoicing of the multitude. On the previous evening, after solemn vespers, the "Litany of the Saints" had been sung in procession by a body of priests and clerks in surplices and copes, in St. Paul's Cathedral. Early masses for God's abundant blessing on the nation were said in almost every parish church. In several of these the visible and distasteful tokens of what had been termed "reform," were carefully removed ; and the old rites and ceremonies were again observed as of old. There was scarcely a sacred sanctuary in the whole of the city and its suburbs in which the Lamp of the Presence had not been suspended and kindled anew. Many hearty prayers for peace and the triumph of Religion rose from bending groups gathered near.

At Islington, Lambeth, and Stratford-Langton—as is on record—images of the Blessed Mother of God had been newly set up. New roods[1] had been re-erected at the parish churches of Barnes, Greenwich, St. Mary's-by-the-Bourne, Stratford-Langton, and at the small church of St. Pancras, in the fields due north of Westminster.

But the House of Lords was the particular spot to which many turned. Rumour had already accurately told the story of Reunion to thousands. The King and Queen had directed the Earl of Arundel, Lord High Chamberlain, together with six knights of the noble order of the Garter, to accompany the Lord Legate from Lambeth to this place. His Grace came in state, attired in his official scarlet robes, and with every token of ecclesiastical authority and legatine jurisdiction borne about him by his officials,—the silver axes, the verges tipped with silver-gilt, and the processional cross—was attended by chamberlain, chaplains, master of the household, and secretaries.

[1] These cases appear to have been early examples of renewed Catholic zeal and private liberality. A little later, Dr. John Storey, a civilian, was formally authorized to see to the re-erection of the Rood and other customary sacred images.

Under a broad canopy of cloth of gold, on a raised platform, sat the Queen upon her throne. The King was placed at Her Majesty's left hand. The Lord Legate, surrounded by his officers, and with the bishops of the two provinces gathered near, to her right. It was a spectacle of solemnity, and there were tears both of sorrow and gratitude on many cheeks ; of sorrow, for the past could not be blotted out, nor its losses duly appraised ; of gratitude, for the long-suffering of Heaven, and that such a day had dawned. The proceedings were opened by prayers said by one of the bishops. In these the favour and benediction of the Almighty, and the intercession of Our Lady and the Saints, were asked upon the special work to be done, amid the hushed silence of all.

Then the Lord High Chancellor, briefly recounting the proceedings already taken in the matter, delivered the Queen's instructions to summon the Commons. On their arrival, the members of both houses were formally asked if they were prepared to, and did, ratify the previous day's work; and if they one and all desired to return to the perfect obedience of the One True Faith. No actual opposition was made ; no word of discord was uttered ; no contention was raised. The Chancellor's proposal was assented to by immediate acclamation and with general applause. The whole assembly, Commons as well as Lords, then rising, the Chancellor presented a petition to their Majesties, setting forth their hopes and wishes.

This Petition, so distinct and unambiguous in its terms, and so entirely worthy of those who presented it, was afterwards embodied in the Statute 1 and 2, Philip and Mary, chap. 8, sect. 2. The leading points of it are here quoted:—

" We, the Lords spiritual and temporal, and the Commons assembled in this present Parliament, representing the whole body of the Realm of England and the dominions of the same, in the name of ourselves particularly, and also of the said body universally, in this our supplication, directed to your Majesties, ... do declare ourselves very sorry and repentant of the schism and disobedience committed in this Realm and dominions aforesaid against the said See Apostolic, either by making, agreeing, or executing any laws, ordinances, or commandments against the supremacy of the said See, or otherwise doing or speaking, that might impugn the same: offering ourselves and promising by this our supplication that, for a token and knowledge of our said repentance, we be and shall be always ready, under and with the authorities of your Majesties . . . . . to do that shall lie in us for the abrogation and repealing of the said laws and ordinances in this present Parliament, as well for ourselves as for the whole body whom we represent, ... set forth this our most humble suit, that we may obtain from the See Apostolic, ... as well particularly as generally, absolution, release, and discharge from all danger of such censure and sentences as by the laws of the Church we be fallen into."

In the first instance this was read by the King and Queen, who, returning the original to the Lord Chancellor, by whom it had been presented, signified their pleasure that it should be again read by him, in the hearing of all.

At its conclusion, the assembly, with the King and Queen at its head, in their own names and the name of the whole Nation, asked that the reconciliation desired might be granted.

Upon this the Legate first desired those portions of the instruments by which the Holy See had empowered him thus to act, to be set forth in the hearing of them all. Then, in a discourse of great power and pathos,—every sentence of which abundantly showed how exactly and accurately he realized the situation, and how well he had been informed of all previous events and recent actions, —the Lord Legate pointed out that their thanks should be heartily and humbly tendered to the High God, the God of Peace and Unity, Who had afforded the present great opportunity for national reconciliation, and for cancelling their past offences.

" The Almighty," he declared, "seemed to look upon this Island with particular favour, having first called its people from the darkness of Paganism to worship the One True God ; and now, when under evil advice, the sheep had been induced to leave their true and tender Shepherd, Almighty God had so pitifully and mercifully given to the people of this nation a true sense and sorrow for their transgressions ; while the people of other nations, who having similarly forsaken the pleasant fold and green pastures, were left in their unhappiness and loss."

He further declared that from the earliest times the English, in unity with whole Christendom, had continued in the Faith of the Church, and had always regarded the See Apostolic with respect and affection.

Kings, from time to time, had gone in person to acknowledge the dignity of the Father of the Faithful; while so great was the proficiency of many of our own countrymen in the literature of religion that, when Charles the Great founded the University of Paris, our countryman Alcuin was specially invited to make a constitution for that body and to guide them in learning and piety.

His eminence then noted that Adrian IV., an Englishman, had been permitted to convert Norway; and, out of affection to his native land, gave to Henry II. the sovereignty of Ireland. England, as a nation, he went on to point out, had been invariably treated with peculiar respect and consideration by the Holy See, of which numerous examples might be given.

But, since the nation's defection from unity, misfortunes had certainly not come singly; while, in common with other countries, grave internal calamities had happened. The same had likewise occurred in earlier centuries elsewhere. Christians of Asia and the Greek Church, after the notable and unhappy schism, soon lost their freedom and empire, sinking under the cruel dominion of the Turks; while in Germany—a fresher example—sects and factions had split up the country, and civil war had both weakened and devastated it.

If the English revolt be faithfully examined, he declared, avarice and sensuality will be seen to have been the principal motives of its first promoters. At the outset it was projected and carried on through the unbridled lust and licentiousness of a single individual; and though vast saving in expenditure, and a great accession of wealth had been promised, yet both these anticipations remained wholly unfulfilled. The Crown was left in debt; the country was impoverished; the poor had become poorer than ever; while, as regards religion, the tyranny with which its new forms had been imposed upon the suffering people, the penalties that had been enforced upon those who disliked and declined it, and the acts of injustice which had been done in consequence, were such that in truth there was far more liberty of conscience left in Turkey than in England.

He then proceeded to touch upon some personal consideration which all would regard and appreciate, and upon certain quite recent and impressive events known to everyone present.

" It is well worth our recollection," he continued, " to consider how wonderfully God has preserved Her Majesty. What contrivances were set on foot to defeat her succession; what numbers conspired against her; what preparations were furnished to destroy her! Yet, notwithstanding the disadvantage of her sex, the surprise of the juncture, the inequality of her forces, she succeeded against her enemies, and made her way to the throne.

" Now, to what can all this unexpected success be attributed but the great goodness and protection of Almighty God? For, humanly speaking, there was nothing appeared in Her Majesty's affairs, but only despair. But the same Divine Providence had established the Queen in her right for recovering the true religion and exterminating error; and, to enable Her Grace the better for the bringing about this blessed purpose, she was now engaged in marriage with a prince of the same belief; that the Emperor, this King's father, had remarkably concerned himself for retrieving the Unity of the Church ; that, though the war's breaking out on all sides had disappointed his purpose, yet it was hoped that what his Imperial Majesty had begun would be carried on to a happier issue by his son.

" To procure this blessing, God had ordained two distinct independent powers, the Civil and Ecclesiastical ; that princes were God's representatives in the first instance, and the Pope in the latter; that the management of the temporal sword was put into the hands of the King and Queen, by immediate commission from God Almighty ; and that they had no superior with respect to secular authority.   As to the power of the Keys and the government of Church, it was delegated by our Saviour to the bishops of Rome, and annexed to the Apostolic See by special prerogative.   And, for proof of this peculiarity of jurisdiction, we have," continues the Cardinal, " the authority of Holy Scripture, and the Fathers from the beginning of Christianity to our own times.   From this See I am sent hither with the character of Legate, and have full powers in my commission.   But, notwithstanding my being entrusted with the Keys, I am not in a condition to use them till some obstructions are removed on your part.   Therefore, before I proceed further, I must solemnly declare to you that I have no prejudicial instructions to any person.   My commission is not to pull down, but to build up; to reconcile, not to censure; to invite, but without compulsion. My business is not to proceed by way of retrospection, or to question things already settled.   As for what is passed, it shall be all overlooked and forgotten."

There is no need in the case of any Christian to stay and point out the wisdom, the charity, and the worth of such acceptable words.

" If their repentance, then publicly expressed," the Cardinal finally remarked, " corresponded to the importance of the occasion and the heinousness of the national sin; at this corporate return of a whole nation, how great must be the joy of the angels, who always rejoice at the repentance of a single sinner ! "

He then rose from his chair-of-state to pronounce the formal absolution, and at the same moment the King and Queen rose too. Their Majesties stood bending towards the legate, while every peer and commoner fell on his knees. In a clear and distinct voice the following form of absolution was uttered by the Cardinal :—

" Our Lord Jesus Christ, who by His most precious Blood hath redeemed and washed us from all our iniquities, that he might purchase to himself a glorious Church without spot or wrinkle, and Whom the Father hath appointed Head over all things, of His great mercy grant you pardon and absolution; and We, by apostolic authority committed unto us by our most Holy Lord Pope Julius III., His delegated Ruler upon earth, do thus absolve and deliver you, and each of you, with the whole realm and dominions thereof, from all heresy and schism, and from all penalties, judgments, and censures in that case incurred; and We also now restore you again to the visible Unity of our Holy Mother the Church, as in our letters shall more plainly appear; in the Name of the Father, and the Son, and the Holy Ghost."

When the names of the Three Persons in the Blessed Trinity were pronounced, and the sign of the cross drawn over the kneeling assembly, the members of it responded with " Amen," or " *Laus Deo*," on all and every side. Queen Mary and others shed tears of joy, for to such it was a day to be ever had in remembrance.

Their Majesties, with the Cardinal, the Lord Chancellor, and the chief of the officers of state then went to the Royal Chapel adjoining; and, having returned thanks to Almighty God for His mercies by a set form of prayer, a solemn *Te Deum* was sung by priests and choristers before the altar.

To commemorate this great national blessing a solemn procession was subsequently ordered by the Cardinal to be made, with the full approval of the Convocation of Canterbury, every year on the feast of St. Andrew,[1] as a solemnity in thanksgiving to Almighty God. During the mass of the festival a suitable sermon, recounting these mercies, was likewise enjoined to be preached.

Although the difficulties in effecting this great work were enormous, yet many considerations of reason and policy had found their weight in the minds and hearts of the people of England in general that corporate action was possible. (1) In the first place the Religion then re-adopted, and the changes so happily made, at once brought the nation into harmony with the ancient Faith of their fathers, and so preserved a true continuity of religious duty and national practice. The Constitution of England, by a slow and steady, but sure, growth, was essentially based on Christianity. Lutheranism and Calvinism had both disorganized and tainted the moral principles of many. (2) In the second place, these last-named opinions, as recently formulated and set forth by two able and powerful heresiarchs, had been previously unknown

---

[1] "It' on S. Andr. d. every yere to come ye shall keep a sol. p'cessio' for a remembr' & thanksg'y to Alm. G. for ye Reconcil. of yᵉ C. of Engl'd fro' Schism to yᵉ Unity of yᵉ Cath [Faith] and yᵉ Pope's Holin. Xᵘ Gen. Vicer and suprem Head of yᵉ same Ch. in Earth, Also on yᵗ and at Masstime a Serm' shall be made by one of yᵉ Canons wherein shall be declar'd unto yᵉ Peeple yᵉ cause of such pr'cession & ye great Recepts of yᵉ Re-come, or an Homely made for yᵗ purpose shall be openly read." —*MS. Epistolæ et Orationes*, Lambeth Library. Wharton MSS. No. 595, fol. 124.

to the nation. **(3)** Thirdly, **the bold** assertion of the innovators **that** God had forsaken His Church, and that His promise to abide by Her until the end of the world had come to naught; that Her worship was idolatry and Her Faith impious **was** deliberately rejected by those who calmly reflected on the past, and looked with **such** dismay on the **reforming-proceedings** of the **two** preceding reigns. **(4)** Fourthly, **the** doctrines **of** Holy Church **were not** only acknowledged to be of the highest antiquity —coming down from the first age and the gathering of apostles in the Upper Room at Jerusalem— but had been marvellously preserved by **an** uninterrupted succession of bishops from those very Apostles themselves, and specially by the actual successors of **St. Peter** in **his chair at** Rome,—one **of** whom, **St.** Gregory **the** Great, had sent hither **St.** Augustine, England's great **missionary**, apostle, and chief **Pastor, to** benefit and bless our beloved country. **(5) Fifthly,** the splendour and dignity, the glory and magnificence **of** the services **of** the Church Universal, **everywhere** performed **and** everywhere alike, with **a** Faith never changing, **and with an** exclusive name, that of " Catholic," which neither **sect** nor faction had ever dared **to** claim, pointed **to** Rome as the true source **of** spiritual authority, **and** to its divinely-preserved bishop as the special guardian of revealed Truth. **(6)** Lastly, **the** legitimate influence of the

L

Bishops of the See of Peter—save by the Oriental schismatics everywhere acknowledged—combined with the acknowledged piety and austerity of the religious orders, the members of which had done so much for true religion and civilization (and the loss of whom, in every English shire, was everywhere being then so severely felt), led to the nation, in its corporate capacity, with one accord and one will, thus deliberately reverting to the Faith of our forefathers.

Here are the words of one who, surveying the situation as it appeared in Queen Mary's reign, wrote more than a century afterwards:—

" The aversion of the nation to Popery was at that time very high, so that tumults were much apprehended; yet the whole work was brought to a final conclusion within two months, without any opposition or the least tumult; so inconsiderable are popular discontents, in opposition to a government well established, and supported by strong alliances."[1]

Admissions of this character admirably serve to bring out the true motives and good desires of all those patriots who were engaged in the great work of national reconciliation and religious peace and

---

[1] " A Letter written to Dr. Burnet, giving an account of Cardinal Pool's Secret Powers," &c., to which are added, " Two Breves that Card. Pool brought over, and some other of his Letters that were never before Printed."—Quarto, p. 40.   London : R. Baldwin, 1685.

concord. Such certainly rank amongst our greatest statesmen.

But of all the subsequent steps taken, some further notice must be recorded in detail, bearing, as many of them do, upon the broad policy of the Lord Legate, and of those who so discreetly acted with him in carrying it out.

For example, the day after that upon which the great work of reconciliation had been thus openly completed, the Lord Mayor and certain Aldermen of the City of London waited upon the Lord Legate at Lambeth House, and desired his Eminence's public attendance in the City. He would, as they confidently declared, be everywhere and on all sides most respectfully welcomed. The chief citizens specially desired his presence. It was determined, therefore, that this should take place on Advent Sunday,[1] and that a public religious solemnity, in which the citizens could join and publicly testify their joy and satisfaction, giving honour to God for His goodness, should be held.

---

[1] " The Devil has made use of two excellent instruments for their restoration; within the Kingdom, the Bishop of Winchester ; without the Kingdom, Cardinal Reginald Pole, created Primate of the Kingdom and Archbishop of Canterbury. He was received with solemn pomp in London at the Holy Cross of the Cathedral of St. Paul. The nobles prostrated themselves at his feet, and as suppliants asked absolution and apostolical benediction from the Beast."—*Henry Bullinger to John Calvin, dated Zurich, January the 18th, 1555. Calvini Opera,* tom. ix, p. 106. Amstelodami: 1667.

It was further resolved that this should take place in St. Paul's Cathedral.

Early on Advent Sunday morning, therefore, Cardinal Pole, in his state barge, left his official residence for the City. He was welcomed by crowds standing on the picturesque piers and landing-stages at Westminster, Whitehall, the Hospital of the Savoy, the " Flete-stairs," and St. Paul's Wharf. At this latter he landed, cheered by a multitude of enthusiastic spectators. Representatives of the ancient guilds, and of the citizens, with the Aldermen and Lord Mayor at their head, formally met him, in their picturesque habits, and with every accustomed mark of respect and welcome. The legatine-cross, the pillars, and silver pole-axes, the processional crucifix, and official verges were borne before him. Surrounded by his own household, and preceded immediately by the Sheriffs of the City, he proceeded to the western doors of the Cathedral, where the officials of that remarkable church duly welcomed him.[1]

[1] " The ij day of Desember dyd com to Powlles all prestes and clarkes with ther copes and crosses, and all the craftes in ther levery, and my lorde mayre and the althermen, agaynst my lord cardenall's commyng; and at the bysshopes of London place my lord chanseller and alle the bysshopes tarehyng for my lord cardenall commyng, that was at ix of the cloke, for he landyd at Beynard Castell ; and ther my lord mayre reseyved hym, and browgth y^m to the Powllse, and to my lord chanseler, and my lord cardenall and all the byshopes whent up into the quer with ther meyturs [i.e., mitres] and at x of the cloke the Kyng's grace

A throng of state officials had gone with the King and Queen, who were then kneeling at their faldstools, and ready to hear mass. This was sung with great effect and celebrated with all the grandeur and splendour of the Catholic rite. The multitude gathered within the Cathedral was very great; while the sermon preached by the Bishop of Winchester is said to have been listened to with interest and anxiety by an earnest and attentive audience.

The Bishop preached from an appropriate sentence in the Epistle for the day—" Now it is high time to awake out of sleep."[1] He compared the state in which the nation had found itself during the two last reigns to a delusive dream, when reason is suspended and imagination becomes wild; when the rich think themselves poor, and the poor believe themselves to be in affluence; when the wretched regard themselves as happy, and the happy as perfectly miserable; but which, when the trance is over, and the deception is made manifest, sorely disappoints and sadly deceives. Pointing out with remarkable clearness the errors into which the nation had been unwittingly led, the public and private calamities which had befallen them, and the wickednesses which had been formally

cam to her mase."—*Cott. Lib. Brit. Museum, Vitellius F. V.*, sub anno 1554.

[1] Romans xiii. 11.

perpetrated, and in which so many had indulged, he congratulated them on the present happy change. He recounted, in touching words of great simplicity, the injustice and cruelty which the Lord Legate had suffered in the death of his near relations, in his own unjust banishment, and in the loss of his fortune and position. Then recalling what Parliament had recently undertaken and effected, he set forth, on the one hand, the corporate action of the nation, by the King and Queen, by the Lords and Commons, in expressing sorrow and repentance for what had been effected, and, on the other, the benevolent action of the Father of the Faithful—the Legate being his official representative—in restoring the nation to visible unity. Thus they had been happily wakened out of their sleep and brought to a true sense of their religious duty. He himself confessing the share which he had borne in the national guilt, desired those who might have followed him in his now acknowledged error to return with him, heart and soul, in his present course of duty.[1]

The effect of this sermon, and the general satisfaction which existed as regards the only rational and secure position taken up in the work just effected, shows not only that the preacher had duly

---

[1] Several records of this timely and eloquent discourse exist. These differ somewhat in detail, but the summary given of it in text will be found to be true and faithful.

realized the situation, but that the citizens in their response obediently and happily followed him.

According to the Canon Law of the Church Universal, the English clergy, either by active or passive action, had incurred certain very grave and serious censures. Some of these were official, others personal, and differed from those relating generally to lay-persons. Hence the Convocation of Canterbury met on the subsequent Thursday, voluntarily acknowledged their sin against God, on their knees—and this on their own behalf, as well as on the part of others officially represented by them—and so received pardon for such irregularities, whether direct or indirect, intentional or the reverse.

There is one fact of the utmost importance, to which particular attention must now be called— viz., that relating to the church and abbey-lands.

The peaceful and blessed revolution which Cardinal Pole had as yet so wisely effected, evidenced on the part of the Roman Pontiff singular wisdom, charity, and discretion. Even his greatest enemies admitted this. For, though there can be no doubt that land given to the Church cannot be taken without sacrilege, and that in this country most heinous and wicked acts of sacrilege had taken place—witness the desecrated churches, the sacred abbeys inhabited by a new and upstart nobility, the poor robbed, and the tithes alienated from their

original purpose and use—yet all these, in the clearest and amplest terms, had been made over to the lay owners who then possessed them.

Here are the exact terms of this transaction:—

" To avoid any further scruple which might arise on account of such possessions, or of the suppression of monasteries and other religious foundations, which were come into the hands of divers persons, either by gift, purchase, or exchange, it had pleased their Majesties to intercede with the Legate in favour of the actual possessors; and that the same Most Reverend Father-in-God had declared that all persons to whom a sufficient conveyance, according to the common laws of the land, had been made of the said lands and possessions, might without any scruple of conscience, enjoy them; *and that they should suffer no molestation, on pretence of decrees of General Councils or of the Canon Law; and that they should be clear from any danger of the Church's censures.*"[1]

---

[1] The Author would here most respectfully point out that if such broad and vast concessions could be properly and benevolently made three and a half centuries ago, as those set forth in the above passage in italics, no real difficulty need exist on the part of Authority in dealing corporately with the Church of England, in view to the restoration of national unity and peace: for the Lord Legate, in his formal instrument, went still further, and distinctly and directly declared that " *neither the possessor of the moveable or immoveable goods of the Church should ever be liable to any censure or ecclesiastical punishment for detaining and not restoring them; that by this Decree all power was taken away*

With the above action—asked for by the King and Queen, sanctioned by the Pope, set forth in irreformable decree by the Legate, welcomed by the then owners of such lands—the English clergy in their convocation fully and altogether agreed, as an important sentence in their Petition to Philip and Mary abundantly declares:—

" Although, in virtue of their character and the respective offices they filled, they were the natural guardians of the rights and possessions of the Church, and therefore it might seem incumbent on them to endeavour to recover what had been lost or scattered in the late schism; yet, after mature deliberation on the whole affair, they frankly confess how difficult and even impracticable such a recovery would be, on account of the many intricacies in which these dealings have been involved, and should such an attempt be made the peace and tranquillity of the Kingdom would be disturbed, and that Unity, which the piety and authority of their Majesties had now established, could hardly be advanced so as to gain its desired end. Wherefore, as they preferred the public quiet to all private

of ever giving a different judgment in these affairs ; and if anything of this kind should be attempted, it was by the present legal instrument declared to be null and void and of no effect." Of course it might even have been argued, in the succeeding reign, that such a broad and far-reaching policy would seem to cover, and might be made to cover, much more than originally could have been reasonably intended.

considerations, and the salvation of souls ransomed by the Blood of Christ to all earthly goods, and did not seek their own profit, but the glory of their Redeemer, they gave their assent to whatever should be enacted in this affair, and besought the Lord Legate not to be reserved or difficult in such dispensations."

As a matter of fact he certainly had not been. The large concession already made was properly balanced by his hearty and earnest suggestion to those who owned church lands or goods, to have before their minds' eye the judgments of God on Belshazzar; and, wheresoever practicable, to restore such to their original purposes. The Legate exhorted all, that from a regard to their own eternal lot, they would provide out of the alienated church lands a due and sufficient subsistence for those who ministered to their flocks, so that these offices might be fully and freely exercised for the benefit of all.

In the Petition of the Convocation of Canterbury one more important point is set forth—a detail of the highest moment—and should not be overlooked, a point which had been carefully embodied in the recent Act.[1]

The independence and high prerogative of the

---

[1] Concilia Mag. Brit., tom. iv., p. 120, transcribed, as is said, from Peter Heylin's " Extracts from the Convocation Registers."

imperial Crown of England against whatever may
seem to derogate from it is therein plainly maintained. The signers of the Petition point out
that after the Reunion of this noble realm to
visible unity with the rest of Christendom it is to
be trusted and hoped that sincere and earnest devotion will increase in the hearts of the people,
and that due and laudable self-denial may induce
many of them to bestow by will manors, lands,
and other possessions to any spiritual body, politic
or corporate, within the kingdom, notwithstanding
the Mortmain Acts.

These sentences and sentiments did but reiterate
what the Queen, the Lord Legate, and the Chancellor were known to hope for and anticipate, and
other of the bishops had openly and strongly
recommended.

As a consequence of this, two colleges were
founded in Oxford, and each was commenced in
this same year, 1555. The actual Letters Patent
concerning Trinity College are dated March the
18th, 1556. Sir Thomas Pope,[1] an Oxfordshire

---

[1] Thomas Pope had obtained considerable lands, by purchase,
from the disbanded and abolished monasteries, *e.g.*, certain
estates belonging to the dissolved Canons of Kenilworth, in
Warwickshire, A.D. 1544, valued at £1,500 13s. 8d. In the same
year he had secured the site of the house of the Franciscan Friars
at Lincoln ; and, jointly with others, the site of the Black Friars
at Beverley in Yorkshire ; together with certain lands sometime
belonging to the Priory of Byeleigh in Essex. The details of

man of a race of gentle-people, sincerely attached to the faith of his forefathers—but who in the course of the recent reforming-undertakings had himself acquired considerable monastic property —set up and endowed Trinity College in that University. It was built on the site of Durham College—then a dilapidated ruin—which had been founded in the latter part of the thirteenth century. Pope, who had been educated at Eton, was a lawyer. He had filled the offices of Clerk of the Star-Chamber, Treasurer of the Court of Augmentations, Master of the Jewel-House, and Warden of the Mint. He died in 1559.

Sir Thomas White,[1] a godly and most munificent Muscovy merchant of the City of London—an influential member of the Merchant Taylors' Company—likewise set up and endowed St. John's College in Oxford. He had been twice Lord Mayor. After conceiving the idea, because of the sermon of Bishop Gardiner at St. Paul's, and in all probability maturing it because of the clear and noble exposition and policy of Pole, he was divinely admonished in a dream to establish it on

these purchases may be found in Sir William Dugdale's " History of Warwickshire, p. 474 ; in Bishop Tanner's work on the Monasteries ; and in Newcome's " Repertorium," vol. ii., p. 610.

[1] Thomas White had rendered signal service to Queen Mary during Wyat's rebellion, in consequence of which he received the honour of knighthood, as is stated in Dr. Rawlinson's MSS. in the Bodleian Library.

a spot where he should find three stately elms [1]
growing out of one root. Such he chanced to
discover in the desolate courtyard of St. Bernard's College, an ancient Cistercian Society, sometime active, but the mansion-house of which was
then decayed, in the Oxford parish of St. Giles.
Sir Thomas White purchased these dilapidated
buildings, with their appurtenances and some
adjacent lands, from the society of Christ Church
in Oxford, and obtained a special charter from the
King and Queen in the same year for setting up
the College. How many it has blessed and benefited can never be known. Sir Thomas White
died in 1567. His funeral sermon was preached
by Edmund Campian, afterwards the celebrated
Jesuit—recently beatified, because of his sufferings
and death on behalf of the old order of things—a
valiant defender, even unto death, of the ancient
Faith.[2]

As a means for further completing the work of
sound Reformation—for such a term is equally
applicable to the proceedings of the Council of

[1] Anthony à Wood states that the tree was living in 1677,
and it is asserted that a younger tree, sprung from that in question, was also at that time flourishing in the gardens of St.
John's College

[2] Decree confirming the honour given to the Blessed Martyrs,
John Cardinal Fisher, Thomas More, and others, put to death
in England for the Faith from the year 1535 to 1583—dated the
29th December, 1886, signed by " D. Cardinal Bartolini."

Trent as to the national synod which the Cardinal held on the 2nd of December, 1555—canons were drawn up at the last-named, under Royal license,[1] to aid in accomplishing this object. These canons —founded on Catholic precedents, and especially on the wise work being effected at Trent, had been submitted by the Legate to the Pope.[2] The synod to consider and discuss them was summoned by

[1] This was a warrant under the Great Seal which gave full power to the Synod to assemble freely and to make decrees, and the greatest freedom to the clergy with regard to the action of each and all in the matter. The two leading questions—(1) of the prerogative of the Crown, and (2) the possibilities of ambiguities in the existing laws, were ably dealt with, the most perfect liberty of action being intentionally allowed to the spiritualty.—*Reginaldi Poli Vita,* folio 6; *Mag. Brit. Concil.,* tom. iv., p. 130. It further appears that similar freedom, by an instrument under the Great Seal, had been given to the Cardinal himself as Legate on returning to his native land.

[2] Cardinal Pole, by formal letter, had informed Pope Paul IV. (John Peter Caraffa, a zealous reformer) of the action of Convocation, and forwarded a draft of the proposed Decrees to be submitted to the National Synod. Of this Holy Father, Sir Richard Morison, whose words are quoted to show the temper and spirit of the innovators, and their hatred of the ancient Faith, wrote as follows:—" This anti-Paul, Paul of the Apostasy, the Servant of the Devil, this anti-Christ newly created at Rome, thinks it but a very small plunder that is offered to him that he is again permitted in England to tyrannize over our consciences, unless the revenues be restored to the monasteries, that is the pig-sties; this patrimony, as he calls it, of the souls which are now serving in the filth of Purgatory. Our ambassadors who went to Rome for the purpose of bringing back this wolf upon the sheep of Christ are now with the Emperor."— *Letter of Sir Richard Morison, Knight, to Henry Bullinger,* dated from Strasburgh, 23 Aug., 1555.

the Bishop of London,[1] as Dean of the Province of Canterbury, who called all the Bishops of both provinces to attend, with the Deans of the various dioceses and the elected representatives of the clergy.

There are no records of ecclesiastical proceedings existing of greater interest to English Churchmen than these. Clear and explicit in their terms, they deal broadly and most effectively with every existing and actively-operating abuse,[2] specially with those which had grown up during the two last reigns; and this with great wisdom and on the soundest principles. There is not a sentence or sentiment throughout which would not commend itself to the instinct of a Catholic. In many respects the various detailed subjects are dealt

[1] Bishop Bonner's Register contains a copy of the writ on folio 394.

[2] The following is a fair specimen of the widely-circulated errors regarding the Sacrament of the Altar, often greedily read by the ignorant, the profane, and the destructionists :—" It becomes us to show our detestation of everything belonging to Antichrist, in all possible ways, both by words and signs; but especially with regard to that extreme and hurtful abomination of the Mass, by which, not only is the whole design of the sacred Supper overthrown, but all benefit of the death of Christ is taken away from mankind. Hence it becomes us to demolish altars ; since, by this kind of furniture the supporters of Antichrist have commended this Mass to the people as a fresh sacrifice of Christ." —*Martin Bucer to Matthew Parker, translated from the Latin.* Parker's MSS., C. C. C. Cambridge, No. 113, folio 41. There is a sentence very like the above on folio 287 (at the back) of Ridley's " Register."

with lucidly, practically, and with extreme wisdom.[1]   In any attempt to restore law and order for the National Church, as at present existing, no more efficient plan than that then adopted could possibly be found; and had the decrees of this National Synod[2] been continously and invariably abided by, instead of having been so unfortunately repudiated, the English nation, as regards Religion, would have been in a far better position than it is at present.   This Synod, in truth, was a turning-point in the history of the Church of England; and if another like it, in all particulars, could be held, and its decrees on all hands accepted, how beneficial and advantageous, how great and lasting

[1] It should be noted, in passing—and the point is an interesting matter of history—that almost every restoration effected in England, through the great Oxford Movement of 1835, is comprehended in the directions and injunctions of these important Decrees of Cardinal Pole; and where such practical reforms have not yet been undertaken, most Christians will admit that such have yet to be effected, in order to complete the good and great work, and to secure Corporate Reunion to the National Church.

[2] The Decrees of this National Synod may be found in MS. Cotton, Brit. Museum, Cleopatra, F. 2, folio 72; and also in a valuable MS. labelled "Synodalia," in the Library of Corpus Christi Coll., Cambridge.   A still more complete copy of the same, with several explanations and additions, was published in Rome, in 1562; and another version issued at Venice, printed by Zileti, later in the same year.   In the 4th volume of the "Concilia" of Wilkins, all these versions seem to have been consulted, for the text of the last-named collection agrees exactly with none.

might be its consequences religiously, politically, and socially!

The Bishops, assembled in Synod, premise that the national evils then existing, arise mainly through the defection of England from the ancient Faith. They begin, therefore, by acknowledging the Divine mercy of the Almighty in having recalled them to this; and to the old rites, by which that Faith was exhibited and taught. Hence they appoint a special collect of thanksgiving to be said daily, and a special solemnity to be observed every year on the Feast of St. Andrew.

The second decree points out that no sooner was obedience refused to the Father of the faithful, than the authority of the laws ecclesiastical, both general and local, was shortly laid aside. In the place of these, false teachers from abroad had been invited hither, and books containing errors of all sorts were generally sought after and studied.

It is perfectly clear that all persons who, on principle, had discountenanced the changes under Henry and Edward, and did their best to restore the nation to Christian Unity and a true Faith, were consistently and persistently slandered by the hired scribes of the " new-men." The literature these writers provided, from the two-paged fly-leaf to the bulky tome, was of a character to destroy authority, reverence in sentiment, decency of worship, and integrity of action. Printed abroad, when with safety and security it could be no longer printed at home, it was secretly imported by hook or by crook, in order to do its work. Hawkers of simple wares, in the country, going from village to village, carried with them batches of these highly-spiced and exciting denunciations, which efficiently kept alive the desire for change, and at the same time fostered that unrest and dissatisfaction with authority, which it was the interest of the innovators to keep alive and render more and more aggressively active. By these means the faith of the people had been corrupted, the sacraments were disparaged; while the discipline of the clergy was disastrously relaxed, and that of the laity fell almost altogether into abeyance. Rapid, most rapid, had been the descent to immorality and disorder. It was, therefore, the present intention of the Lord Legate and the Bishops to recount, and to call once again into active use, the decrees of general and provincial councils, all of which were to have the same weight as they had of old, before the national schism.

Importing and reading heretical books are consequently distinctly forbidden. These are to be judged as to their character by the decrees of the Council of Florence, which had dealt distinctly with the doctrine of the Sacraments. And, as all that naturally flows from these decrees is to be piously and dutifully regarded, the Lord Legate added various practical directions concerning the Reservation of the Blessed Sacrament, totally disused in recent times ; *i.e.*, under Edward VI.   Orders and directions were here likewise set forth for due and careful observance of the annual feasts of dedication.

But, as reform should begin with the shepherds of the flock, all neglect and disorder among such were so far as possible to be banished. The clergy were exhorted to disengage themselves from worldly concerns ; and, as so many of them appeared only to consider the temporal advantages of their benefices, or failed to reside amongst their flocks, penalties were to be inflicted for such breaches of the ecclesiastical laws.

Unless, however, those who had the cure of souls did their duty by preaching, which was particularly enjoined upon them on every Sunday and festival of obligation, such sound reform and solid progress as were desired by all persons of good-will, would never be properly attained.   None, nevertheless, are to preach but those duly ordained and formally licensed ; and, in order that sound teaching should be easily had, certain *Homilies* [1] are to be at once set forth.

---

[1] Drafts of some of these Homilies, together with a systematic and excellent *schema* for the whole series, are to be found amongst the Parker MSS. in C. C. Coll., Cambridge. Four volumes, it appears, were to have been issued. 1st, A series in

Example, however was always better than precept. Hence the Bishops, dignitaries, and all the clergy were solemnly urged to live soberly, piously, and chastely. They were to avoid all undue pomp and superfluity in their habits, equipage, and the furniture of their official residences ; their table was to be frugal, and recommended by hospitality, charity, and Christian conversation. Where it was possible, the relief of the necessitous, the education of the poor, and the general practice of works of piety and charity were to be attempted. The Bishops more especially were enjoined to show themselves openly as fathers of the indigent, and of widows and orphans, protectors of the weak and oppressed, and true and faithful shepherds of the whole flock of Christ. Moreover, they were to be assiduous in the study of Holy Scripture, and of the Catholic Fathers and Sacred Canons; to discharge their episcopal functions with eminent care and attention; to refrain unduly from meddling with worldly matters, and in all things to become patterns for their flocks, and to lead pure

which controverted questions were to be treated (such as those then so fiercely in contention) ; 2ndly, A series on the Apostles' Creed, the Ten Commandments, the "Our Father," the "Hail Mary," and the Seven Sacraments of the Church Universal; 3rdly, A series adapted for simple expositions of the Epistles and Gospels for the Sundays and Festivals throughout the Christian Year ; and, 4thly, A series dealing with the various rites and ceremonies of the Church, and with the vices and virtues.

and blameless lives. Like care, *mutatis mutandis,* was expected from the inferior clergy. According to their means and opportunities, and in their various degrees, these, in such goodly words and works, were to follow the chief rulers of the Church. And, so that none should live in ignorance of their obligations and actual duty, these formal directions of Authority were to be published and set forth anew from time to time and duly distributed.

In recent times—the six years of Edward's rule—the scandalous living and laxity of the clergy—bishops as well as priests—had created grave and great disorders, and had been at once irregular and indecent. The clerical tonsure and habit, therefore, were to be henceforth restored, the Divine offices of the *Portiforium* were to be duly recited according to the Canons, while the clergy were solemnly enjoined to give themselves up cheerfully and willingly to sacred learning. Those in holy orders who had descended to vile and disreputable employments—and such were not a few—were urged to repentance and immediate amendment.

The greatest care, it was further enjoined, was to be taken in the matter of ordination. This was all the more necessary, as many unordained persons without the smallest authority, had taken to the explication of Scripture and to preaching during the last reign. All who presented themselves, therefore, to the bishops for the sacred ministries were to be (1), clear of all errors as regards the Faith ; (2), they must be able to give distinct proof of having been born in lawful wedlock ; (3), they must likewise have attained to the canonical age ; (4), they must, moreover, be free from all undue physical blemishes, which most properly exclude from the sacred ministry ; (5), their life and conversation must have been, still further, sound and praiseworthy ; while finally, (6), their learning must be suitable to the order and rank in the ministry to which they aspired.

As regards institution and collation to benefices, the canons of old, as formerly in force, were to be duly put into operation ; while all unnecessary dispensations regarding the same—certain of which had been unjust to Englishmen, advantageous to Italians, and other foreigners, and in themselves scandalous—were to be directly avoided. Residence in the Prebendal House, Vicarage, College, or Rectory, as the case might be, was to be insisted on. Vacant benefices were to be promptly filled up ; while, in the meantime, every parish altar was to be duly and efficiently served. Furthermore, no benefice was to be promised before it was vacant ; and all simony and simoniacal transactions were distinctly forbidden ; and if discovered, were to be promptly and efficiently punished. The oath to be taken at institution or collation was made most clear in its terms, and was intended in perfect good faith to avoid all such heinous and shameful irregularities as had been recently tolerated.

The fabrics of the churches were, furthermore, to be kept in good order ; true inventories of Church lands and goods were to be made, lawful debts to the Church were to be put on record, and attested by proper witnesses ; and such documents were to be carefully preserved. What was wanting as regards the canonical *instrumenta ecclesiastica* was, as soon as possible, to be provided. At the same time—and in accordance with what had been openly decreed—the following provision, sanctioned by Ecclesiastical authority, was to be fairly and faithfully had in mind and regarded :—

" As to those Ecclesiastical possessions which were formally taken from the Church, and confirmed by the Holy See to their present owners, these are expressly excepted from this Decree, and it is our will that they should in no ways be affected by it."

Then follow full directions for the due education of youth for the priesthood ; and how sufficient means are to be procured for carrying this out. It was to have been mainly done in connection with the Cathedral Churches, and by those beneficed therein. A small charge on the incomes of all the clergy was at the same time to be made, while efficient teachers from various quarters were to be provided for the special object in view.

Parish Churches were to be personally visited from time to time by the bishops ; the sacrament of Confirmation was to be periodically administered ; and any criminal cases needing the consideration and judgment of the diocesan in his court, were to be promptly heard and faithfully adjudicated upon, without needless delay or undue costs.

As regards the interiors of the Parish Churches, the old rules and customs which had grown up during eight hundred years—customs of expressive solemnity and of singular beauty and value— were everywhere to be restored and regarded. The baptismal water was to be carefully secured from all irreverence ; the holy oils were to be kept in a secure aumbrey ; the tabernacle[1] for the Blessed Eucharist was to be of suitable material, and to be duly furnished and preserved by lawn veil, rich silk coverings, and lock. The Holy Sacrament was to be often renewed, and whenever borne to the sick, it was to be so borne with all the customary marks of worship—lanterns, canopy,

---

[1] It is believed that in England a receptacle in the form of a dove was commonly suspended over an altar for this purpose. Sometimes, however, a metal Tower or Sacrament-house was in use, placed above or behind the altar. Occasionally the Holy Sacrament was preserved in an Aumbrey or cupboard within the sanctuary and close to the altar. The custom varied.

incense, and hand-bell. Banns of marriage were to be duly published; while a record of those baptized, of the sponsors at bishopping, of the married and of the faithful departed, were to be kept in separate MS. volumes.

Unconsecrated altars were at once to receive consecration. If any had been profaned, such were to be carefully purified and blessed anew. Special inquiry was to be made, and action taken, so that nothing should be lacking for the due and reverent ministry of the altar. Chalices, patens, *ciboria*, *corporalia*, priestly vestments, and authorized service-books, were to be procured at once. The Christian Sacrifice was to be duly offered with all proper reverence and devotion. One clerk at least, vested in a surplice or rochet, was always to serve the priest, and to be able to make the customary responses, and to minister accurately, with recollectedness and reverence. Everything in the church itself, moreover, was to be clean, pure, wholesome, and safely kept. The churchyard was to be enclosed, the graves to be preserved in decent order; and all needful repairs both of church and churchyard-fences to be carried out as soon as possible.

Everything that could be done to render the change then taken efficient, was thus to be attempted and carried out; and nothing pertinent nor important seems to have been forgotten or neglected. The learning, the discretion, the wisdom and the firmness of the Lord Legate were at once notable and noted. Here was the Finger of the Almighty. At this momentous crisis in the nation's history the intercessions of the old Saints, and the patronage of the Blessed Mother of God seem to have proved both potent and efficacious.

As regards the work of the clergy, Divine service, Christian teaching, the goods of the Church, the mischievous influence of evil-livers, the observance of Advent, Lent, Rogation-tide, and the solemn fast and feasts, all was duly had in consideration.

Moreover, the bearing of the people in Church during Divine service, the due government of hospitals, charities, and schools; the position of collegiate and prebendal churches; the subject of residence by Bishops and dignitaries, the duties of Archdeacons, Vicars-General and Commissaries, were one and all fully dealt with, and this in a true spirit of piety, justice, and wisdom.

Nothing seems to have been wanting in what was thus attempted; and while almost all the Injunctions set forth by this Synod were in accordance with the decrees and canons of Ancient Councils, both national and general—for novelties were of course eschewed—no one could fail to have seen that the experience which the Cardinal Legate himself had obtained during the Sessions of the Council of Trent,—in which His Lord's Grace had exercised so important a part, and which referred to the Church throughout the world—was then specially applied for the advantage of the people of his native country : for the national Church in its corporate capacity, then efficiently restored to Catholic Unity, and for the greater honour of Almighty God.

CHAPTER V.

DEATH OF THE QUEEN AND THE CARDINAL-ARCHBISHOP OUR NATION'S LOSS.

CONTENTS OF CHAPTER V.

Death of the Queen and the Cardinal-Archbishop our nation's loss.—Policy of Persecution.—Exaggeration and fables.—Teaching of the Lollards.—Disastrous influence of Cranmer.—Pleads guilty of high treason.—And denies the Faith.—The Fires of Smithfield.—Fundamental Innovators.—Their fiery rhetoric.—Impiety and contention.—Cardinal Pole's charity.—Exercised again and again.—Cranmer spiritually censured.—Queen Mary no persecutor.—Shows forbearance and conciliation.—Laws of the age severe.—Lollardism a pest.—Treasonable publications.—Well-deserved punishments.—Diseases of Body and Soul.—Character of the Middle Ages.—Beneficent influence of the Church.—Dignity and power of the clergy.—Obedience and Patriotism practised.—The Cardinal's knowledge of the Past.—Appointed Archbishop of Canterbury.—Consecration of Cardinal Pole.—His MS. Register-Book.—Pole deals with existing scandals.—Marriage of the clergy.—Visitation of Canterbury Cathedral.—Success therein of the Cardinal.—Abbot Feckenham's testimony. Further Honours for the Cardinal.—His vigilance and zeal.—Sarum Service Books reprinted.—Bishop Gardiner's ability.—His edifying death.—Restoration of tithes.—St. Edward's shrine.—Old Foundations restored.—Thomas Stafford's Rebellion.—Courts of France and Spain.—Cardinal Pole recalled.—The Queen's bold action.—The situation in England.—Pole's letter to the Pope.—His moderate and reasonable opinions.—The innovators retire abroad.—And create confusion and disorder.—Sedition-mongers and heretics at home.—Proclamation against such.—Irreligion and disorder.—The Edwardine Ordinations.—Profanities of the innovators.—Influence of moral gloom.—Heresy a distinct crime.—Queen Mary's sufferings.—Her attachment to the Faith.—Her duties as Queen.—Her edifying death.—Personal appearance.—Character and accomplishments.—Her death a national misfortune.—Her funeral Sermon.—Her Burial at Westminster.—Cardinal Pole's death.—His position and characteristics.—Prince of the Church and diplomatist.—His work worthy of imitation. — Personal appearance and character. — Existing portraits of him. — His systematic industry. — His learning and eloquence.—His particular treatises.—High and noble private character.—Foresight, prudence, and charity.—His burial at Canterbury.—Concluding reflections.

CHAPTER V.

OTHING could have been more disastrous, as regards the important religious
work which Cardinal Pole had in so
great a measure effected, than the
course of those national events which led, in due
time, to the punishments inflicted upon Cranmer
and so many of those who agreed with him. Perhaps, on the whole, it is at once wiser and safer, as
well as more just, to refer the evil to the age
itself in which such was done. For it is obviously
impossible, with any show of justice, to lay the
blame of this course of proceeding upon any single
individual, whether accuser, judge, sheriff, or hired
executioner. Neither the King, nor the Queen,

nor the Lord Legate can be properly blamed. Nor, indeed, can Gardiner, the Lord Chancellor, nor Bonner, the Bishop of London.[1] The policy, to many persons, evidently seemed the only one at hand and available. For the evil was great and momentous enough; and the burden of meeting and overcoming it vast and pressing. That several officials should have co-operated in carrying that policy out, is most unfortunate; for it has left, it is to be feared, an uneffaceable impression upon the people of England, which is still fresh and marked.[2] It is of no avail, in extenuation of any individual, to point out exactly what the laws then in operation were; and that in process, judgment, and action, little or nothing actually illegal was done. When it is abundantly shown that the

---

[1] "It is obvious, even in the most partial accounts of the treatment of the people who were brought before him upon grounds of religion, that he [Bonner] behaved to most of them at first, not merely with good temper, but with a great deal of seeming kindness. He tried to smooth down their ruffled feelings, to win upon their regard, to coax them into relinquishing their peculiar opinions. Over and over again we find him appealing to them so kindly and forcibly as to draw thanks and tears from bystanders interested in their fate."—*Letter of John Bruce, F.S.A., in the* "*Athenæum,*" Oct. the 27th, 1855. See also "Essays on subjects connected with the Reformation in England," by the Rev. S. R. Maitland, D.D., pp. 386-576. London: 1849.

[2] Regarding Ridley's and Latimer's death, Mr. C. W. Boase, Fellow of Exeter College, thus recently wrote:—"The horrible sight worked upon the beholders as it has worked since, *and will work while the English Nation survives.*"—*Historic Towns, Oxford*, p. 120. London: 1887.

State, and not the Church, in every case, carried out sentences to which the laws gave sanction, scarcely anything material is effected by such a statement of the fact. It is of little use, moreover, to show—as truly enough it can be shown in abundance—that similar punishments were inflicted on their victims by the innovating party. The methods adopted by those of this faction, who undertook to inform and instruct Posterity—methods, in their results, not to be credited without investigation and inquiry—have certainly served the purposes of their not too-scrupulous authors. For, over and above the actual facts, unfortunate enough in themselves, the falsehoods, exaggerations, inventions, and fables in use have always been numerous, and have been carefully handed on from writer to writer—none of such falsehoods and fables being properly examined—in order to stifle inquiry in the interests of Truth, to perpetuate false traditions, and to vilify honest and zealous men.

Before this narrative is continued, it seems necessary to revert to what had taken place a century and a half previously. For such—it should never be overlooked—has a distinct bearing upon the events of Queen Mary's reign, and serves to show how Cardinal Pole's policy was subsequently brought to nought.

In the early part of the fifteenth century, Archbishop Arundel, and others who, at least, may be presumed to have had the interests both of Church and State at heart—however much their judgments may be thought to have been erroneous—desired to combine for the efficient maintenance of the Faith, and for the welfare of the nation. True Religion seemed in danger. The teaching of the Lollards — so directly bearing on political and social life—had been most mischievous and disturbing;[1] but it had found bold advocates in the then Earl of Salisbury, Thomas Latimer, William Neville, and other persons of considerable influence. Both Lords and Commons had deliberately petitioned for the statute, by which an obstinate and impenitent heretic, duly convicted before the Spiritual Court, was to be handed over to the secular officers and burned; while all heretical books were to be destroyed.[2] Whether the enactment of this well-known statute against these heretics was wise and politic is an open question.

---

[1] "In the fact that he [Wickliffe] was permitted to reside unmolested at Lutterworth, and enjoy the income of that living, we have reason for agreeing with the impartial Historian who urges that, 'if we allot to *him* the praise of courage, we cannot refuse *them* the praise of moderation.' It was only when rebellion and outrages of all kinds were becoming every day more and more common, that the severer penalties of measures of coercion were introduced to repress the disorders which an unrestrained license of thought and speech had brought into existence."—*Centenary Studies*, by Edwin de Lisle, M.P., pp. 38, 39. London : 1884.

[2] Wilkins' "Concilia," vol. iii. pp. 252, 254, 262, 267, 328.

Looked upon and judged by a nineteenth-century taste, it certainly was not.

To the words and works of Thomas Cranmer, several incidental references have already been made.   He it was who had invited hither the revolutionary wretches from abroad, by cant and falsehood to spread their moral poison throughout the length and breadth of the land.   Of his disastrous and malign influence under Henry and Edward there could have been no doubt.[1]   It has been pointed out what followed from his action in endeavouring to set aside the claims of Mary to the Crown.   His name stands at the head of those who most falsely and iniquitously denied that she had been born in lawful wedlock.   He it was who had

---

[1] How weighty had been Cranmer's influence and responsibility—the man who had invited hither the foreign heretics—is apparent from the speech of Dudley, Duke of Northumberland, on the scaffold.   After having acknowledged the justice of his sentence, and " being allowed an entire freedom of speech, he called God and all who were present to witness that he suffered for a cause in which he had been engaged by other persons, whom he asked God to pardon.   He took this opportunity of declaring to them that for some time before the death of King Henry, and ever since, he had been led astray by the Reforming Preachers, which had been the principal cause of his misfortunes.   He therefore cautioned them to beware of these profligate and seditious persons who had opened the book of error, and knew not how to close it.   That ever since these new doctrines had been set on foot, God had given them up to themselves, and inflicted on them the severest punishments—war, sedition, riots, rebellion, plague, and famine.   He therefore exhorts them to obedience to the Queen, and to return to the true Catholic Faith."

actively co-operated in the usurpation of Lady Jane Grey. In the document sent to Queen Mary, she was commanded to desist from any pretensions to the Crown, and was ordered by those who signed the instrument to retire into private life— a distinct act of treason.[1]

Now, at Cranmer's trial, it should be remembered that he pleaded guilty to the indictment, and submitted himself to his Sovereign's mercy. On this he was regularly attainted of high treason, and the sentence was duly confirmed by Act of Parliament. In consequence of this, the See of Canterbury had at once become void in law. Yet, be it remarked, it was not authoritatively de-

---

[1] So early as the year 1397, King Richard II., by and with the assent of the Lords spiritual and temporal and the Commons, carefully defined the four points of treason, and this even more clearly than these had been done forty-seven years previously. (1) Everyone who compasses and purposes to secure the death of the King; (2) Everyone who purposes to depose him, or to surrender his leige homage; (3) Everyone who raises and stirs up the populace against the King; (4) and everyone who sides against him to make war in his realm, and who is thereupon duly attainted and judged in Parliament is held to be guilty of high treason.   In the reign of Henry VI., several new treasons had been created, while that of Henry VIII. is notable for the large and needless increase of such.   The legislation of Queen Mary, however,—of which Cardinal Pole had by letter distinctly approved,—was remarkably lenient, for by a single Act of Parliament she swept away these unjust and disastrous enactments. The new treasons, præmunires, and felonies created in the two preceding reigns were directly abolished by Statute 1 Mary, chap. i.

clared vacant ; and, until Cranmer was officially degraded according to ecclesiastical law and custom, he was still looked upon as Archbishop.

There is no necessity to add to what has already been briefly set forth in regard to the disputations concerning the Holy Eucharist which were held at Oxford. Suffice it to point out that Cranmer, at their close, distinctly and categorically denied the Faith concerning the Sacrament—he had already declared that its author was the Devil himself[1]— maintaining at the same time several other heretical tenets, which had been invented by Luther, Calvin, or some other heresiarch ; and, after being called upon by the deputation from the Convocation of Canterbury to retract, was formally and faithfully declared to be a heretic. This occurred no less than two whole years before his execution. It cannot be asserted, therefore, that the door of repentance was in any degree closed to him. His superiors and judges—like their Master

[1] The following is taken from his archiepiscopal Manifesto regarding the Eucharist :—

" As the Devil is a liar, and the father of lying, so he has now stirred up his servants to persecute Christ and His True Religion. That whereas the great abuses of the Latin Masses had been reformed in the two late reigns, and the services in the Holy Supper performed agreeably to the institution of our Saviour and the practice of the Apostles, so now the Devil endeavours to restore the Latin satisfactory masses—a thing of his own invention and device."—*Manifesto of the Archbishop*, made in September, 1552.

—pitiful and merciful enough, could not, however, forget that justice should never be wanting.[1] The method of punishment, be it remembered, moreover, was not exclusively theirs. It belonged to the English Nation.

That it tended, indirectly it may be, but efficiently, to rob England of the spiritual advantages which Cardinal Pole had secured is very certain. For when a change in the Sovereign took place—when Mary died and Elizabeth Boleyne succeeded her—those opposed to Unity, Peace, and Catholicity—with such sad events to dwell upon, and having always an effective batch of lies in their right hand whenever such seemed to be needed in addition—never wearied of telling of the fires of Smithfield in all their terrible details, or of dwelling upon the sufferings of three men[2] who,

---

[1] The same was the case with Latimer, who was kept in confinement for nearly three years in the hope of his repentance. He had been notoriously guilty both of treason and sedition, and was found to be in direct and constant communication with the foreign stirrers-up-of-strife and their English allies. " At Westminster the xiii. day of September, 1553. This daye Mr. Hugh Lattymer clercke appeared before the Lordes & for his seditious demeanor was comitted to the Towere, there to remaine a close prisoner, havinge attendinge upon him one Anstey, his servant." *Harl. MSS.*, Brit. Museum, No. 643, folio 8. b.

[2] The teaching and temper of one of them may be gathered from the following address, which needs to be better known than it is. It is part of Ridley's farewell to the City :—

" Oh, London, London ! to whom now may I speak in thee, or whom shall I bid farewell ? Shall I speak to the prebendaries

so far as man can see, died without repentance at the stake—though with some fortitude—outside the north wall of the City of Oxford.

That these fundamental innovators, and the persons both at home and abroad with whom they consorted and co-operated, eventually but dis-

of Paul's? Alas! all that loved God's word, and were true setters forth thereof, are now (as I hear say) some burnt and slain, some exiled and banished, and some holden in hard prisons, and appointed daily to be put to most cruel death, for Christ's Gospel sake. As for the rest of them, I know they would never brook me well, nor I could never delight in them. Shall I speak to the See thereof, wherein of late I was placed almost, and not fully, by the space of three years? But what may I say to it being (as I hear say I am) deposed and expulsed by judgment, as an unjust usurper of that room? Oh, judgment, judgment! can this be just judgment to condemn the chief minister of God's word, the pastor and bishop of the diocese, and never bring him into judgment, that he might have heard what crimes were laid to his charge, nor never suffer him to have any place or time to answer for himself? Thinkest thou that hereafter, when true justice shall have place, that this judgment can be allowed either of God or of man? Well, as for the cause and whole matter of my deposition, and the spoil of my goods which thou possessest yet, I refer to unto God, which is a just Judge; and I beseech God, if it be his pleasure, that that which is but my personal wrong be not laid to thy charge in the latter day—this only can I pray for.

" O thou now wicked and bloody See, why dost thou set up again many altars of idolatry, which by the Word of God were justly taken away? Oh, why hast thou overthrown the Lord's table? Why dost thou daily delude the people, masking in thy masses, in the stead of the Lord's holy supper, which ought to be common as well (saith Chrysostom, yea, the Lord himself,) to the people as to the priest? How darest thou deny to the people of Christ, contrary to his express commandment in the gospel, his holy cup? Why babblest thou to the people the

tinctly overthrew the Old Religion and founded another, is quite certain.[1] No special pleading of the professional advocate nor act of historical

common prayer in a strange tongue? wherein St. Paul commandeth, in the Lord's Name, that no man should speak before the congregation, except it should be by and by declared in their common tongue, that all might be edified. Nay, hearken, thou whorish bawd of Babylon, thou wicked limb of Antichrist, thou bloody wolf; why slayest thou down and makest havoc of the prophets of God? Why murderest thou so cruelly Christ's poor seely sheep, which will follow none other but their pastor Christ his voice? Thinkest thou to escape, or that the Lord will not require the blood of his saints at thy hands? Thy God, which is the work of thy hands, and whom thou sayest thou hast power to make, that thy deaf and dumb god (I say) will not indeed nor cannot (although thou art not ashamed to call him thy Maker) make thee to escape the revenging hand of the high and Almighty God. But be thou assured, that the living Lord our Saviour and Redeemer, which sitteth now on the right hand of his Father in glory—he seeth all thy wicked ways and cruelty done to his dear members, and he will not forget his holy ones ; and his hands shalt thou never escape. Instead of my farewell to thee, now I say, Fie upon thee, fie upon thee, filthy drab, and all thy false prophets ! " To the above rhetoric may be added a record of the following facts :—

At the degradation of Bishop Ridley and Latimer, Brooks, Bishop of Gloucester, allowed him only to be degraded from the priesthood. On this Bishop Jeremy Collier wrote : " The reason why Ridley passed for no more than a priest may be better conjectured. For this prelate, being consecrated to his See of Rochester several years after the Pope's supremacy was discarded, the kingdom was then suffered to be in a state of schism, and by consequence the Bishops had no authority to consecrate and ordain. This was the sense of most of the governing clergy of this reign."—*Ecclesiastical History*, by Jeremy Collier, vol. vi. p. 122. London, 1846.

[1] " Henry VIII. had rather destroyed the Papal dominion in this country than established anything else in its place. His

jugglery can alter the fact, which may be gathered even from the Church's enemies. Moral force could never have accomplished such works; but unjust laws, violent legal outrages in the form of law and tyrannical cruelties—within the space of fifty years—did the dark deeds all too efficiently. Impiety dominated public life; contention was everywhere indulged in ; the discipline of the Redeemer was laughed to scorn.[1] Furthermore, let it be noted that truth and error were constantly

amiable and short-lived son was the real Founder of the Protestant Church of England. From the chaos of conflicting opinions and practices prevailing through the land, he formed a church, on doctrines purely scriptural, and in its ceremonial retaining only such ancient rites and observances as are authorized or not forbidden by Scripture, and which were at the same time agreeable to the taste and manners of the People."—The Reform of England by the Decrees of Cardinal Pole, by Henry Raikes, M.A. 4to. p. v. Chester: 1839.

[1] As Calvin wrote to Cranmer, "The hireling dogs of the Pope are barking unceasingly, that the pure word of Christ may not be heard. *Impiety is everywhere boiling forth and raging with such licentiousness that Religion is little better than an open mockery.*"—Original Letter, dated "Geneva, 1552."

"The same *spirit of contention is raging here, which was the origin of so many evils amongst ourselves;* of not only I might say perpetual dissensions among the true disciples of Christ, but of *an infinite contempt of all the discipline of Christ and of the Sacred ministry.* For Satan, when he cannot retain his chief idol, the Mass, and the remaining superstition and idolatry of this Sacrament, comes amongst us by the spreading of these evils, in order that he may at once bring discredit on the whole salutary administration of the Sacred Supper, and may render it despicable."—*Letter from Martin Bucer to Peter Martyr. Scripta Anglicana,* p. 546. Basil, 1577.

confounded in the centuries that succeeded, both being artfully distorted; while grave writers and shallow leaders-of-the-blind alike united to teach the pitiable people of this duped nation—which at length came to accept the teaching as true—that the Church was their enemy, and that negation-mongering and misbelief were the only true means of salvation.

During Cranmer's confinement, both in London and Oxford, the Lord Legate had done all that was possible and politic to bring him to a sound mind. Again and again the time of punishment had been postponed; again and again earnest endeavours had been made to induce him to accept the Faith. Repentance and obedience were both pressed upon him in pity and with earnestness. A long and closely-reasoned Letter from Cardinal Pole on the doctrine of the Eucharist, addressed to the heart as well as to the head, is one most pleasing instance of this. But where Bishop Fisher had failed, it was not likely that anyone else would succeed.

This did not, however, prevent the Lord Legate from pointing out—as his office bound him to do—that the grave and deadly errors into which Cranmer had fallen were at once the effect and punishment of the moral and doctrinal disorders of his past life. He had notoriously been raised to the episcopal office in order to gratify the passions of Henry VIII., and this shameful purpose had been at all times effected. Pole, at the same time, takes notice of the complex and interminable evils endured by the nation which Cranmer's prevarications concerning the Faith, his perjuries and sensuality had directly and distinctly brought about.[1]

In another Letter—calling God to witness his sincerity—the Cardinal declares that "his concern for him (Cranmer) and the desire of his welfare were such that were there any available means of rescuing him from that terrible sentence of death, which, unless he returned to his right mind and duty, must surely affect both soul and body, he would most willingly prefer it to all the honours and emoluments which can befall any man in the life that now is."

Cranmer, as we have seen, had been already condemned for treasonable practices against his Sovereign's person, rights, and title, and had received sentence of death confirmed by the Legislature. His errors and heresies, so obstinately persisted in, had been examined by a spiritual tribunal, which all eyes had recognized and respected; and it had been duly found that his eccle-

---

[1] The original of this Letter, in Latin, was formerly preserved in the French King's Library, MS. No. 10,213, folio 43. It may be found printed *verbatim* in Cardinal Quirini's "Collection of Pole's Correspondence," part v. p. 238.

siastical offences had been destructive of True Religion, and entirely deserved censure and punishment. The actual sentence, after pointing out Cranmer's general heresies, went on to declare that "particularly he had held and taught a doctrine concerning the Sacraments of the Body and Blood of Christ and of Holy Orders, contrary to what had always been taught and believed ; . . . . that he had revived the peculiar errors of Berengarius and of Wickliffe,[1] and had aided and abetted those of Luther. To all these he remained firm, obstinately repudiating the necessity for repentance. For these valid reasons, therefore, he is excommunicated and anathematized, at the same time —according to custom, precedent, and law—he is deprived of all his ecclesiastical rights and privileges; his effects are confiscated, and he is ordered

[1] Wickliffe, it may be here pointed out, taught that bishops have no pre-eminence over simple priests—a " view " which the present Bishop of Durham, before he was appointed to this prelatial office, *mutatis mutandis*, appears to have proclaimed as an original discovery of his own. Wickliffe also maintained that all ecclesiastical powers are in abeyance during mortal sin ; that man, whether he wills it or not, is bound to sin ; that God undoubtedly approves of sin ; that confession of sin is quite useless and supererogatory, and that the temporal prince should at once cut off the head of any ecclesiastic who sinned. This man's works, in which these " views " are exhibited, have recently been reprinted ; for there appears to be no ancient or modern heretic too absurd or too wild in his notions who may not obtain a band of noisy admirers amongst the shallow sentimentalists and fadmongers of the present day.

to be at once degraded and delivered up, both as a traitor and a heretic, to the secular power for punishment.

This in detail need not be dwelt upon. Sufficient reference has been already made thereto on a previous page; and other writers have dwelt upon it both impressively and at great length. Nor need any fresh or newly-stated accounts be set forth of similar punishments endured by similar transgressors. John Foxe, the author upon whose printed words so many persons rely for their history of this complex period, is not to be depended on for his fiery and lurid descriptions, which are uniformly either false, romance-like, misleading, or greatly exaggerated.

If Queen Mary—instigated by Cardinal Pole, as has been said, without any sufficient or solid basis of truth—were a persecutor, it was certainly not by virtue of any tenet of her religion that she became one; for, from the period at which she attained to the English crown, and for nearly two years afterwards,[1] she had invariably declared herself openly and frankly an adherent of the religion of St. Augustine of Canterbury and St. Gregory

---

[1] "Many of the reformed, who had neither outraged the Papists nor appeared for the Lady Jane, had either the liberty to go beyond sea, or, if they happened to be seized, were dismissed without much difficulty at their friends' intercession."— *Ecclesiastical History*, by Jeremy Collier, vol. ii., 375, 380.

the Great, which every well-informed Christian knows to be the True Religion; to which, at the period in question, eleven-twelfths of the people of England still adhered, and which, moreover, never sanctioned, nor sanctions, Persecution.

With equal frankness, both by private letters to Cardinal Pole and to the Emperor Charles, and by public utterance at home, she entirely disclaimed every degree of force and violence against those who had been seduced into heresy and schism. Her private virtues, and specially her regard for the poor and erring, were notorious. Moreover, in all the ordinances and decrees issued by ecclesiastical Authority, and made use of by Pole, for visibly restoring the kingdom to the Unity of the Faith, charity, forbearance, prudence, and conciliation[1] are always and ever found to be the watchwords of their policy and action. Herein Gardiner, too, was always at-one with them.

As regards the Cardinal's own words and works, in distinct and forcible terms he again and again expressed himself directly in opposition to all extreme and rigorous measures. But neither Queen, Cardinal, nor prelate could alter ancient or existing laws.[2] There they were on the statute-book.

---

[1] Cotton MSS., Brit. Museum, Titus B. II., folios 170-176.

[2] *E.g.,* The " Act of the Six Articles," proclaimed April the 28th, 1539, condemned all proved heretics who denied the Real Presence, to be burnt. This was the special work of Henry

They belonged to the age, and were quite in harmony with its sentiments and convictions. In these struggles and contests all parties used them. If duly put into force, the practical inconveniences of such laws could not be removed, until such had been legally repealed.

No one, furthermore, can deny that the eloquent and charitable Spanish chaplains of King Philip openly condemned needless persecution and cruelty, as being (this has already been shown) not only directly and notoriously opposed to the Catholic Faith, but exceedingly detrimental to the interests of True Religion.

When, after two years' reign—during which malign treason, insolent cant, artful duplicity, attempted murder,[1] and open rebellion had in

---

VIII. The Commission *ad inquirendum de heretica pravitate,* empowered to act by Edward VI. in 1549 (Rymer's " Foedera," xv. 182) was exactly to the same purpose; while subsequently Elizabeth's warrant, addressed to the Lord Keeper Bacon in July, 1575, to burn two Anabaptist heretics, are proofs that the " Supreme Headship," whether assumed by female or male, to put the point mildly, was no particular blessing to the people of England.

[1] For example, one William Thomas, a disciple of Goodman, the Protestant preacher, plotted the murder of the Queen, for which he was most properly and righteously executed. Two well-known Christian preachers at St. Paul's Cathedral, when instructing the ignorant—Dr. Bourne, afterwards a bishop, and Dr. Pendleton—were openly assaulted, one by having a sharp dagg hurled at him with great force, and the other by being fired at with a pistol, the bullet of which grazed his person. Similar aggressions were made in other places.

turns been tried by the enemies of order and law —several of the plotters and sedition-workers laboured from abroad, it was found absolutely necessary to revise the ancient statutes against that old and well-known pest, Lollardism.[1] The scandalous principles of the new men, their dishonest tricks and contrivances to mislead the populace,[2] their preachments and plots, their threats to take the Queen's life—were directly incompatible with the due and proper security of

---

[1] See " Centenary Studies," by Edwin de Lisle, M.P., London, 1884, a most able tractate, in which the false and dangerous principles of Wickliffe and Luther are concisely and powerfully exposed.

[2] An artful contrivance was managed by which mysterious or meaningless words and decisions on disputed subjects were heard to come forth from a thick and solid wall in Aldersgate Street. The Protestant preachers—no doubt knowing their true origin —unctuously declared these to be the audible utterances of the Holy Ghost. When some on-looker in the street cried out, " God save the Queen " [Mary] there was no response, but when another exclaimed, " God save the Princess " [Elizabeth] a shrill and loud " Amen " was heard. All kinds of controversial propositions were dealt with by question and answer—the replies often involving coarse and seditious language, and invariably gross heresy. Religion, the sacraments, the Christian sacrifice, the Queen's proposed marriage, were all dealt with. It is on record that no less than twenty thousand excited persons visited the spot in the course of two days, so that the City authorities were obliged to interfere. The Lord Mayor, as a practical act, ordered the wall to be demolished, which, being done in the sight of the astonished populace, a young girl of eighteen, named Elizabeth Croft, was found in a carefully-made recess. She not only publicly confessed the fraud at St. Paul's, but named the persons who had incited her so to act.

her government, or in truth of any efficient government at all. Books of the most offensive and treasonable character, *e.g.*, John Knox's " Blaste against the Monstruous Regimen of Women," [1] Goodman's volume entitled " The Superior Magistrate, etc.," and John Poynet's " Treatise on Politic Power," printed abroad, were circulated on all hands. Full of the most irreligious assumptions, foul slanders, and mischievous teaching, it was essential and most desirable promptly to curb the base actions of the scheming men who wrote them. Such utterances could not be discreetly ignored. Secure in their foreign retreats, these literary agitators egged on any hair-brained fanatics and sentimental heretics at home—always in the forefront in times of confusion and turmoil—who

---

[1] " There were interspersed in this publication atrocious and horrible calumnies against the Queen of England, whom Knox called at one time ' the wicked Mary,' at another time a ' monster.' And he exasperated King Philip also by language not much less violent. When men had read this infamous libel, attached as they are to true religion and to our church, they considered it neither profitable nor safe to ourselves that Knox should be received with favour by our church. . . . . You cannot but be aware how unbecoming it would have been in us impotently to rage in half-muttered abuse against magistrates ; not, perhaps, because they do not deserve it, but because of the office imposed upon them by God. This we can assure you, that that outrageous pamphlet of Knox's added much oil to the flame of persecution in England. For before the publication of that book not one of our brethren had suffered death."—*Letter from David Whitehead and others*, dated Frankfort, 20th Sept., 1555.

could be found to resist the law, and endeavour to bring discredit upon the policy of the Queen and her advisers.

When calmly and without prejudice the various cases are carefully examined, however—and when they are compared with the acts of Henry, Edward, and Elizabeth[1]—it is found that in most instances, after a fair and legal trial according to existing laws, the persons punished thoroughly and entirely deserved what they received. It might have been better, perhaps, terminating their sufferings more promptly, that the axe or the halter, rather than any sharper or severer form of punishment had been invariably adopted. There is, it must be acknowledged without any contention, something very revolting and repulsive to the sensitive in

[1] " Henry VIII. and his successors for many generations inflicted fines, imprisonment, and death on thousands of their subjects for denying the spiritual supremacy of the temporal sovereign. This galling Inquisition lasted for nearly three hundred years, and the severity of its decrees scarcely finds a parallel in the Spanish Inquisition. Prescott avows that the administration of Elizabeth was 'not a whit less despotic and scarcely less sanguinary' ('Ferdinand and Isabella,' vol. iii., p. 202) than that of Isabella. The clergy of Ireland under Cromwell were ordered, under pain of death, to quit their country, and were obliged to pursue their studies in foreign seminaries. Any priest who dared to return to his native country forfeited his life. Whoever harboured a priest suffered death, and those who knew his hiding-place and did not reveal it to the Inquisitors had both his ears cut off."—*The Faith of Our Fathers*, by James Gibbons. D.D., Bishop of Richmond, p. 244.   Baltimore : 1877.

that frightful doom—punishment by fire. The red-hot ploughshares of old, the branding of poor beggars on the cheek, the kindling faggot, and the chained-criminal in his dying agony, are sickening sights from which most persons would certainly desire to avert their gaze. The same, too, may be said of flogging with a seven-thonged whip, strangling with a hempen rope, or cutting off a man's head with an axe. Pity, a ray of sunlight from heaven, of course is a beautiful moral quality, and acute suffering is ever sad to witness and still sadder to bear; but those who have to administer the law for the general good of the community know well at the same time that Law must be ever upheld, and that Justice should never be disregarded. Under over-much disorder, contention, and repudiation of lawful authority, social security for each and every individual may suddenly cease to exist. What has been, may be. There were very painful duties to be done at this period, it is true; and it must be admitted by all who hold that diseases of the soul are at least as malignant as diseases of the body, that such duties were not done inefficiently; though some persons have maintained (the Author is unable to agree with them) that, if done at all, the scale adopted was possibly inadequate for effectually meeting the deeply-seated and ever-extending evil with which our beloved nation was then first cursed. The sweating sickness of old, as well as virulent small-pox, the incomprehensible cattle-plague and hydrophobia in these recent and enlightened days, have had and have to meet the practical and perhaps efficient policy of what is termed "stamping-out."

Whether, after all, Religion is more practical and potent now ; whether the close of one era, and the commencement of another, was on the whole beneficial to England, are interesting problems, quite open to discussion, but perhaps not so very easy to be solved.

Throughout those "middle ages" in England, which are so caricatured and defamed by some, the influence of the Church upon the nation and people had always been most advantageous and beneficial. It stood, in the Name of God, between the weak and the strong, with no fear for the latter, and with all due consideration and charity for the former; so that Justice might ever be done faithfully, and Truth and Right and good government might be always firmly upheld. The more this attractive subject is directly and indirectly examined, the more clearly does this leading truth distinctly stand out. For the social life of the people was then everywhere touched and tinctured by the Christian Religion ; and, as a consequence, was everywhere abundantly blessed from above, and hallowed below. The Crucifix, artfully sculptured with the arms of the Redeemer outstretched

in mercy beside cross-roads ; the Madonna and
Child in the wayside shrine, the churches and cross
of every village, the market-cross of every town,
the dead Christ in the arms of His Mother, wrought
in stone, where the faithful departed slept, were one
and all telling and expressive tokens—in a measure
sacramental tokens—of this great truth.   Again :
the active Ecclesiastical power, distinct and domi-
nant, invariably preserved that which was wholesome and beneficial, and tended to bind all classes
together by religious and social bonds for the
common good.   The landed property of the higher
ecclesiastics, held in trust for God and the people,
the local possessions of the beneficed clergy, the
lands, farms and their appurtenances of the Cathedral
chapters, as well as the tithes, in almost every case,
touched in one way or another each parish of the
realm.   On hill-slopes, in peaceful hamlets and
valleys, within walled cities, and in every country
town, the picturesque spires of parish churches or
of monastic corporations rose heavenwards—their
mellowed bells day by day calling the people to
worship and prayer.   The religious orders, whom
our ancestors reverenced, had, as all knew, by the
patient labour of centuries, and by abounding
perseverance, turned barren tracts into smiling
pastures ; and, with Heaven's blessing of dew and
sunshine, of cold and heat, had made rich and
golden corn-fields wave under many a July's

cloudless sky.   In a very practical and important
matter, the Cistercians had well fostered the growth
of sheep-farming—by which English wool brought
plenty or abundance to thousands, both yeomen
and hinds.   Such religious orders, owning but a
life-interest in their lands and properties, were
almost always just and benevolent landlords; and
seldom turned away their faces from their poor
neighbours in any case of distress or sorrow.   For
such owned common interests.   At the open grille
of the monastery-gate, a benevolent, welcome, and
acceptable dole—without any questions or many
words—was always to be found.   In the parish
church or monastic sanctuary, such woe-stricken
wayfarers invariably found a place of temporary
rest.   These well-furnished churches were the poor
man's second and brighter home.   Then—to take
a wider sweep of the situation—the beneficial
power of the clergy in the State was more than
considerable.   From their cultured ranks were
selected all the great officers of the State : for
bishops and abbots ranked with the barons and
earls.   These prelates and their clergy, regular
and secular, worked devoutly and devotedly for
the general welfare of the community, when each
member of the State was baptized, and when all
the people of every class—duly heeding the call
to Mattins and Mass, to Vespers and Rosary—
turned to the Church for aid and sustentation, as

a child turns to its mother's breast. Loyalty, at the same time, was kept alive and healthy by the ordinary every-day lessons of Christianity. For all power comes from God, and the powers that be are ordained of God. Obedience, by the same principle, and in the two independent spheres, was alike rendered to the Father of the faithful and to the Sovereign. Patriotism everywhere flourished. Order was everywhere secure. True, the wealth of the Church created some jealousy, as wealth ever does : so that base men—with no fear of God, nor any regard for man before their eyes— prepared to secure for themselves, by any means, the opportunity for an application of robbery and confiscation. The attacks of the Wyckliffites on the Church's temporalties in a previous century, no doubt, prepared the way for the dissolution of the religious houses under Henry VIII. The constant drain of money to Rome, however, the cost of Legations, the payment of heavy fees and fines, the difficulty and tediousness of appeals for justice, the expense of necessary dispensations and licenses ; and the general delay in obtaining prompt settlements of ecclesiastical causes and just judgements, all tended indirectly, but efficiently, to cripple and render unpopular the clergy of England. Much zeal and money thus spent—as so many saw for themselves—brought in return little or no apparent advantage. Moreover, it seems to be perfectly clear that the policy, then so popular in Italy, of filling our Prebendal and Cathedral Churches with foreigners, who, from their distant homes, secured the revenues, but left the official work either undone or only performed by a cheap substitute, tended greatly to make the Tudor revolution possible. All this may be gathered, indirectly perhaps, but still it may be gathered from the official correspondence of Cardinal Pole with his friends and contemporaries. To judge from what therein may be found, little of interest and importance in the then recent History of England had escaped his notice, if it appeared to bear in any way upon the great national work, which, by God's mercy, he had been permitted to complete.

But to proceed with a narration of such further facts as may tend to throw a light upon the history and policy of the great prelate, whose words and works are under consideration.

The Pope, on December 11th, 1555, had appointed him to be administrator of the See of Canterbury, and at the same time created him Cardinal-Priest. The Bulls originally granting him full legatine powers had been issued on the 8th of March, 1554. Four months afterwards, *i.e.*, on the 6th of July,[1]

---

[1] 1554, July 6, " S^{mus} concessit privilegium Card^{ll} Polo, legato in Angliâ, Ecclesias aliaque disponendi et episcopos intrusos tempore schismatis rehabilitandi, et dispensandi cum ipsis in

he received special and additional powers for accomplishing the work in hand ; and, in the year 1555, still further specific and exceptional authority for rehabilitating those bishops who had been irregularly intruded into English Sees during the period of division ; with abundant power to dispense them from the consequences of all irregularities contracted in that unhappy state.

Subsequently, he was duly and regularly nominated Archbishop of Canterbury.

The following discreet sentiments on the subject of that Primacy, confidentially set forth for the Pope, are deserving of note :—

" I have received from your Holiness the decree by which I am nominated to the See of Canterbury ; and at the first consideration of it, may most truly say that the greatness of the charge in question gave me a just distrust of my sufficiency to acquit myself of it, and would have altogether deterred me from making such an undertaking my own choice. I reflected afterwards, however, on the Princes at whose recommendation I was designated for this post of honour, on the Vicar of Jesus Christ who has given an illustrious testimony in my favour ; and on the assessors,[1] by whose approbation I had been chosen, and those whose

omnibus irregularitatibus quas tempore schismatis contraxerat."
—*From an authentic Transcript of the Original.*

[1] The Dean and Prebendaries of Canterbury Cathedral.

welfare I was to superintend ; and lastly, that I was to perform this duty in my own native land, which is, as it should be, most dear to me. On these considerations I did not dare to say even a single word to refuse the burden." [1]

Cardinal Pole was, by consequence, consecrated a bishop at the Church of the Grey Friars at Greenwich on the 22nd of March, 1556,[2] Nicholas Heath, Archbishop of York, being the consecrator, assisted by six other prelates. Three days later the accustomed ceremonies at Bow Church in Cheapside took place, at which High Mass was sung by the Bishop of Worcester.

Every legal formality having been completed, both in accordance with Canon Law and Catholic custom, the Lord Legate was enthroned, and became Cardinal-Archbishop of Canterbury. In this high and holy office he continued to complete and consolidate the great work of his life—Reunion.

His official MS. Register-book, still preserved

[1] From the fifth volume of Pole's Letters.

[2] " The Sonday xxij day of Marche [A.D. 1555-1556] was at the Gray-ffrers at Grenwych was my lord cardenelle Polle was consecratyd, with x byshopes mytyred the iij yer of the quene Mare."

" The xxv day of Marche was owre Ladyday, the Annunsyasyou, at Bow chyrche in London was hangyd with cloth of gold & with ryche hares [*i.e.*, arras] and cossens [*i.e.*, cushions] for the commynge of my lord cardenall Polle ; ther dyd the bysshope of Vorseter did synge he [*i.e.*, high] masse mytyred."— *Cott. MSS., Brit. Museum*, Vitellius, F. v.

amongst the archives of Lambeth Palace, and containing sufficient evidence of the weight and value of such labours, is of vellum, large folio in size, and was probably bound in rough calf, as it now appears, during the last century. It certainly does not contain all the documents which might have been therein preserved. Several are wanting. No reference is made to the peculiar cases of re-habilitation of bishops and of the conditional or absolute ordination, if any, of the ministers made under Edward VI. It comprises only eighty-two parchment leaves, the various entries being made in some official scribe's handwriting. Possibly they were originally made on single skins of vellum. These leaves are usually covered with matter on both sides, the initial commencement of new paragraphs being in black letter. On the first page is a large shield of family arms of eight quarterings,[1] surmounted by a cardinal's hat and

---

[1] These arms, with the quarterings just as they appear, were likewise to be found displayed in the east window of the Founder's Chapel at Magdalene College, on the north side of the sanctuary, at the period of the official visitation by Richard Lee, Portcullis, in 1574 (MS. in Queen's College Library, H. 33, and Harleian MSS., British Museum, No. 1412). Here is the record, with the names added within brackets:—Quarterly of eight. 1. Quarterly France and England, over all a label of three points Erm., each point charged with a canton gules. [Plantagenet.] 2. Per pale or and sa. a saltire engrailed counterchanged. [Pole.] 3. Gules a saltire argent, over all a label of three points gobony, ar. and az. [Nevill.] 4. Gules a fesse between six cross-crosslets

tassels, with a shield of the arms of the See of Canterbury, surmounted by a precious mitre below. At the foot of the page stands the name of the probable illuminator, " Jo. Mulcasterus." On the second folio an elaborate letter " R.," with which the word " Reginaldus " commences, drawn with consummate art in black ink, is admirably designed, and still in the most perfect preservation.

Throughout his episcopate the Lord Legate was constant in his labours and most earnest in effecting all such improvements as were possible and practicable. The scandals created by the married clergy, for example, had been numerous and keenly felt: none more so. Women of chaste lives and good repute, if approached, declined any communication with the lapsed regulars or loose-living seculars, who turned to a lower moral plane. Such persons, however, were treated by the Cardinal with charity, firmness, and discretion.[1] The

or. [Beauchamp.] 5. Checquy ar. and azure a chevron ermine. [Newburgh.] 6. Argent three fusils in fesse gules. [Montacute.] 7. Or. an eagle displayed vert. [Monthermer.] 8. Quarterly first and fourth, or three chevrons gules [Clare]; Arg. and gules, on the second and third quarters a fret or., over all a bend sa. [Norreys.]

[1] " THE FORM OF THE RESTITUTION OF A MARRIED PRIEST.

" Whereas I Richard Karsey, prest, late Curate of Beddington within the dioces of Winton being ordered a preste abowt 21 yeres agonne having ministrid as a prest in all kind of prestly

astonishment and disgust of the laity at Cranmer's irregularities, and at the marriage of the clerics—witness Sir John Bourne's stern expostulation—

function and ministration of and in Sacraments and Sacramentals as the office of a prest appertayneth, have sithens that time contrary to the state of myne order, decrees of the churche and laudable customes of the same, married one Elizabeth ——, a single and solute woman, and with her in one howse as man & wief have cohabited and dwellid, to the offense of my christen brethren and breach of the unitie of Christe said Church, I. the said Richard do now lamente and bewaile my lief past and th' offences by me committed inteuding firmly by Goddes grace hereafter to leade a pure chast and continent lief according to such grace as almighty god of his mercy uppon myne humble petition and prayer shall graunte me, and I do heare before you my competent Judge and Ordinary most humbly requier absolution of and from all such censures and paines of the Lawes as by my said offeuces & ungodly behaviour I have incurred and deserved, ffyrmely & solemnly promising and professing before you in this present writing never to returne againe to the saide Elizabethe as to my wief or concubine, but from henceforth to abstein from her . . . . . and also from all other women according to the Lawes and Constitutions of our Mother the Churche and as myne Order also requireth. In witnes of this myne advised and deliberate mynde promise & profession I have to the same in this writing subscribed my Name with Myne owne Hand. Geven the 10th day of July in the yeare of our Lord God a thousand five hundred fiftie and sixe.

" Per me Richardum Karsey."

" Read before M' Thomas Stympe L.D. Custos of the Spiritualties of the vacant diocese of Winchester, in his Court beside the north door of St. Paul's Cathedral in the presence of John Incent, notary public, & Anthony Huse.

"The said Richard was absolved from the sentence of Excommunication, suspention, interdict & other censures & pains, & was restored to the sacraments & sacramentals & to his own presbyteral order, as is here formally set forth."

—*Cardinal Pole's MS. Register*, folio **41 a**, Lambeth Library.

was as great as might occur now-a-days if the Anglican bishops and clergy—restoring primitive polygamy for those waxing unusually uxorious—should think it seemly and right to take to themselves two or three wives *at the same time.* Though the complex and varying difficulties which constantly faced the Cardinal were ever changing and presenting themselves in new forms, yet, acting in the spirit of the decrees of the great Council of Trent, he cheerfully went forward, endeavouring to remedy all existing breaches of law, Catholic custom and discipline, and to restore the Church of England to that happy position which it had held for so many centuries. Not only in his own diocese, but in every portion of his province, such endeavours were made, and in some cases—notably in those of Winchester, Worcester, and Hereford—with great success.[1]

At the formal Visitation of his Cathedral Church

---

[1] See "Injunctions given to the Cathedral Church of Hereford by the V. Rev. F. in God, Richard Bp. of Wourcester to ye M. Rev. F. in God Raynald Pool Card. & L*d* Legat to ye K. & Q. Ma'ty & to ye hole realm of Engl' from the Pope's Holin' & ye See Ap'call of Rome ye 17 d. of July in ye y* of o* L*d* G. 1556 inviolately to be observ'd under ye peine of contempt." In these " Injunctions " external tokens of reverence are enjoined at the *Sit nomen Domini* and *Laudate pueri*, and the clergy and others are ordered to bow their knees at the *Et incarnatus est* and *Homo factus est.* The 27th of these Injunctions stands thus :—" It' y' ye D. & ye Ch.' shall receive no Bastard or priests' children to be Queristers."—*MS. Epistolæ et Orationes*, Lambeth Library, Wharton MSS., No. 595, p. 123.

of Canterbury, all who were officially connected therewith were summoned. On the list which occurs set forth in his Register (following the forma. Citation on page 42) stand the names of Nicholas Wootton, the Dean; Richard Thorndon, Bishop of Dover; together with those of eleven Prebendaries, six "Preachers of the Word," twelve minor canons, thirteen vicars-choral, ten choristers, fifty-one boys being taught at the Grammar School, two sub-sacristans, two vergers, four bell-ringers, &c. Local visitations in several independent rural-deaneries were subsequently held; and His Grace's Visitation-articles—so concise, complete, and admirable—are set forth at length upon these vellum folios.

That the Cardinal-Archbishop was to a great extent successful in his work of restoration may be gathered from various sources. On the other hand, every effort on the part of the "new men,"[1]

---

[1] What these men desired to see effected may be gathered from what they actually and ruthlessly accomplished when they obtained the power as well as the will. Nothing could well be more sickening, however, than a contemplation in detail of their words and works. In the present day some of the latter seem almost incredible, while the former are invariably either canting or blasphemous. For instance, Bishop Horne, of Winchester, in the year 1570, in his official capacity wrote to the President and Fellows of Trinity College thus:—" Whereas I am informed that certain monuments tending to idolatrie & Popish or devill's service, as crosses, censares and such like filthie stuffe used in the idolatrous temple, more meeter for the same than for the House of God remayneth in your College undefaced. . . .

though directed against such works, was made with demoniacal intention and disastrous zeal. Yet—to provide a pregnant testimony—Abbot Feckenham, in a speech delivered in the House of Lords early in Elizabeth's reign, pointed out the true state of the nation and people under Queen Mary in the following luminous sentences:—

" Your lordships may remember how quiet and governable the people were. It was not then their custom to prescribe to Authority, to run

I very earnestly forthwith upon the receite hereof, will you to deface all manner [of] such trashe, as in the churche of Christe is so noysome and unseemlie," etc., etc.—*Register of Trinity College, Oxon*, folio 138, b.

This bishop at a visitation of his cathedral 2nd October, 1571, ordered " the rood lofte in the bodie of the Church to be mured upp:" " images in the glasse windowes, or other places of the churche to be putt oute & extinguished, together with the stone crosse in the churchyarde." (Folio 83.) He also ordered " that the organes be no more used in servyce-time & that the stipende for the orgayne-player . . . . be hereaffter torned to some other godlye use & necessary purpose in the colledge chapel " (folio 88), while at an official visitation of New College, amongst other scandalous changes, ordering the images of the saints in the choir to be burned—" omnes et singulae imagines ibidem olim stantes igni committantur." Still further (" Register," folio 65)—" Neque socii, scholares, aut ministri chori, se convertant in divinis, more papistico, ad orientem, cum cantatur *Gloria Patri*." When this man, Robert Horne, was Dean of Durham the destruction he wrought was wholesale, and his method most scandalous and sacrilegious. Vestments, MS. service books, hangings, ancient monuments, and the whole life and miracles of St. Cuthbert in stained glass in the Cloisters were ruthlessly made away with.—*See "Ancient Rites of the Church of Durham,"* London, 1671.

before the laws, nor to disobey the Proclamations of their Sovereign. There was then no sacrilegious rapine, no plundering of churches, no blasphemous outrage and trampling the Holy Sacrament under their feet. It was none of their way to tear down the pix, and hang up the knave of clubs in the place. They did not hack and hew the Crucifix in those times. They were better observers of discipline than to eat flesh openly and fill their shambles with butcher's meat in the holy solemnity of Lent. In the late reign [Queen Mary's] the generality of the people, and particularly the nobility and those of the Privy Council, were exemplary for their public devotion; it being the custom to go to a church or chapel to beg the protection of God before they entered upon the business of the day." [1]

But to return to what relates more especially to the personal position of the Cardinal-Archbishop.

When Sir John Mason—a firm favourer of the Edwardine innovations—resigned the Chancellorship of the University of Oxford, Cardinal Pole had been chosen to occupy that exalted office ; as, upon Bishop Gardiner's untimely death, he was selected to fill the like dignity in the University of Cambridge.

The Oxford electors officially declared that he

----

[1] Cotton MSS., British Museum, Vespasian, D. 18, folio 8.

had already and formerly been a credit to the University, both at Corpus Christi and St. Mary Magdalen Colleges, but that now he was an honour to the whole kingdom, and an ornament to the English Church.   They notice more particularly his increasing vigilance, careful zeal, and fatherly care, in repressing all error and in maintaining the unchangeable Truth.   They greatly rejoice over his labours in the cause of peace and unity; and recount at the same time his singular good-will to this his own English University, of which so many daily proofs bear clear and abundant testimony.

The Queen herself[1] co-operated in every due and efficient manner with the Cardinal-Archbishop. Their policies of restoration were one.

Such acts as these, concerning both Universities, serve to intimate how popular was the Lord Legate's policy, and in how sincere and earnest a manner his great labours for Corporate Reunion were appreciated by those who had thus welcomed him to his new dignities.

In the celebration of Divine Service, and in the

---

[1] " Queen Mary took pains to restore the splendour of the University of Oxford. . . . . . She not only contributed large sums for rebuilding the public schools, but, moreover, granted the University three considerable impropriations. In her charter reciting these benefactions, she declares it to be her determined resolution to employ her royal munificence in reviving its ancient lustre and discipline, and recovering its privileges."—*Life of Sir Thomas Pope*, by Thomas Warton, B.D., pp. 148, 149. Oxford : 1772.

various rites and ceremonies of the Church, the greatest practical difficulty had been experienced, because of the want of service-books. So wide had been the destruction of these—destruction as wicked as it was wanton—that old printed copies were everywhere unattainable; while vellum MSS. were rarer still.   Hence, with the distinct sanction of Authority, not less than fourteen or fifteen examples of the old Salisbury Use from the presses of Berthalet, Regnault, and Kingston, were issued in Paris, London, and elsewhere.[1]

---

[1] The following English Service Books—which the Author has personally examined—were printed during this reign :—

𝔐𝔦𝔰𝔰𝔞𝔩𝔢 𝔞𝔡 𝔲𝔰𝔲𝔪 𝔦𝔫𝔰𝔦𝔤𝔫𝔦𝔰 𝔈𝔠𝔠𝔩𝔢𝔰𝔦𝔢 𝔖𝔞𝔯𝔦𝔰𝔟𝔲𝔯𝔦𝔢𝔫𝔰𝔦𝔰, Parisiis, folio : 1555.   Red and black.   Three foliations.   Two engravings at the Canon on vellum.   In the frontispiece, the arms of France and England quartered, crowned and supported by Angels, the Rose with I.H.S. in the centre crowned : below, St. George and the Dragon.   [I. Amazeur pro G. Merlin.]

𝔐𝔦𝔰𝔰𝔞𝔩𝔢 𝔞𝔡 𝔲𝔰𝔲𝔪 𝔦𝔫𝔰𝔦𝔤𝔫𝔦𝔰 𝔈𝔠𝔠𝔩𝔢𝔰𝔦𝔢 𝔖𝔞𝔯𝔦𝔰𝔟𝔲𝔯𝔦𝔢𝔫𝔰𝔦𝔰, etc.   Red and black.   In frontispiece, the Arms of England in a Garter and crowned.   Vivat Re. and " M.R." between two pillars, on whose bases are the initials I.D., i.e., Iohn Day.   (The last edition of this Missal printed in England.)   Londini, folio: 1557.

𝔓𝔬𝔯𝔱𝔦𝔣𝔬𝔯𝔦𝔲𝔪 𝔰𝔢𝔲 𝔅𝔯𝔢𝔲𝔦𝔞𝔯𝔦𝔲𝔪, 𝔞𝔡 𝔦𝔫𝔰𝔦𝔤𝔫𝔦𝔰 𝔖𝔞𝔯𝔦𝔰𝔟𝔲𝔯𝔦𝔢𝔫𝔰𝔦𝔰 𝔈𝔠𝔠𝔩𝔢𝔰𝔦𝔢 𝔲𝔰𝔲𝔪, etc. 4to.   I. Kingston and H. Sutton.   Londini : 1556.

𝔥𝔬𝔯𝔢 𝔟𝔢𝔞𝔱𝔦𝔰𝔰𝔦𝔪𝔢 𝔳𝔦𝔯𝔤𝔦𝔫𝔦𝔰 𝔐𝔞𝔯𝔦𝔢 𝔰𝔢𝔠𝔲'𝔡𝔲𝔪 𝔲𝔰𝔲' 𝔖𝔞𝔯' 𝔱𝔬𝔱𝔞𝔩𝔦𝔱𝔢𝔯 𝔞𝔡 𝔩𝔬𝔫𝔤𝔲𝔪, etc.   8vo.   Rothomagi : 1556.   [The Woodcuts in the Kalendar represent the Twelve Ages of Man.]

𝔥𝔬𝔯𝔢 𝔞𝔡 𝔲𝔰𝔲𝔪 𝔖𝔞𝔯𝔲𝔪.   8vo.   Parisiis : 1556.

𝔓𝔬𝔯𝔱𝔦𝔣𝔬𝔯𝔦𝔲𝔪 𝔰𝔢𝔲 𝔅𝔯𝔢𝔲𝔦𝔞𝔯𝔦𝔲𝔪 𝔞𝔡 𝔲𝔰𝔲𝔪 𝔈𝔠𝔠𝔩𝔢𝔰𝔦𝔢 𝔖𝔞𝔯𝔦𝔰𝔟𝔲𝔯𝔦𝔢𝔫𝔰𝔦𝔰 castigatum, etc.   16mo.   Rothomagi : 1556.   Printed by R. Valentin.

𝔓𝔬𝔯𝔱𝔦𝔣𝔬𝔯𝔦𝔲𝔪 𝔰𝔢𝔲 𝔅𝔯𝔢𝔲𝔦𝔞𝔯𝔦𝔲𝔪 𝔞𝔡 𝔲𝔰𝔲𝔪 𝔈𝔠𝔠𝔩𝔢𝔰𝔦𝔢 𝔖𝔞𝔯𝔦𝔰𝔟𝔲𝔯𝔦𝔢𝔫𝔰𝔦𝔰.   4to.   Londini : 1555.   In the Colophon " per F. Regnault in alma

Bishop Gardiner, practically an ally of the Cardinal-Archbishop in all that might conduce to the spiritual welfare of the kingdom,[1] did much— as has been already pointed out—in co-operation with His Grace towards making adequate provision for the clergy, and in recommending them and their cause to the consideration of both Houses of Parliament. As the Legate himself testified in a letter to King Philip—then absent from England —the Lord High Chancellor had surpassed himself from his official seat in the ability, eloquence, prudence and piety of his great speeches made

Universitate Parisien."   Originally issued twenty years earlier.

Proccessionale ad usum insignis Ecclesie Sarisbu' observandos accomodum, etc.   Red and black.   4to.   Londini: 1555.

Prymer in Englysshe and in Latin sette out alonge : after the use of Sarum.   Red and black.   8vo. ; paged.   Rothomagi: 1556.

Pystles and Gospells of ye Sondayes and Festyuall dayes, etc.   8vo.   Londini: 1555.

Corona beate Marie uirginis.   4to.   [Qy.? Londini: 1556.]

Hore beate Marie Uirginis sec' usum Sar'.   16mo. Parisiis: 1557.

Proccessionale ad usum insignis Eccl'ie Sar', etc.   Impressum Londini: 1555.   [Belonging to Rev. W. J. Blew, M.A..   Qy.? Has this a new title-page ?   Was it the earlier edition of 1537 ?   On fol. xv. the office of St. Thomas of Canterbury is re-introduced.]

[1] So far as the Author has discovered, the jealousy which some writers assert to have existed between Pole and Gardiner, is based on imagination, and not on fact.   In the Cardinal's confidential letters to King Philip—written for the King's eye alone and not for publication—the most just and generous appreciation of the Lord Chancellor is everywhere apparent; and they contain sentences of remarkable point and power, utterly inconsistent with any such notion of jealousy.

with this aim. But these were amongst his latest
efforts. The evening shadows of his day were
lengthening and growing deeper. His life was
evidently drawing towards its close. Worn and
weary with the noble struggle in which, for so
long a time, he had been engaged: often disappointed, sometimes elated; always, however,
acting for the greater glory of God and the good
of his countrymen; his physical frame was found
to have become so debilitated, and his lofty spirit
so broken, that he soon withdrew to his chamber,
and, warned by increasing weakness, began to prepare for death, and to make a good end. Nothing
could well have been more edifying to those in
waiting or attendance than his patient bearing, his
due recollectedness, his earnest preparation for his
path across the dark valley. Mass was said in his
chamber by one of his chaplains every morning.
" He desired," as the record stands, "that the
Sacred Passion of our Saviour might be redde to
hym, and when they came to the denyal of Peter,
he bidde them there staye; for, saithe he, I have
sinned with Peter, but have not yet learnt to
weep bitterly with him." In due course he received the Sacrament of Extreme Unction with
excellent dispositions, and was furthermore fortified by the Food of Angels for his last extremity.
He died,[1] lamented by the Queen and all good

[1] Bishop Gardiner's official gold ring. with which he was

men, and was buried in Winchester Cathedral. A man of great ability, a bold and wise statesman, he was likewise an ecclesiastic of learning, piety and power.

Owing mainly to Gardiner's influence and labours —but with Pole's active co-operation—the tenths and first fruits, appropriate-benefices, glebe-lands and other lands, which since the twentieth year of Henry VIII. had been annexed to the Crown— producing yearly no less a sum than sixty thousand pounds—were formally resigned by the Queen and placed at the Cardinal's disposal for the maintenance of True Religion. Special benefactions for masses for the dead [1] were regarded and restored to the benefit of those for whom they had been made. Her Grace took an active and personal part in this noble and godly act. She openly expressed her wishes to deputations of both Houses of Parliament, so that in the Lords the Bill for accomplishing those wishes was passed with only two dissentient voices; while in the Commons the measure was carried by 193 votes to 126. No

buried, was taken out of his coffin, and is now in the keeping of the Dean and Chapter of Winchester. It is set with an oval intaglio on plasma, with profile head of Minerva; at either side of the bezel being a square facetted ornament set with small rubies.

[1] "Apologie of priuate Masse, spred abroade in writing without name of the authore . . . . . with an Answere, etc. 8vo. London : 1562.—*Library of Hartwell Park, Bucks*, (now dispersed.)

sooner had it received the sign-manual than the Cardinal saw that it was at once put into operation. It proved a distinct and remarkable blessing.

As Lord Chancellor, Dr. Nicholas Heath,[1] first Bishop of Worcester, afterwards Archbishop of York, succeeded Bishop Gardiner; and in every respect proved himself a worthy and efficient successor.

About the same time Mary restored the shrine of St. Edward the Confessor in Westminster Abbey,[2] honourably and most reverently re-shrining his sacred relics, and re-established the Hospital of the Savoy in the Strand,[3] re-endowing it with abbey lands; while the ladies of her household, moved by

---

[1] John Story writes to the Earl of Devonshire from London, 23 Feb. 1556. Therein he prays for his lordship's personal prosperity, so useful in the future for the Christian religion and his native land. The Queen and Cardinal Pole have the spiritual and civil matters of the realm in contemplation. Justice is reduced to order by the activity and energy of the present Lord Chancellor, Dr. Nicholas Heath, Archbishop of York.—*State Papers, sub anno* 1556.

[2] "The xx day of Marche was taken up at Westmynster agayn with a hondered lyghtes King Edward the Confessor in the sam plasse wher y[s] shryne was; and y[u] shalle be sett up agayn as fast as my lord abbott can have y[u] done; for it was a godly shyte (*i.e.*, sight) to have seen y[t], how reverently he was cared from the plasse that he was taken up wher he was led (*i.e.*, laid) when that the abbay was spowlyd and robyd; and so he was cared, and goodly syngyng and sentsyng as has bene sene, and masse song."—Cotton MSS., Vitellius F. v.

[3] The Hospital of the Savoy was re-established by royal warrant, dated June 15, 1556, from St. James's; when Ralph Jackson, clerk, was appointed Master of the same.

her example, furnished it at their own cost. It was the only religious foundation of this Queen's which subsequently escaped destruction under Elizabeth Boleyne. At Westminster, John Feckenham was appointed Abbot, not for life, but for three years, in accordance with certain continental traditions. Some writers assert that only fourteen monks were associated with him, but by a letter from the Lord Bishop Priuli to Beccatelli, it appears that exactly double that number had been brought back to St. Peter's Abbey Church.

When Sion House had been dissolved, and the inmates sent adrift, most of the nuns returned to their families; though some are said to have passed their days, following the rule of their order, in a cottage near their old home. Under Edward VI., several others, having had their pensions stopped, and being persecuted, were threatened with death, retired to a House of their Order at Dermond, in Flanders. They had chosen one Katherine Palmer for their Superior. Here Cardinal Pole found them, and under Queen Mary they were brought back to England; only, however, to be scattered again in the subsequent reign.

Towards the end of the month of May, 1557, Queen Mary issued a Proclamation complaining of having been ill-used by the French King. There can be little doubt that she had solid and excellent reasons for this complaint. The treasonable rebellions of Northumberland and Wyat had no doubt been known to him ; while Dudley and Aston, who actually conspired together in the French ambassador's London mansion, were afterwards welcomed and entertained at the French Court.

The Queen, though often induced actually to declare war with France, declined to do so until her own state had been attacked by a force fitted out by the Protestant refugees in France. Thomas Stafford, in the month of April, 1557, had landed with many foreign adherents in Yorkshire, and, with the aid of the disaffected there, had seized Scarborough Castle. Upon this he issued a counter Proclamation, most insulting in its terms to the Queen, and took upon himself the office of " Protector of the kingdom." He was was soon taken, however, brought to London, with certain of his French associates, and beheaded for treason on Tower Hill. It is clear that Stafford had been abundantly furnished with men, money, arms, and ammunition with which to invade Her Majesty's dominions. In the Queen's Proclamation, consequently, she forbad her subjects to trade with the French, and declared the King an enemy to herself and the country.

It is probable that Queen Mary would still have borne in patience and silence aggressions like these, had not the Pope induced the King to determine the truce between himself and King Philip. Hereupon—and, instead of awarding blame, upright persons will give praise—the Queen reasonably enough stood firmly by her husband. War was declared against France on June 7, 1557.

Soon afterwards King Philip took leave of the Queen, and embarked for the Continent. On the 10th day of the month of August, he gained a great battle at St. Quintin's in Picardy. The bravery of the English troops which he commanded, fighting side by side with the Spaniards, rendered his success complete; for many French prisoners, and some of high rank, were taken. Soon after this, to add to the complications of Mary's Government, the French incited the Scots to invade England.

The Pope was much vexed with the outspoken words and unmistakable action of Queen Mary, and, as some authorities say, equally annoyed with Cardinal Pole, who had always, and most consistently, aimed at removing the differences existing between the Courts of France and Spain. His Eminence had even gone so far as to suggest, with the most obvious respect, that the Holy Father himself should become an active mediator between these Powers. But such a proposal did not harmonize with the then policy of the Court of Rome. Cardinal Pole's interference, therefore, was so resented that his legatine commission was actually recalled, and he himself cited to appear before the Congregation of the Holy Office to give explanations, and offer excuses, either for inaction or too great activity.

And not only this, but William Peyto, a Friar Observant, subsequently Bishop of Salisbury, was created Cardinal and Legate in his place.

The Queen, on hearing this from her confidential agents abroad, was grievously and heartily vexed and disappointed. Obedience led her to say little; but duty to God and the nation she governed compelled her to act. To this end she enjoined that all the English ports, by which messengers could arrive, should be closed to them, and that no one coming from Rome should be admitted. Should any papers or despatches be discovered, such were at once to be sent on to the Council. She at the same time wrote to her ambassador in Rome, pointing out that if Cardinal Pole were to lose his position of legate, and be recalled, the interests of the Church of God in England would directly and severely suffer. His Eminence owned two distinct offices—Lord Legate and Archbishop of Canterbury, to which See the legatine privilege, out of regard to the British monarch, had been throughout antiquity attached. The Queen further pointed out to the Holy Father that old and unchanged usage had tended to leave it unquestioned; and that, furthermore, it had become a part of the

English constitution. That she looked upon the having a Lord Legate in England as portion of her royal prerogative; that by her coronation oath she was bound to maintain all the Christian privileges of the kingdom; and that none of these—more particularly that in question—could be relinquished without damage to the nation and ignominy to herself. Even if the Peers and Commons were disposed to abandon the old position, the Queen, she added, with singular dignity and Christian boldness, would be wholly and altogether unable to concur with them.[1] In fine, the sacred trust, solemnly committed to her at her coronation by the Almighty, could neither be tampered with nor abandoned.

In answer to this ably-argued despatch, the Pope informed the English ambassador at Rome that he had specially-important information to communicate to Cardinal Pole himself; making, at the same time, other comments upon the Queen's contention; and that he personally desired to see the English Legate. This, His Holiness declared, sufficiently explained his desire. And of this he wished the Queen to be duly informed.

---

[1] "Life of Reginald Pole," by Becatelli, from which, and from a copy of the document, the above is faithfully paraphrased. See also "Vita Reginaldi Poli, Britanni, S. R. E. Cardinalis, et Cautuariensis Archiepiscopi." Venetiis, M.D.LXIII., Ex officina Dominici Guerrei and Ioan. Baptistæ fratrum. By Andrew Duditius, pp. viii. 49.

Cardinal Pole's Letter to the Pope, in which he indirectly defended himself against several ungenerous attacks, and set forth the true position of the situation in England, is of some moment, and demands more than a mere passing allusion. That situation had somewhat changed and was still changing. There can be no doubt that the relations of foreign state to state, and of kingdom to kingdom — the contentions and struggles of foreigners—materially affected that home policy which the English Cardinal had deliberately adopted. Public men often appeared to be at cross-purposes. Malice and misinformation again and again did their work.[1] In Cardinal Pole's case, envious and designing persons, as a last

[1] Though Cardinal Pole had probably been deprived of his position as *legatus a latere* in favour of Peyto, yet he still regarded himself, being a Cardinal, as *legatus natus*. See his Letters, vol. v. 144. On p. 102 of Mr. Oswald J. Reichel's concise and most able book, " The Elements of Canon Law," he states that of old the Archbishop " was (1) Archbishop of the See of Canterbury, (2) Metropolitan of the Province of Canterbury, and (3) Primate of all England and born Legate of the Pope." But he cites no authority, either foreign or English, for his last assertion. It is said that James I. claimed some kind of similar position for Archbishop Abbot, and that the idea was referred to in the proceedings for suspending that Archbishop by the King, as Supreme Head of the National Church ; but still no definite authority either then or now seems to be forthcoming for the existence of such a dignity and position. Whether any Archbishop of Canterbury, who was also a Cardinal, may, *honoris causâ*, have been rightly styled " legatus natus " appears to be undetermined.

resource in their application of aggressive methods, had deliberately cast a slur upon his orthodoxy. He was said to have secretly favoured the Lutheran faction, or certain of their immoral phantasies; but, when informed of this, the Lord Legate modestly and mildly remarked that, if his past conduct did not satisfy his critics, he had nothing further of any importance to add in his defence.

"If I stand in special need of comfort," he wrote, "and expect it from His Holiness—no less than St. Augustine expected it from St. Gregory—I am conscious to myself of a similar diligence and goodwill in procuring the advancement of the Christian cause in this kingdom, to that which St. Augustine exerted; and I certainly exert it under far more difficult circumstances, for I daily discover for myself that it is an easier work to inform untaught minds than to unlearn those who have imbibed erroneous doctrines . . . . . All that remains to us, is to send up our common petitions to God that He may be pleased to dispose all things to the advantage of Holy Church, the reputation of the See of St. Peter, and the honour of the Sacred College."

This has been written of as "a remonstrance."[1]

---

[1] It is said that Cardinal Pole penned a systematic explanation and expostulation in regard to what Rumour had asserted; that this explanation was addressed to the Pope; that the Cardinal had some intention of publishing it : but that, on reflection, and in the interests of Peace, the MS. of it was burnt.

But such a term appears inapplicable. It was a mere statement of the truth as regards his position and action, remarkable alike for simplicity, dignity, and good temper, and it evidently had its due influence on the Holy Father.

Pole continued to act as Legate in England, consequently : no further action in the matter, bearing adversely against him, being taken at Rome. He was systematic and zealous in the administration of his diocese—witness the various details which his MS. Register-book contains on record—and at the same time found all his suffragans equally active in co-operation with him throughout the Province of Canterbury.

As regards the work of punishment by imprisonment, faggot and fire, there can be no doubt that it was impossible for him, a single individual, however influential, to avoid or override the then existing law. This fact should never be lost sight of, nor disregarded by those so ready to give judgment in all causes and upon all persons. His private letter to the Cardinal of Augsburg abundantly sets forth his own moderate and reasonable sentiments on the subject. He will not, he says, deny—and what sensible and reasonable being would deny?—that there may be men, themselves so addicted to grievous and pernicious errors, and so apt to entrap and mislead others, that they may justly be put to death, in the same manner that an unsound limb is sometimes amputated to preserve a whole body. But even this he maintains to be an extreme case, holding that all reasonable remedies should be first applied. The Bishops, as shepherds of their flocks, should ever remember that they are Fathers-in-God as well as judges, and should be always and invariably tender and true to their erring children. This, he declared, was the policy of the Fathers of Trent; and it had been scrupulously followed by himself, and by all over whom he possessed any influence in England.

Those of the "new men," who watched the action of Authority, thought it discreet—and for such, practically, it *was* discreet—to take themselves abroad, and out of harm's way, at the earliest opportunity. Though not numerous, such were tolerably compact in their co-operation and action, and exceedingly bold in their assertions. Some, on the other hand, were so earnest in their extraordinary and eccentric errors, and so zealous and fearless in disseminating them, that they seemed to court immediate punishment. Such they received, and thoroughly deserved. Those, however, —and no one can blame them,—who had wisely sought refuge abroad in Strasburg and Zurich, at Antwerp, Frankfort, and Basle, were safe if not welcome. There, nevertheless, out of the way of actual and pressing danger, they at once began to differ widely amongst themselves; and, amid much wrangling and jangling, to consolidate Chaos. Sometimes the veriest trifles—questions relating to official habits, and postures of sitting, walking, or standing, at what they termed " diets," " assemblies-of-the-saints," and " exercises," were solemnly and long-windedly discussed by men who held themselves to be somehow or other inspired : at others, the fringe of the deepest and most mysterious subjects of Revelation, of Christian philosophy, and of Catholic morals afforded topics for coarse controversial chatter, and the display of vulgarity, arrogance, and self-will. Disagreements, contentions, reproaches, and harsh judgments, set forth in Scriptural phraseology, were everywhere rampant ; while the moral confusion and social disorder that reigned, and the misery which came of such, can hardly be adequately described.

In the meantime, it was being all too-plainly discovered by those who had the interests of the nation very sincerely at heart, that no further progress had been made in the work of consolidating the religious unity of the kingdom; and that, owing to the deeply-seated heresies[1] of the new men—many of which appealed directly to their

---

[1] As early as June, 1555, a formal Proclamation, printed by Cawood, had been published against printing, importing, reading, selling, or keeping heretical books. The need for such a warning was everywhere apparent, for the wildest theories and the craziest social and theological propositions had been long

lowest instincts, and were thus readily popularized —divers evils remained altogether unsuppressed while others were obviously extending. Pipers, ignorant preachers, prattlers of error, together with sedition-mongers, conspirators, wandering ballad-singers, and heretics of all kinds, were actively engaged in destroying the Old Faith. Their daring impudence was only equalled by their distressing profanity, devilish art, and disastrous success.

Further action—perfectly necessary and eminently wise, and not adopted one day too soon—was taken, therefore, by Commissioners, as the following interesting State document[1] sufficiently sets forth :—

"For as much as divers devilish and clamorous persons have not only invented, bruited, and set forth divers false rumours, tales, and seditious slanders against us, but also have sown

bandied about and discussed by the foolish and fanatical. Amongst the writings of notorious foreigners enumerated were certain treatises by Calvin, Luther, A'Lasco, Zwingle, Melancthon, Bullinger, Erasmus, and Bucer; amongst the treatises of Englishmen were various books by Cranmer, Latimer, Hooper, Bale, and Hall the Chronicler, which, obscuring, denying, or perverting Truth, both with art and malice, had wrought many evils and ruined many souls.

[1] It is dated February the 8th, 1557. The Select Council had previously issued Orders against strolling players and pipers, who wander about from town to village, disseminating seditions and heresies.—*State Papers*, dated May 7th, 1556. At Westminster 6th Sep. 1557, a letter was addressed to the Lord Mayor ordering that no Players be allowed to play any plays between All Saints' Day and Shrove-tide; and then only such as have been seen and allowed by the Ordinary.

divers heresies and heretical opinions, and set forth divers seditious books, within this our realm of England, meaning thereby to move, procure, and stir up division, strife, contentions, and seditions, not only amongst our loving subjects, but also betwixt us and our said subjects; with divers other outrageous misdemeanours, enormities, contempts, and offences daily committed and done, to the disquieting of us and our people; We, minding and intending the due punishment of such offenders, and the repressing of such like offences, enormities, and misbehaviours, from henceforth, having special trust and confidence in your fidelities, wisdoms, and discretions, have authorised, appointed, and assigned you to be our commissioners, and by these presents do give full power and authority unto you, and three of you, to enquire, as well by the oaths of twelve good and lawful men, as by witnesses, and all other means and politic ways you can devise, of all and sundry heresies, heretical opinions, Lollardies, heretical and seditious books, concealments, contempts, conspiracies, and of all false rumours, tales, seditious and clamorous words and sayings, raised, published, bruited, invented, or set forth against us, or either of us, or against the quiet governance and rule of our people and subjects, by books, letters, tales, or otherwise, in any county, city, borough, or other place or places, within this our realm of England, and elsewhere, in any place or places beyond the seas; and of the bringers-in, users, utterers, buyers, sellers, readers, keepers, or conveyors of any such letters, books, rumour, or tale; and of all and every their coadjutors, counsellors, consorters, procurers, abettors, and maintainers, giving to you, and three of you, full power and authority, by virtue hereof to search out, and take into your hands and possession, all manner of heretical and seditious books, letters, writings, wheresoever they, or any of them, shall be found, as well in printers' houses and shops, as elsewhere; willing you, and every of you, to search for the same in all places, according to your discretions. . . . . And also to enquire and search out all such persons as obstinately do refuse to receive the blessed sacrament of the altar, to hear mass, or come to their parish, or other convenient places appointed for divine service, and all such as refuse to go in processions, to take holy water, or holy bread, or otherwise to misuse themselves in any church, or other hallowed place, wheresoever any of the same offences have been, or hereafter shall be committed within this our said realm.   Nevertheless, our will and pleasure is, that, when, and as often as, any person or persons, hereafter to be called or convented before you, do obstinately persist or stand in any manner of heresy, or heretical opinions, that then ye, or three of you, do immediately take order, that the same person, or persons, so standing, or persisting, be delivered and committed to his ordinary, there to be used according to the spiritual and ecclesiastical laws.   And also we give unto you, or three of you, full power and authority to enquire and search out all vagabonds, and masterless men, barrators, quarrellers, and suspect persons, vagrant, or abiding within the City of London, or ten miles compass of the same; and all assaults and affrays done and committed within the same City and compass."

What had actually taken place during the last reign is well known, and cannot be misunderstood. It was clearly enough seen by Cardinal Pole and all other far-sighted Christian people, that unless prompt action were taken to crush such innovations, True Religion must die out.   The moral disorder was so vast, and the irreligious poison scattered under Edward VI. and his " superintendents" had been so deadly in its effect, that prompt action was essential for the well-being of the State. Under that youth, ministers, preachers, and these " superintendents " had taken the places of the old prelates, priests, and deacons.[1]   Altars had been

---

[1] The position of the controversy concerning Orders—a position which ought to be surveyed and known—is here not unfairly or unfaithfully set forth, from the ancient standing-point :—" Though the consecration of bishops and priests in Henry's VIII.'s reign (after the schism happened, and a general interdict and excommunication was pronounced against the

broken down to wean the people from divine service and the Ancient Faith. A contention at once arose as to the shape of the new wooden tables. Were they to be square or oblong, placed on a solid frame, and attached thereto, or were they to consist merely of a few loose boards on trestles? Some were placed at the upper end of the church, others in the middle of the choir, east

whole ecclesiastical body) was esteemed uncanonical, and annulled as to jurisdiction, yet, all the time, during the said reign, the validity of their consecrations was never contested by the Catholic party. But, in the succeeding reign of Edward VI., a considerable alteration being made in doctrinal points, and among other things, a new Ordinal established, their ordination was not only looked upon as uncanonical, but also as invalid, upon account of the errors and omissions, which declared the insufficiency of their Ordinal. The reformers not only struck out the article of obedience to the see of Rome (which rendered their consecration uncanonical, and deprived them of all spiritual jurisdiction), but the most of them renewed the error of Aërius, and made no essential difference between the episcopal and sacerdotal character. To these errors they added several others, which were directly incompatible with a valid ordination : that ordination was not a sacrament instituted by Christ, but only a mere ceremony, to appoint a ministry for religious performances; that all power, both temporal and spiritual, was derived from the Civil Government, and, mainly, from the King : that those of the episcopal character, could perform nothing effectually towards the validity of their character, without the King's mandate or letters patent : that those of the sacerdotal character had no power to offer sacrifice, to consecrate the Holy Eucharist, or to absolve from sin. This was the constant belief both of the consecrators and of those that were consecrated according to the new Ordinal : to which may be added, that, though they had held the orthodox points above mentioned, they made use of a matter and form, that was insufficient, and not capable of con-

and west, with long benches around them; for
"the Supper" was partaken of sitting.[1] Stowe
the Chronicler gives several examples of profane
indignities perpetrated in the desolated sanctuaries;
and there are other revolting records in existence,
the perusal of which brings a blush to the face of
the reader. Neither font nor table was free from
the reforming atrocities then perpetrated, many of
the repulsive details of which are not fit to be
printed.

At the Court of the King and Queen — it

ferring that power, which essentially belongs to the episcopal
and sacerdotal character ; and that, having at the same time
no intention to confer any orders, but such as were conformable
to their errors, which were destructive of Christ's institution,
their ordination was, *ipso facto,* null and invalid.   These are the
considerations Dr. Harding and others went upon, when
they denied Jewel's character, and represented the whole body
of such of the reformed clergy to be no other than laymen, ex-
cepting such as were consecrated in Henry VIII.'s reign, before
the new Ordinal, or any other erroneous ceremony of ordination
was made use of. For the same considerations, the learned
divines of Queen Mary's reign, nay the Convocation, and even
the legislative power in parliament, declared the aforesaid
bishops and inferior clergy to be invalidly consecrated ; and
actually caused all those to be reordained, in whom they found
any essential defect. In the following reign of Queen Elizabeth,
the divines of the Catholic party continued in the same opinion
concerning the invalidity of Protestant ordinations ; and all
were reordained that came over to them, notwithstanding any
pretended consecration among themselves."—Dodd's *Church
History of England.*

[1] This arrangement remains even now (A.D. 1887) at Upper
Winchendon, co. Bucks, in the diocese of Oxford—a small
church about to undergo the work of restoration.

should now be put on record—were to be found men of mark and spirit, of strong wills and of noble aspirations—statesmen and warriors, poets, ecclesiastics, and painters. Of statesmen Reginald Pole was by far the ablest and most remarkable. His distinct genius none could doubt. He towered above all. Amongst the first, likewise, was Alva, ever handsome in person, but perhaps over-vigorous in deed; amongst the last, Hans Holbein, a limner of wonderful power and fidelity. Fleming, Count Egmont, the Flanders Protestant, Ruy Gomez, the accomplished Spanish statesman, Emmanuel Duke and Prince of Savoy (who subsequently was reported from abroad to be about to marry Elizabeth Boleyne, but who, upon a later visit to England, and upon nearer acquaintance with such a unique virgin, discreetly declined the questionable honour), and King Philip's vigorous and successful opponent in the future, the Prince of Orange.

Under lowering clouds and lurid skies, a series of cold seasons, followed by fevers and famines, occurred almost every year during this reign. That moral gloom which often overshadows the multitude during times of rapid social change and great political upheaval, took possession of very many minds ; some of whom beheld in various very strange, if not supernatural, occurrences, witnessed from time to time, obvious tokens of the displeasure of Heaven. These were taken up by the "new men" as very useful and timely for their own purpose, in pointing out that God had evidently forsaken the people of England, because of the Spanish marriage and the punishment of evil men and misdoers. By the astrologers and nativity-casters, by several mumbling prophets and mouthing preachers of the "new gospel," the presence of a Roman Cardinal in England—though a noble Englishman, a great prelate, and a far-sighted statesman—had blighted the grain, clouded the skies, murrained the cattle, and brought sickness and sadness to the multitude. Moreover, the common people were in addition artfully taught—and many of them learnt the lesson readily enough—that any punishment for any transgression of the law was an act of inherent injustice; that no Court of Inquiry nor Inquisition of any kind must be set up, and that each and every individual in matters of religion and morals should have the fullest licence to freely put into operation the "blessed grace of obstinacy," and the personal charms of self-choosing and self-pleasing.

Heresy, however, during the times in question, was regarded, as it always had been regarded in every well-ordered Christian nation, not only as an offence against Religion, but as a crime against the State. The policy of Cardinal Pole and Queen

ry could not alter this fact. Heresy, therefore,
s punished accordingly. This was the case in
gland and Switzerland, as well as in Spain and
ly. Henry VIII. and Edward VI. most cruelly
nished those of the Old Faith, just as Jews and
homatans had been proscribed in Spain. The
quisition of the last-named country was not in
y true sense an ecclesiastical, but was distinctly
political and royal institution. The sovereign
solutely nominated its chief rulers and officers,
ether clerical or lay, and dismissed them at his
ll. Their jurisdiction was exclusively from the
ng ; while the emoluments accruing from all
ney payments, fines and confiscations, were
ariably paid into the monarch's treasure-house.
e Inquisition consequently, as cannot be denied,
s a political tribunal. Its authority began,
tinued, and ended in the Crown.

But, to return to a consideration of the actual
uation. There can be little doubt that foreign
nplications—in which the King was interested,
the one hand, and the general feeling against
ilip of the English nation, on the other—caused
at anxiety to the Queen, always a sufferer from
lily weakness. The death of the Emperor was
st keenly felt. The loss of Calais was a sharp
d severe blow. Her husband's treatment of her
s open to the gravest animadversion. Anyhow,
regards the restoration of the Ancient Faith,

the grand feature of her reign,[1] she had co-operated most earnestly and sincerely with her kinsman the Cardinal ; while Gardiner and Bonner, Heath, Lord Paget of Beaudesert, and Lord Dacre of Gillicsland—with others, most worthy in themselves, and most patriotic in their whole course of action, did all that seemed possible and politic to remove or punish the evil-doers, to bless and benefit their country, and to uphold the Nation's weal. Such labour, however, was often marred by severity or failure, and constantly hindered by opposition. Those who were near the Queen at the same time realized that her manifold sufferings had long marvellously weakened her power of endurance, and that the end was surely at hand. And so it was.

Queen Mary died early in the morning of the 17th of November, 1558, at St. James's Palace. She was forty-two years and nine months old ; and had reigned exactly five years, four months, and eleven days. Throughout her serious illnesses she had displayed a beautiful patience and calm resig-

[1] " Her unshaken attachment to her Mother's Faith, and the unfortunate circumstances in which she was placed on assuming the sceptre, to rule over a people then convulsed by a revolution so momentous as the abolition of their religious creed, added to the false principles of intolerance urged by her Councillors—all conspired to cause her failure, and to throw a shadow over her reign no argument could have power to remove."—*Privy Purse Expenses of Princess Mary*, by Sir F. Madden, F.S.A., p. cxvi. London : 1831.

nation, perfectly saintly. As during the whole of her life she had been instant in prayer, and constant in reading Holy Scripture[1] and other sacred writings, so it was until its close. Enduring much pain, both bodily and mental, at that period—with many sad memories of the past, which still lingered, and of carking disappointments which had been more than ordinarily bitter—her duties as Queen were never neglected. At Philip's direct suggestion, she had been induced to recognize her half-sister, Anne Boleyne's daughter, as her successor—though this must have added

[1] "To make a practice of reading the Scriptures ought, in the eyes of the Bishop (Gilbert Burnet, who, perpetuating the lying traditions of John Foxe, attacks Mary on every occasion, and by every unworthy weapon), to have been reckoned neither bigotry nor superstition ; and it is mentioned by Lord Morley, a layman, in terms of admiration, that she was accustomed to read over every day with her chaplain the daily service. [See " Praise of the Virgin," by Erasmus, MS. Reg. No. 17, A. xlvi.] So differently do men judge of what is superstition and what is not ! Mary, in truth, felt most conscientiously that the first duty required from man is to worship his Creator ; and if she has been censured or sneered at for her piety, it must be ascribed to the wickedness or weakness of her calumniators."—*Privy Purse Expenses of Princess Mary*, p. cxxxi. London : 1831. One of her Prayer Books, a Book of the " Hours of the Virgin," is preserved at Stonyhurst College. The volume is bound in crimson velvet, studded in centre and corners of each side with silver-gilt letters, which together make up the name MARIA REGINA. On the obverse cover the centre letter R is ensigned with a crown, on either side of which is a Tudor Rose and a pomegranate—the badge of Katherine of Arragon, Mary's mother; in the centre of the reverse cover is a shield, upon which are enamelled the royal arms, ensigned by a royal crown.

many a sharp and stinging pang to the stroke of death. She sent presents of jewels to Elizabeth by the Countess of Feria (Jane Dormer), and charged her not to fail in paying all those lawful debts which had been contracted by privy seals. This noble lady's devotion to her Sovereign and to the Ancient Faith are worthy of special note.

Mary's last end was that of a true Christian monarch. Mass had been said in her chamber every morning; and Extreme Unction was administered as the end surely approached. At daybreak of the 17th, when she had become almost speechless, she was able only to adore her Redeemer at the Elevation of the Host[1] by a look of devout resignation and trustful confidence; and then, when the benediction had been given, her spirit, blessed and benefited by divine grace, passed peacefully to her Maker's keeping.

Michele, the Venetian ambassador,[2] thus carefully and faithfully described Mary's person—a description exactly borne out by a very striking and well-painted contemporary portrait, still exist-

---

[1] " At the levacion of the sacrament, yᵉ strengthe of her body and vse of her tong being taken awaye, yet nevertheless she, at the instante, lifted vp her eyes, *ministros nuncios devoti cordis*, and in the benediction of the churche she bowed down her hedd, and withal yielded a mylde and glorious spirite into yᵉ Hand of her Maker."—Cotton MSS. Brit. Museum, Vespasian, D, xviii. folio 104, b.

[2] His record in Italian is preserved in Lausdowne MSS. Brit. Museum, No. 840, A, folio 155, b.

ing :[1]—" She is of low stature, but has no deformity in any part of her person. She is thin and delicate, and altogether unlike her father, who was tall and strongly made ; or her mother, who, if not tall, was somewhat stout. Her face is well-formed, and her features prove, as well as her pictures, that when younger she was not only good-looking, but more than moderately handsome." [2]

[1] In the Library of the Society of Antiquaries, Burlington House ; bequeathed by the late Rev. Mr. Kerrich, who purchased it in 1800 from the collection of Mr. Smith of Lincoln. It has upon it the initials " H. E. 1554," and is believed to have been painted by Lucas Van Heere.

[2] A careful consideration of the best-known portraits of Queen Mary, leads the Author to place implicit reliance on the graphic description given in the text. The picture at Burleigh House, representing her very late in life, and after severe illness, with those in the possession of the Duke of Northumberland (sometime belonging to the family of Phillips of Ickford, Bucks), Mr. Wenman Martin, and the portrait in the family group by Holbein at Hampton Court, however, all tend to support this judgment. So, likewise, do the striking and remarkable portraits by Sir Antonio More, at Madrid—of which he has seen a copy—and that at Woburn Abbey, by the same artist; and another at Trinity College, Cambridge. It may be here added that no less than thirteen portraits in oil, representing her as Princess, are known to exist, of which the Author has inspected eight; and twenty-five portraits in oil (either on canvas or panel), representing her as Queen, of which he has examined thirteen. One portrait of her as Princess, at Burleigh House, is engraved in the great work of Mr. Lodge. In the original she has brown hair, large open hazel eyes, full red lips, and an excellent complexion. It is possibly the same picture as is described in Troughton's " Narrative," as existing in 1553 in the house of a gentleman named Featherstone, at Stamford. (See " Archæologia," vol. xxiii. p. 38.) In addition, there are said to be at least four original and valuable portraits

The Spanish Secretary of the Duke de Nájera—not entering into details, but giving a very distinct general opinion—likewise reported that Mary was very pleasing in person, and so remarkably popular as to be almost adored. Amongst other points of praise he remarks, that " she knows so well how to conceal her requirements—no small proof of true wisdom." [1] This was penned in 1543, when she was exactly twenty-eight years of age. Antonio Guidi was even more complimentary, and perhaps a little flattering. [2] Ordinary English traditions have certainly ignored his judgment ; but then, such are not always to be depended upon.

Mary, when studied in the light of historical Truth, was a beautiful character. Her solid education had been such that it had long previously impaired her health. Mistress of five languages, she could converse fluently in four. She spoke Latin with perfect grace and ease : [3] and translated Erasmus's " Paraphrase on St. John's Gospel "

of this Queen in Scotland, viz., at Duff House, Bannffshire, at Inverary Castle, Argyleshire ; at Dalkeith House, Midlothian ; and at Innes House, Morayshire.

[1] " Archæologia," vol. xxii. p. 353.

[2] " Sed quid ego de pulcherrimis illius et suavissimis moribus dicam ? Quibus illa sibi omnium mentes animosque devinciebat? Quid de excellenti totius corporis pulchritudine ? Cum quidem formosissimum illius os, et venustos pilaresque oculos is pudor et verecundia honestaret, ut eam omnes supra humanam speciem admirarentur."—*Oratio Anton. Guidi*, 4to.   Rom. 1559.

[3] Lansdowne MSS. No. 840, A, folio 156.

into English. She wrote and spoke her own tongue with remarkable elegance; and could play on the virginals, regals, and lute. Her royal duties were done with regularity and efficiency. She was fond of animals and singing-birds—a pleasant feature, evidencing kindness of heart; while her love for, and condescension towards the poor,[1] her charity to her dependents, her unvarying consideration for her servants, made her greatly beloved. Nowhere in English history has so touching a character been besmeared and besmirched by the ordinary scribe, who so delights in defaming and descrying the Faith of his forefathers.

The death of the Queen was indeed a misfortune for England. By it all the restorations of law, order, and morals, through Cardinal Pole, were practically brought to naught, while the irreligious disorders of the reign of Edward VI. were subsequently restored and renewed.

The patience, devotion, charity, and other noble qualities[2] which Queen Mary owned and

---

[1] "At Hampton Court ye xvi. day of Sep'. 1554.—A letter from the Kinge and Queen's Highnes to the Lord Treasurer, autherisinge him to dissolve the Parkes of Maribone and Hide, and havinge bestowed the Dere and Palle of the same to their Maties use, upon a due Survaye of the ground of the said Parke, soe to distribute the Parcelles thereof to the Inhabitants dwellinge thereabouts as may be most to theire Highnes advantage and comoditie of their lovinge Subjects."—Harl. MSS. No. 643, folio 35, b.

[2] "She had," as Bishop White of Winchester formally and

exhibited, would have made her beautiful name and works continuously venerated, had it not been for the severe punishments which were inflicted by then existing laws upon heretics, socialists, and other perverse and misguided people, during that disturbed period—and which, with singular art, have been largely exaggerated by John Foxe and his numerous romancing followers and literary partizans.

As Sir Frederick Madden so well and truly wrote:—" There have been brighter characters in history, but few would bear so strict an examination in regard to the irreproachable and unblemished tenor of private life. Mary in this view must be ranked amongst the best, although not the greatest of our sovereigns." [1]

Be it reverently noted at the same time, that the sins of the people generally, had been of so dark a dye, while the innumerable sacrileges of Henry VIII. were of such an awful character,

---

publicly declared, " in all estates the feare of God in her harte. I verylye beleve the poorest creature in all this Citie feared not God more than she did. She vsed singuler mercye towardes offenders. She vsed much pitie and compassion towardes the poor and oppressed. She vsed clemencie amongst her nobles. She restored more noble howses decayed then ever did prince of this realme."—Cott. MSS. Brit. Museum, Vespasian, D, xviii., folios 103, 104. See also Lansd. MSS. 840, A, folio 156, for a most touching description of her religious character and virtues.

[1] *Privy Purse Expenses of the Princess Mary*, by Sir Frederick Madden, F.S.A., p. clxx. London : 1831.

that of course such might not be easily expiated. The Boy-King had died, possibly by poison, as a mere youth, and the Nation was thus well rid of his cant and priggishness. No child might be born of Queen Mary, who, probably for the transgressions of others, thus in a two-fold manner keenly suffered ; firstly, in that, to her bitter disappointment, she bare no offspring, and secondly, in the saddening and sickening knowledge that her kingdom would pass at once under the rule of such a bastard and dissimulating heretic as must bring a devastating plague upon the State, and abounding and abiding disaster to True Religion.

She was buried in Westminster Abbey,[1] on the north side of Henry VII.'s Chapel. The funeral rites, which took place on December the 10th, were those of the Catholic Church. During the whole of the reign of the woman who succeeded her, however, not the slightest mark of respect to Queen Mary's memory, either by record or monument, was ever shown. But King James I., later on, erected a single monument to Mary and Elizabeth.

The Will of Queen Mary, a most touching document,[2] rife with charity and religion, affords

---

[1] The details of the Burial of Queen Mary are given in a MSS. in the College of Arms, I. 14, folios 19 to 30.

[2] Harl. MSS. No. 6949, folio 29, &c. (Transcribed from the Original by the Rev. George Harbin, M.A., Chaplain to Thomas, Lord Viscount Weymouth.)

a true and most interesting insight into her character. Its provisions, however, were totally disregarded by her successor.

Cardinal Pole, smitten by fever—the seasons having been very unhealthy—and for several weeks lying ill at Lambeth House, did not long survive his royal mistress and kinswoman. Anxious, worn and weary, he had been duly informed of her death, and within two days himself likewise passed away.

As was then quaintly, but accurately[1] chronicled :—

" The xix. day of November [1558] ded betwyn v and vj in the morning my lord cardenall Polle at Lambeth, and he was byshope of Canturbere; and ther he lay tyll the Consell sett the tyme he should be bered, and when and wher . . . .

(Dec. 10.) The sam mornyng my lord Cardenall was . . . . . from Lambeth, and cared toward Canterbury with grett . . . . . blake ; & he was cared in a charett with . . . . . rolles wroth [*i.e.*, wrought] with fine gold & gret baners . . . . . & iiij baners of santes in owllo [*i.e.*, in oil]."

The Lord Legate had thus lived to see some of his fairest hopes realized, and others roughly dashed to the ground and destroyed. He could

---

[1] Cotton MSS. Brit. Museum. Vitellius, F. v. (parts of the volume have been much damaged by fire).

look abroad, however, throughout the shires of his native land, and see that at all events very much of his labour had not been altogether in vain.[1] Several efforts of Christian foresight and wisdom had been blessed; for the old order in many favoured places lived and energized anew. He had likewise found many good men and true ready and willing to co-operate, under the Queen, in the great work of religious restoration and unity; but unanticipated events and adverse circumstances were apparently too strong to be successfully turned to his purpose. The great cause for which he had lived and laboured had, on the whole, apparently failed. As he humbly resigned His soul into His Maker's hands, so he obediently resigned that most holy cause (still undetermined) in which he had been permitted to take so leading and remarkable a part on earth, and for which, no doubt, he still makes intercession in a better place. His memory as a Peacemaker is blessed.

But, to recall his position and to sum up briefly his characteristics: After a more than usually solid and brilliant education, he had obtained considerable experience as Envoy at Paris and Brussels; while his connection with Padua and Venice, in his early days, and his frequent intercourse with leading

<hr>

[1] The last entry in Cardinal Pole's Register bears date the 9th day of Nov. 1558, when the record that David Cotton, clerk, had been duly instituted to the vicarage of Boughton, occurs.

contemporaries exercising a similar office at each of these cities, gave him advantages of the highest order. He had been Ambassador to the King of France; he was also Legate of Viterbo, and took a leading part in the work of the great Council of Trent.

So great was his influence in the College of Cardinals and with rulers and diplomatists abroad, that he had been more than once named as likely to be elected Pope; but complicated circumstances overbore his claims and were against his success.[1] He is said to have been actually elected Pope in the room of Alexander Farnese, Paul III., but, disliking the proceedings in one act of voting, and asking for a fresh election, the Cardinal de Monte was then chosen, who took the title of Julius III. About this time Pole spent some time at a Benedictine monastery at Verona. His labours for England have already been recounted.

[1] Thomas Martyn writes to the Earl of Devonshire, on May 31, 1555, from Staple Inn, Calais. "He has moved the Lord Chancellor for license for him to go to Milan or Naples. The Bishop of Orleans and Monsieur Viglius have arrived. Four persons are named for the vacant Popedom—vacant through the death of Pope Julius III.—but Cardinal Pole is likely to be chosen."—State Papers, Record Office, *sub anno* 1555. "When the Cardinals met in the chapel to pay their obedience to the new Pope [Julius III.], and Cardinal Pole, presenting himself with the rest, as the custom is, to kiss his feet, the Pope rose up, and embracing him, with tears told him it was to his disinterestedness that he owed the papacy, which he frequently repeated."

The great work of the Cardinal's life, however, — for which birth, education, experience and Christian principle served so well to fit him—was, let it be remembered, the restoration of the National Church of England to Catholic Unity. His Injunctions, the Decrees of the National Synod over which he presided, and the Constitutions he officially set forth, one and all exhibit his sound principles and sterling wisdom.

These solemn documents and ecclesiastical instruments, the heritage of every English Catholic, can never be safely altered nor wisely added to, for they all comprehend the divine wisdom of the Universal Church set forth for actual guidance. The two Convocations of Canterbury and York, as well as the informal Lambeth Synods,[1] might corporately study them, and then profitably accept them for the benefit of the Church and People of England and her colonies. Wheresoever such have not yet been practically re-adopted and followed, by those who have endeavoured to carry on the work of Keble, Newman and Pusey, commenced at Oxford in 1835, something important and essential seems still evidently wanting, though many of the Cardinal's suggestions have been already actually completed. No modern " reformer "—in the best sense of the word, and acting in the spirit

---

[1] Popularly but barbarously styled " Pan-Anglican Synods."

and teaching of the Council of Trent—can neglect the whole of the sound and solid work of Cardinal Pole ; while every Anglican Archbishop and Bishop, if such should desire to complete and crown the Oxford movement and to secure Corporate Reunion for our isolated and consequently weakened communion, should devoutly and discreetly follow in his footsteps. His Eminence's works stand as a monument of his charity and a memorial of his true greatness as a wise and prudent ecclesiastical statesman.

Of his personal appearance and character [1] something must now be said. His features were refined and regular, his countenance frank and open, his eye keen and pleasant; [2] giving at once an indication, perfectly accurate, of his great general abilities—firmness, decision, integrity, and bene-

---

[1] The Rev. Thomas Phillips, of Ickford, Bucks, thus described the Cardinal :—" He was of a middle stature, and of a healthy rather than robust constitution ; though he was sometimes subject to a defluxion which fell on his arm and caused an inflammation in his right eye. His complexion was fair, mixed with an agreeable vermilion, and his beard and hair in his youth, of a light colour, his countenance was open and serene, enlivened with a cheerful and pleasant eye, the index of his mind, which was unsuspecting, honest, and benevolent."

[2] " He was a man of great learning and of great humanity, very modest and obliging, and very well qualified for publick employ. He was of a midling stature, fresh-colour'd, and had eyes very lively and sparkling, and a cheerful look."—*History and Antiquities of the Cathedral Church of Canterbury*, by J. Dart, p. 169. London : 1726.

volence. A list of portraits and engravings of him will be found at the end of this chapter. That which appears as the frontispiece of this volume is taken from an old *replica* of the well-known picture at Wardour Castle, and represents him towards the close of his life. Probably the two most authentic portraits in existence is that in the drawing-room of Lambeth Palace,[1] and that which was formerly in the Casa Grimani at Venice, now in private hands. The former is on panel, not painted with any remarkable art, but no doubt a good likeness, taken from life, and a perfectly genuine picture. His Grace is repre-rented in cassock, a crimped rochet with wide sleeves, scarlet silk *mozetta* and ancient limp biretta of the same colour. His features are well-formed, regular, and of some vigour, and he wears both beard and moustache, by which that most expressive portion of every face, the mouth, is too much hidden. His hair and beard are light auburn, his skin is fresh and pink-looking, and there is a general dignity about this quaint picture which is notable. The other portrait, in the Guard-room at Lambeth Palace, is of a far higher stamp as a picture, being exceedingly well painted, with an easy pose, and great dignity, but representing him at a later period. Whether it was ever so good a

---

[1] Formerly hung in the Archbishop's Sacristy, to the north-east of the Chapel.

likeness as the other is open to question. The
Venice portrait is possibly a reproduction of the
ancient one on panel at Lambeth, though the hair
and beard are darker; or possibly it is another
original by the same artist. The various existing
engravings of the Cardinal are of very varying
interest: in some scarcely a trace of the likeness
to those here described can be observed. There
are several portraits in oil in Rome,[1] but, as has
been said by a competent judge of such, none of
any remarkable artistic merit.

And now to add a few concluding words as to his
personal character. His systematic industry was
notable, while his constant application to work was
a marked feature in his ever-busy life. He despised
the foolish opinion of common people, who so often
hold and declare that unprofitable laziness is the
exclusive privilege of persons of blood and rank;
whereas, to put the truth plainly, nothing can be
more entirely foreign to the nature of those of noble
extraction, whose watchwords are " Duty and
honour," than indolence and mere ease. And this
was exactly the case with Cardinal Pole—ever
labouring by mind and pen for the good estate of

---

[1] Two in the Vatican Collection, one in the English College,
and three others in private collections,—one of which, as the
Author is informed, belonged formerly to Cardinal Aldobrandini,
and another, a large three-quarter length portrait in *cappa
magna*, to Henry Benedict Stuart, Cardinal Duke of York.

mankind, for the welfare of his country, and the honour of God.

His learning and eloquence were remarkable, while his perfect knowledge of the Latin language was unique. If certain critics have regarded his style as somewhat diffuse; others, again, admit that, even when he was wrong,[1] it was so perfect and graceful alike in its simplicity and force, that it scarcely seemed capable of improvement.

The long list of his works, which stands at the close of this chapter—many of them exceedingly rare—proves that both in dogmatic and moral theology, in history, biography, politics, and law, he was a very master in the Church Universal. Few prelates of his day did more to undermine error and stablish and settle his readers in the Faith. His great and chief treatise, " On the Unity of the Church," a very masterpiece of reasoning, is full of divine wisdom, carefully set forth with perfect truth, much skill, and the greatest prudence. In the " Preface," afterwards added, and specially addressed to Edward VI., the whole method is admirably clear and the matter of the utmost importance. Specially useful at a crisis, it is interesting for all time. His books, " On the Nature of a General Council," and " On the Papacy," are like-

---

[1] Longolius, Christophorus. " Epistolarum Libri quatuor : item Pet. Bembi, Jac. Sadoleti, Gul. Budæi, D. Erasmi epistolarum ad Longolium liber unus." 8°. Basil, 1533.

wise of considerable value; while the indirect reply to the too-popular policy of Machiavelli, embodied in his "Apology to Charles V.," is an able contribution to the study of true Christian politics. Nor is his "Essay on Peace," addressed to the two great political potentates of the day, the Emperor and the French King, of any less interest. His other lesser writings, "On Unity," "On the Baptism of Constantine," "On the Return of England to Catholic Unity,"[1] and on certain details of the life of our Blessed Lord, are one and all full of research and divine wisdom; while each of those publications specially penned and issued to promote the cause of Corporate Reunion and the efficiency of the Church of England—Canons, Decrees, University Statutes, Provincial Constitutions, and Diocesan Injunctions—are entirely worthy of his rank and ability.

He was totally averse to flattery, always delivering his opinion, whether official or private, with such grace and kindness that those who differed from him could never take offence at the frankness of his bearing and the plainness of his speech. In ordinary conversation, however, always careful and reticent, he was particularly circumspect that nothing unbecoming his person or dignity should ever escape his lips.

---

[1] Published only in Italian, and exceedingly rare.

As a diplomatist, he invariably carried all these admirable characteristics into actual practice, desiring to secure nothing but what was true and righteous, just and honourable, for those whom he served and represented.   His labours in England as Lord Legate can never be forgotten.

Few Archbishops of Canterbury before him and none, save perhaps that great prelate, William Laud,[1] after him, ever planned a nobler work than that which he had conceived to be both possible and probable of accomplishment.

Retiring in his manner, equable in his temper, dignified amongst his equals, and condescending to his inferiors, his obvious virtues were exceedingly notable.   Unenslaved either by anger or envy,[2] by avarice or lust, he was at the same time always merciful in judgment,[3] kind in manner, and ex-

---

[1] It is the present fashion to disparage and decry the work of Archbishop Laud, and with this the noble character and truly patriotic policy of King Charles I. Nothing has more tended to emasculate and destroy the monarchical principle amongst Englishmen than the artful and persistent misrepresentation and disparagement of this unfortunate monarch and his great Archbishop by certain flippant and shallow English writers during the past thirty years. Seldom or never has history been more deliberately or steadily perverted than by the members of this mistaken, jaundiced, and malignant gang.

[2] "To his credit, it may be added, few men have left a character so free from private vice, or acts of individual oppression."—*The Reform of England by the decrees of Cardinal Pole*, &c., by Henry Raikes, p. x. Chester 1839.

[3] No volume has ever been penned which contains more ridicu-

ceedingly patient under any misunderstanding or reverses. Generous, benevolent, and charitable, he ever showed a true nobility of character; while, during his archiepiscopate, he invariably distinguished himself by his foresight, prudence, wisdom, and charity. So that the Church of England should certainly bless his memory. His benefactions and legacies to the Cathedral of Canterbury alone were worthy of a Christian prelate and a Prince of the Church; while his other gifts in charity were numerous. He seems to have formed a favourable opinion of the character of Sir William Cecil.[1]

He was buried in his own Cathedral,[2] near to

lous and unjust assertions than the "Life of Pole" in Dean Hook's "Lives of the Archbishops of Canterbury." If such be History, I ask what is Fiction? Here are two sentences from it:—"The master-passion to which Reginald Pole succumbed was his abhorrence and detestation of Henry VIII. . . . . . Instead of combating his (Pole's) malignant passions, Pole encouraged them; and, as has been the case with better men than Pole, he mistook malignity for zeal; impatient for revenge, he supposed that he was animated by a desire to do God service."—Pp. 3, 4.

[1] Bishop Aloysius Priuli, on Dec. 9, 1558, from Lambeth, writes in Latin to Sir William Cecil, sending him a silver inkstand left to him by the late Cardinal Pole some days before his death. —*State Papers Record Office, sub anno* 1558.

[2] "He was buried fourty Days after his Death in a Leaden Coffin on the North-side of *Becket's* Crown, where is a Table-Monument of Brick Plaister'd over and Painted, and against the Wall a Painting of the Resurrection, a Sepulchre, twelve Angels, our God in Hebrew written, and Angels supporting the Cardinal's

the place where his saintly predecessor, St. Thomas, had been martyred for the Church's liberties. On his tomb are engraved the words : " Depositum Cardinalis Poli," and over it, " Beati mortui qui in Domino moriuntur." That monument, however, was mean and quite unworthy of so high and eminent a character. Moreover, in the half-century that followed, his labours were soon forgotten, and his name scarcely mentioned.

To the destruction of the Altar under Edward and Elizabeth—with the loss of independence by the spiritualty, and of their lawful possessions by the poor,[1] let it be specially noted—followed the over-turn of the Throne under Charles I., and a Civil War for eighteen years. To these evils was added that of the destruction of the ancient national constitution under James II., when England was successfully betrayed into the hands of an ambitious and deter-mined Dutchman, by a craven and degraded nobility

Arms."—*History and Antiquities of the Cathedral Church of Canterbury,* p. 171. London : 1726. In Dart's plate of this Tomb, engraved by J. Cole, a large painting of St. Christopher appears above.

[1] " The great sin of the Reformation was the confiscation of so large a portion of the property of the Church for the aggrandize-ment of temporal ambition, and the enriching of the nobility who had taken a part in the struggle. Almost all the social evils under which Great Britain is now labouring, may be traced to this fatal and most iniquitous spoliation, under the mask of Religion, of the patrimony of the poor, on the occasion of the Reformation."—*History of Europe,* by Sir Archibald Alison, Bart., vol. xii. p. 384. Edinburgh : 1854.

and a dull-minded and deluded populace. Now, alas! there is little left either of the shadowy authority of the monarch, the privileges of the peers, or the ancient individual rights of the people. Each has gone in fact, and lives mainly in rhetorical sound or in cherished memory. The once beneficial influence of the Established Church has given place to a mere concern for its supposed interests—henceforth to be considered and determined, with those of other important national institutions, by the new and noble principle of carefully counting the noses, and considering the varying but notable noises whensoever articulate, of the Rabble-multitude:—at once, as some think and boast, a national position of true religious dignity and great political security.

Though, as we have seen, Cardinal Pole laboured to remove the chief and deep-seated cause of this series of national evils, though he laboured with some success, yet was not all-successful in so labouring; he has, nevertheless, left behind him in his works a monument of wisdom, and in a remembrance of those labours an example, which, if humbly followed in the Present or Future, must inevitably bring down the blessing of the Peacemakers upon those who, in earnestness and reverence, seek faithfully and hopefully to merit the same.

Fide et constantiâ.

E (Reginaldus, *Cardinalis et Archiep*-
ntuar.) ad HENRICUM OCTAVUM BRITANNIÆ
GEM PRO ECCLESIASTICÆ UNITATIS DEFENS-
NE libri quatuor, sm. folio, VERY FINE COPY *in*
rk red morocco extra, gold tooling on sides, gilt
ges, by Rivière, £8. 10s

Romæ, apud A. Bladum, s. a. (circ. 1536)
This interesting work in which Pole tried to prove to
enry VIII. that he ought to follow the Clergy, not to
rcede it, gave him great alarm and Cranmer was commanded
reply to it. The cardinal promised Henry not to publish
e book, and it is most probable Pole privately printed it
r distribution to his friends only. Brunet states that it
as become rare because the author suppressed as many
opies as possible. From whatever cause the book is
undoubtedly rarely found, and Harley, Earl of Oxford,
uring the last century, searched in vain for a copy. Lord
uildford's sold for 24 guineas in 1829.

ADDITIONAL NOTES TO CHAPTER V.

No. I.—List of the Published Works of Reginald Cardinal Pole.

Polus Reginaldus.   R. P . . . . ad Henricu' Octavum Britanniae regem pro Ecclesiasticae Unitatis defensione, Libri quatuor. Folio.   Romae.   [Qy. ? 1535.]

Another folio edition was issued at Strasburg in 1555, and a third in folio, "Ingolstadii. 1587."

Polus Reginaldus.   De Concilio Liber.   De Baptismo Constantini Magni [Edited by P. Manutius].   4to.   Romae, 1562.

Polus Reginaldus.   De Summo Pontifice Christi in terris vicario, eiusque officio et potestate Liber . . . . in modum dialogi co'scriptus.   8vo.   Lovanii, 1569.

Polus Reginaldus.   Discorso di pace di Mons. R. Polo Cardinale Legato a Carlo V. Imperatore, et Henrico II.   Re de Francia.   [Qy. ? Romæ, 1556.]

N.B.—Other editions of this were published at Rome, in 4to, in 1555, at Venice, in 4to, in 1558, and at Milan, in 8vo, in 1560.

Polus Reginaldus.   Reformatio Angliae ex decretis R. P. Sedis Apostolicae Legati, anno 1556.   4to.   Romae, 1562.

Polus Reg^{dus}.   A brefe overture or openyng of the legacion of . . . . Cardinall Poole . . . . with the substance of his oracyou to the Kyng & Quenes Majestie, for the reconcilement of the Realme of Englande to the unitie of the Catholyke Churche. 8vo.   [Qy.? 1555.]

Polus Reginaldus, Oratione della pace.   4to.   1558.

Polus Reginaldus.   Longolii vita ab ipsius amicissimo quodam [i.e., R. Polus] exarata.   4to.   1524.

Polus Reginaldus.   Copia delle Lettere del Re d'Inghilterra & del Card. Polo . . . . sopra la reduzione di quel Regno alla unione della . . . . Chiesa, etc.   4to.   [Qy.? 1557.]

Reginaldi Poli, Cardinalis Britanni Ad Henricum Octavum, Britanniæ Regem, pro Ecclesiasticae Unitatis Defensione, Libri quatuor.   Ingolstadii, 1587.

Oratio, Caesarem accendens in eos, qui nomen Evangelio dederunt; cum Scholis Athanasii.   4to.   1554.

Libri duo, viz.: De Concilio, de baptismo Constantii et de reformatione Angliae. 8vo. Dilingæ, 1562. (This was published also at Venice in the same year.)

De Concilio, Liber Reginaldi Poli Cardinalis.   Romae, MDLXII. Apud Paulum Manutium Aldi F.   (pp. 64, quarto.)

Reformatio Angliae ex decretis Reginaldi Poli Cardinalis, Sedis Apostolicae Legati, anno MDLVI.   (pp. 30, quarto.)   Romae, MDLXII.

Vita Reginaldi Poli Britanni S. R. E. Cardinalis, et Cantuariensis Archiepiscopi.   (pp. 48, quarto.)   Venetiis, MDLXIII.   Ex Officina Dominici Guerrei, &c.

Oratione in materia di pace.   (Quarto.)   Nell' academia Ven. 1558.

Polus Reginaldus.   Oratione in materia della pace a Carlo V. 4to.   1562, 1567, 1569, and 1575.

Polus Reginaldus.   Consilium de emendanda Ecclesia, etc. Signed by Pole and others.   4to.   1555.

Polus Reginaldus.   Epistolarum R. P. . . . . . et aliorum ad ipsum.   Vita Cardinalis, &c.   4to.   Brixiae, 1744.

Polus Reginaldus.   Liber de Concilio.   Eiusdem de baptismo Constantini Magni Imperatoris.   Reformatio Angliae ex decretis einsdem [With Preface by P. M.—i.e., P. Manutius.] 8vo. Venetiis, 1562.

No. II.—PORTRAITS AND ENGRAVINGS OF CARDINAL POLE.

Cardinal Pole.   Three-quarter size, seated; costume as cardinal, paper in right hand; Latin Motto to the right. By Titian (?). On canvas, 44 in. by 35.   In the Dining-room of Lambeth Palace.

"A curious ancient painting on board [measuring 21½ by 17½ inches] being a portrait of Cardinal Pole, and from the circumstance of the place in which it is fixed and the inscription on it, probably a genuine resemblance of that celebrated churchman. The style of execution in this painting is rather hard and

stiff, like most ancient portraits, but there is much of character.
On one side of the Cardinal's head are his arms, impaled with
those of Canterbury.   Above them the following inscription:—

> " Reginaldus Polus, R. E. Cardinalis
> " Collegii Corporis XP. Oxon olim Socius
> " Electus in dict' Collegiu' 14 Feb.

And some words beneath, now totally defaced and illegible."—
History and Antiquities of the Parish of Lambeth. By Thos. Allen,
pp. 207.   London, 1827.

Cardinal Pole.   A half-length miniature, seated;   scarlet
biretta, rochet, and mantle.   Panel, 13 in. by 8 in.   By Titian.
This portrait belonged to the family of the Rocci, and was last
purchased from the Colonna family.   Belonging to Lord
Arundell of Wardour.   (See Frontispiece.)

Cardinal Pole.   Three-quarter size, seated, long grey beard,
dark biretta, rochet, and mantle; book to his left; green curtain
behind.   Canvas, 45 in. by 36 in.   Belonging to the Earl
Spencer, K.G.

Engraved Portraits.

Effigies Reginaldi Poli Cardinalis (in an oval), with his arms
and prelate's hat below.—Part I., fig. 9, *Historia Overo Vita di
Elisabetta.*   Amsterdamo, 1703.

Cardinal Pole (in an oval), Raphael pinxit [not Raphael, but
Sebastian del Piombo].   Major sculpt. A.D. 1767.   In the Crozat
Collection, dispersed in 1771.

Reginaldus Polus.   8vo., in the " Heerologia."

Reginaldus Polus, Cardinalis; small, in Imperialis's " Museum
Historicum."   4to.   Venice, 1640.   Oval, with a rose in a tri-
angular ornament in each corner.

Reginaldus Polus.   Larmessin sc.   4to.

Reginaldus Polus, Cardinalis, natus An. 1500, Maii 11.
Card. St. Mariae in Cosmedin, 1536, Maii 22, &c.   Copied from
Imperialis's "Museum."

Polus.   Vander Werff, p. P. à Gunst sc.

Cardinal Pole.   8vo, printed in colours from a curious ancient painting in Lambeth Palace.   W. Maddocks sc.   From a painting on board preserved in the Vestry, in "Lambeth Palace Illustrated," 1806.

Cardinal Pole; In Imagin. XII. Card. 1598.   T. Galle

Cardinal Pole.   Pernetus.

Cardinal Pole; in "Albi Eloges Cardin."   F. Wyngard.

Cardinal Pole.   C. Picart sc., 1816.   From the original by Titian, in the Collection of Lord Arundell of Wardour; in Lodge's "Illustrious Portraits."

Cardinal Poole.   Small oval (with three others).   London : Printed for Richard Chiswell.

Reginaldus Card. Polus, an etching, in outline.

Another, without title or lettering (Brit. Museum).   From the Cracherode Collection.

Cardinal Pole, *The Pope's Legate*, and Arch Bishop of Canterbury.   Engrav'd for the Universal Magazine, 1749, for J. Hinton, at the King's Arms, in St. Paul's Churchyard, London.

Portrait du Cardinal Polus.   D'Après le Tableau de Raphaël, ou de Fra Sebastién del Piombo, qui est dans le Cabinet de M. Crozat gravé par Nicholas de Larmessin (rectangular line engraving, imperial 8vo.).   This is copied again in Phillips' "Life of Pole."

Cardinal Pole, line engraving, small 8vo, oval.   J. S. sculpt. Apparently copied from the above, only reversed.

Cardinal Pole, with coat of arms, rectangular.   From the painting on wood in Lambeth Palace.   4to.   London, 1810.

Pole, the Papal Legate.   Oval mezzotint ; copied from the above, coat of arms omitted.   London, 1817.

Cardinal Pole, ob. 1557.   Engraved by H. T. Ryall, quarto, rectangular, with an ornamental border, and a single shield above.   From the original of Titian in the Collection of Lord Arundell of Wardour.   Published by John Tallis & Co., London and New York.

Cardinal Pole, small 8vo. (a smaller copy of the same oil-painting).

Polus.   Folio, in an oval, between two Doric pillars, with a prelate's hat over a shield of arms.   Adr⁰ Vander Werff pinx. P. à Gunst sculp.   (This differs slightly from that in the British Museum.)

Effigies Reginaldi Poli Cardinalis.   Oval, within a rectangular figure ; Tweede Deel, fol. 477.   8vo.   (With shield of 8 quarterings, and prelate's hat below.)

Another, large octavo.   Engraved by P. S. Simms.

Another, large octavo.   R. White sculp.   Printed for Rich. Chiswell, at the Rose and Crown, in St. Paul's Churchyard.

Reginald Pole, Cardinal.   Rectangular, line engraving, unlettered, large folio.   Brit. Museum, Cracherode Collection.

Reginald Pole.   Oval in rectangular figure, 8vo, line and mezzotint, unlettered.

O Lord, we know that all who love Thy Name
    Are one in Thee ; Thy Spirit's quickening fire
Has wrapt their torpid nature into flame,
    And given them oneness of intense desire
    To mount towards Thee higher still and higher.
Yet are they widely severed to their shame
    In outward worship : discord in the choir
Brings on their glorious Faith the sceptic's blame.
O turn we, therefore, schism-torn to Thee,
    And ask that Thou would'st make us whole again,
Not only in the Spirit's unity,
    But in a visible communion ; then
The Holy Catholic Church indeed will be
    Thy home, thy tabernacle among men.

JOHN CHARLES EARLE.

CORPORATE REUNION:
A PRACTICAL EPILOGUE.

EPILOGUE.

I.—The Order of Corporate Reunion : Founded Anno Domini 1877.

II.—The Order of Corporate Reunion : A Reply to " The Month," A.D. 1881.

III.—The Movement for Corporate Reunion : An Address delivered at a Public Conference in 1887.

IV.—Scheme for Public Lectures on Reunion.

V.—Practical Suggestions on Corporate Reunion.

Dona pacem, Domine.

PRACTICAL EPILOGUE.

I.—The Order of Corporate Reunion, Founded a.d. 1877.

That they all may be One.

IT has long been felt that there is need of united action for the purpose of supplying certain defects, opposing certain abuses, and carrying out certain objects in the Church of England ; and this feeling has led to the formation of various Societies, more or less numerous and influential. Such are—The Society for the Propagation of the Gospel; the Church Missionary Society; the English Church Union; the Guild of St. Alban ; the Home Reunion Society; the Confraternity of the Blessed Sacrament; the Society for the Maintenance of the Faith, and the Association for the Promotion of the Unity of Christendom, all of which extend their operations as far as possible over the entire Anglican Church.

But a new crisis has arisen with which these Societies are powerless to deal; for now it is found, to the sorrow and shame of many, that the Spiritual freedom of the Church, together with the actual jurisdiction of its Episcopate, is practically extinct. And, having been forced by the invasion and active power of these evils to investigate more closely the whole history and condition of the Established Church since the Tudor changes, certain other defects and abuses have become evident to the Founders of this Order, which urgently call for remedy. The attention of Catholic Churchmen, therefore, is especially invited to the ensuing brief statement of its object and the method by which it desires to work.

The evils deplored, and which have to be contended with, are these :—

1. Extreme confusion in organization and discipline.
2. Grave diversity of doctrinal teaching.
3. Lapse of spiritual jurisdiction.
5. Loss of the spiritual freedom of the Church.
4. Uncertainty of sacramental status,[1] arising

---

[1] This, of course, need not mean that Church-of-England people question their own sacramental status or Episcopal suc-

from the long-continued prevalence of shameful neglect and carelessness in the administration of Baptism, contrary to the directions contained in the Book of Common Prayer.

6. Want of an unquestioned Episcopal Succession.

All these defects and evils have been carefully examined into ; and, after long and prayerful deliberation, adequate remedies have, by the help of God, been secured. The rulers of this Order are in a position to satisfy every person who may desire further information, that nothing which is needed for a sound dogmatic basis,—actual power of Jurisdiction for the Rulers of the Order, spiritual freedom to worship and serve God Almighty as did our forefathers, and certain integrity of all sacraments,—is wanting to the same.

cession ; but that other persons do—a notorious fact, which cannot truthfully either be gainsaid or denied. On the other hand—as a sign of rapid doctrinal declension and official disorganization—it cannot now be overlooked that Wesleyan and Baptist preachers sometimes read the Lessons in our parish churches ; that, as at Westminster Abbey and elsewhere, Presbyterian ministers and ordinary laymen, and even Unitarians, deliver Lectures in such consecrated places ; and, in the case of the Bishop of Rochester, the Rev. Dr. A. H. K. Boyd, of St. Andrew's, in Scotland, is said to have preached a series of discourses to the candidates for ordination in the Bishop's chapel of Selsdon Park House, Dr. Boyd being a Presbyterian Minister.

Not only have the Rulers succeeded in obtaining all these things, but they have carefully done so without adding to the existing confusion, without infringing upon the lawful rights of any, and without hastening that disintegrating and destructive process which is rapidly going on around, and which they so unfeignedly deplore.

They therefore affectionately invite all faithful Catholics in the Church of England to examine and study the principles of action of the Order. This can be done by perusal of their *Pastoral Letter*, and by personal application to their duly-appointed officers. That the work of the Order should be conducted in accordance with the methods laid down, it is necessary that those only should be made acquainted with the details, who may be practically concerned in them. As it is desired to interfere with no one who is not willing to co-operate, so it is the strong and solemn determination of the Rulers of the Order not to allow any-one not concerned to interfere with them in any way. If this great work be of God, as it is believed to be, then by His help it will prosper. If not, it will soon enough come to nought without the intervention, opposition, or contrivance of man.

Finally, attention is called to the fact that certain defects and misunderstandings which have hitherto beset the path of Churchmen have constituted very serious obstacles and hindrances to the attainment of Corporate Reunion with other portions of the One Family of God. These defects and misunderstandings are now, thanks be to the Blessed and Adorable Trinity! entirely obviated in the persons of all who enter this Order. For twenty years thousands of faithful Christians have been unceasingly praying for the Restoration of Corporate Reunion to the Churches of Christ; so that many cannot but regard the formal foundation and successful institution of this Order as a direct answer to these prayers.

Ad majorem Dei gloriam.

II.—The Order of Corporate Reunion: A Reply to "The Month."[1]

OUR comments, Sir, in "The Month," upon my article on the Order of Corporate Reunion, which appeared in the "Nineteenth Century," are certainly not wanting in vigour. The adjectives you have selected for use are both strong and numerous; while your final condemnation is very severe. For

---

[1] The Editor of "The Month," in courteously sending a copy of that serial containing his comments to Dr. Lee, wrote, on Nov. 30th, 1881, as follows:—"I hope you will not think that I am adding insult to injury in sending you a copy of the current

myself, however, I do not object to plain speaking or plain writing, as I occasionally use both; and, as you are so kind as to remark, on p. 569, of myself, "If we misunderstand him, we hope he will set us right," I send this short reply to endeavour to do so.

Firstly, then, let me put on record a needful and interesting historical fact:—

Seventeen years ago, at the suggestion of some distinguished English Catholics, two Italian bishops were anxiously and carefully considering the Anglican position and the movement for Reunion in the Church of England. With this latter, including much of its literature, they were thoroughly cognizant. One of these prelates—personally acquainted with the late ex-Archdeacon Robert Wilberforce—is now in a position of eminent dignity and

number of 'The Month.' You will believe me when I say that I have written it with outspoken plainness, at least in the most friendly spirit. I hope my words speak for themselves. If I have at all misrepresented, or if you would desire to say anything in answer, I shall be very glad to insert a Letter from you."

To this Dr. Lee at once replied, sending the above Answer in manuscript.

That Answer was returned to him on the 14th of December, with the following:—"It is impossible for me to put it in, and I return it to you with many thanks." And again, in a second Letter, dated the 16th of December:—"Do allow me to assure you that my desire always is to show you all possible courtesy and respect, and that I returned your Letter only because you had asked that if it was inserted it should be printed entire, and this was unfortunately out of my power."

I make no comments on this.

great authority. What they said on the subject and practically recommended was then put on record. Part of that record, in which both prelates agreed —quite sufficient for my present purpose—is before me as I write:—" Were the Anglican body, by reason of unquestioned and valid orders, in a similar position to that of the Greeks, a movement from amongst Anglicans of good-will, for obtaining Corporate Unity, could no doubt be readily approved and properly assisted."

My friend the late Bishop of Kerry wrote to Rome to the same effect in 1865, and the Very Rev. Dr. Smith, at that time a Professor at the Propaganda (as I was informed by Bishop Moriarty, whose letters are before me), heartily agreed with those bishops.

Since then various independent but obviously providential circumstances have enabled the above practical suggestions to be carried into effect. Of course, at first sight, this may appear remarkable. So it is. But it is nevertheless true. Characterizing the action of the O.C.R. as " not merely a delusion on the part of its promoters, but a fearful sacrilege," you, of course, look at the movement from a standing-point of your own. So do I. Perhaps in the future we may each be enabled to vary our opinions somewhat on the subject, without making harsh criticisms or random charges, and so come nearer to an agreement. However this may be, Sir, I will endeavour to follow you in writing unambiguously and plainly, so that we may at least secure the common and obvious advantage of understanding each other.

"We are quite willing," you remark, "to concede to Dr. Lee that the administration of Baptism is not only *janua sacramentorum*, but also *janua Ecclesiæ*, that no one is a member of the visible Church who has not been lawfully baptized" (p. 572). So be it then. And so let it be. Now, as all members of the O.C.R. have certainly been lawfully baptized, I do not at all understand your previous categorical statement: "Unfortunately they [members of the O.C.R.] will not enter in by the door, but seek to climb up some other way into the fold" (p. 569). If there be but one door, as there certainly is, and no other (saving, of course, the baptism of desire and the baptism of blood), and as they have already entered by that one door, and have never been put out of the One Church, into which they thus entered; how in the name of all that is good and true, can they rightly and righteously be charged with being non-Catholics? Or how can the due and careful administration of baptism by its clergy make the O.C.R. "a new sect," and its founders and authorities the authors of a "new schism?" Again, on p. 575, you wrote, Our Lord's "Sacred Blood is consumed by those whom He. . . . . recognizes as none of His;" whereas you have already distinctly admitted the exact contrary.

Let me here further explain myself. A man, in comparison with other men, may be a lax Catholic, or a wayward Catholic, or cowardly or disobedient, or wanting in patience or perseverance, or given to prevarication, or morally limp and indolent, and yet not cease to be a Catholic. Unless such an one deliberately and of intent and malice apostatizes by rejecting the Faith, or has been formally and righteously cut off from the Church of God—after accusation, charge, trial, defence and sentence by competent Authority—he is, without any shadow of doubt, still a member of it. An ordinary parish priest may impose on a sinner a sharp and long penance, or refuse absolution altogether, or may postpone communion; but he cannot properly declare such a person to be no Christian at all; and if he did his personal decree would be mere words and vapour,—contrary to obvious fact. Even the righteous application of a sharply-defined rule and severe principle in ecclesiastical courts is frequently modified by circumstances, and marked by recognized and acknowledged exceptions. This is not only in perfect accordance with all Canon Law and Church tradition, but with Common Sense and the most elementary principle of ordinary justice. The Church of God being guided by the

Spirit of God, cannot in its supremest court, and in the long run, do an act of inherent and intentional injustice, and I am perfectly certain will not.

Yet you write—" Others (of the O.C.R.) we know "—not "we fear," "we suspect," or "we think it probable," but "*we know* "—" will go on throwing their stones at Catholics, Ritualists, and Puritans alike, and to the end of the story will remain intruders into the sanctuary of the Most High " (p. 579). To this I take leave to reply that no member of the O.C.R. has thrown any stone at any Catholic, or, as far as I know and believe, has any wish or intention to do so, or to do anything of the sort; and that no baptized person who by baptism has been made a member of Christ, a child of God, and an inheritor of the kingdom of Heaven, should be looked upon as an intruder. " The Spirit and the Bride say Come, and let him that heareth say Come, and let him that is athirst Come, and whosoever will let him take of the water of life freely." In lieu of such an invitation, I find a sentence which, by its severe terms, leaves me no loop-hole for not pointing out that it seems like a distinct disregarding of the Divine command—" Thou shalt not bear false witness against thy neighbour."

Sir, we claim to be Catholics by right of our regeneration, our Faith, and our sacraments. Nowhere does the Established Church tell us to believe in ought else than in the Catholic Church.

This I look upon as distinctly providential. The
Established Church, like all local churches, as
everyone must admit, is not a subject of faith at
all. When, therefore, we daily confess that we
" believe in the Catholic Church," we do not mean
by this that we believe in some abstraction, some
idea, or some corporation which once existed centuries ago, and does not exist now. On the contrary, we believe in that Divine body which was
set up at Pentecost—owning now as much power
to further define or explain the One Faith as it
possessed at Nicæa or Ephesus. We know that it
is One, Holy, Catholic and Apostolic, and we believe and accept all the reasonable corollaries,
authoritative expositions, and obvious consequences
of such a belief. The Church of God is of course
indefectible and infallible, for it directly represents the Almighty, and is ever endowed and en-
dued with His Blessed Spirit. If it were not thus
Divine, there would be no heavenly Teacher in the
world at all; and man would be thrown back on
his own disorganized and often weakened conscience, on his personal conceptions of history, or
on some temporary blending or combination of
ever-changing human opinions, or on other mere
vain and worthless human expedients. Members
of the O.C.R., I repeat, have a direct part
and lot in the Church by right of their baptism,
as well as by the soundness of their Faith, and

the spiritual reality and divine grace of the sacraments.

Our members know that the Church of God is Catholic and not national; and that consequently such a stilted though common phrase as you put into our mouth—" He need not forsake the Church of his baptism, or stoop his neck to the yoke of a foreign ecclesiastic " (p. 568), could never proceed from the mouth of any member of the O.C.R.   St. Peter, the first Pope, and the inspired author of a part of the New Testament, was " a foreign ecclesiastic ; " and if in political affairs our degraded ancestors, at the instigation of Whig peers, were so anxious " to stoop their necks " to a Lutheran Dutchman, their descendants, who have already had a Scotch Archbishop, need not demur as regards ecclesiastical affairs to recognize in Peter's successor a holy and righteous Italian Pontiff.   If the Church of England be inherently and exclusively national, the Church of God is Catholic, embracing, as of old, Jew and Gentile, barbarian, Scythian, bond and free.

We of the O.C.R., therefore, have deliberately concluded that independent National Churches, apart from the Church of God, though sometimes founded on Christian sentiments, are in themselves anomalies.   They are seldom able to maintain the Faith, they bear no charmed life, and in due course cease to be.   Fluctuating and indistinct in their teaching, changeable in their belief, they are one and all built on shifting sand. Hence their rulers seldom grasp principles, and can never resist revolutionary change. The plea of the necessity for reformation (on which they may have been first set up) is always ready to be used by restless persons for further change. The varying will of the People eventually dominates everything; so that wherever the necessity arises, Creeds, Canons, and true Traditions are to all intents and purposes rudely put aside or efficiently trodden out.

The present position of the Church of England, both as regards laxity of doctrine and the enmity of its foes, is dangerous in the extreme; and this all true patriots must deplore. It is letting slip its chief doctrines and sinking deeper and deeper into the slough of doctrinal indifference. Practically, indeed, its faith is indefinite, for there is no living authority to determine what is of faith or what is error. For instance, no person can authoritatively tell me what the Church of England teaches as regards Baptism. Moreover, the now-exploded policy that every beneficed cleric should follow the bishop over him, is simply unworkable and essentially ridiculous. If this policy were now in vogue, in one diocese the Athanasian Creed would be scornfully rejected; in another the principles of the condemned " Essays and Reviews " would be accepted and applied; in another the very notion of a Christian priesthood would be ridiculed and cast out; while any clergyman roving from place to place, and ready to attempt such summersaults, would have to change his religious creed with his geographical longitude and latitude—a position of no slight moral and intellectual difficulty.

To show that National Churches are quite unable to maintain the Faith, let the present alarming state of Oxford be considered. It is tolerably well set forth in a recent sermon by Canon King, reported in the " Oxford University Herald." It is one of a series of sermons to undergraduates, of which Mr. Jowett of Balliol and Dr. Percival were the preachers during the present term— " gentlemen of different Schools of Thought," but all tolerated, and all beautifully and benevolently acting together. Canon King certainly begins at the beginning. Of the University he truly enough declares :—" The restrictions, compulsions, penalties, almost everywhere done away with, *very little Authority is exercised to keep you in the right Faith.* You have parted with home and its thousand tender, protective, authoritative influences; and here, when you seek to rest, your head rests, it may be like Jacob's, on a pillar that is hard as stone; and *you find us with old things very much broken up, brought back to the consideration*

*of the first principles of society and individual life,
discussing even the existence of a soul and God.* You
have come among us at a time when there are
difficulties and dangers close at hand, all around
you. It is a great and serious time, but there is
abundance of power for you, and it is a day of
splendid and increasing opportunities." Though
a Christian " Professor " of something or other,
he himself does not presume to teach. For he
appears to have no authority on which to rest his
teaching. He asks his hearers to teach themselves
to become or remain Deists. His practical suggestion, and in his own words, is as follows:—" I
do wish this morning to make the venture, and to
ask for your help, to ask you to protect for the
common good that which is beautiful beyond all
comparison with all created beauty, and more
effectual for man's happiness than all the flowers
of Paradise—*I mean even a belief in God Himself.* I
want to ask you all to help in this, to help in the
maintenance of the belief in God." Of course the
political co-operation of Tractarians and Ritualists
with Radicals, Know-nothing-arians, and Atheists
has brought about this awful state of affairs.

And in our dangerous position of ecclesiastical
isolation there seems no human probability of
things being mended. For Authority comes from
above, not from below. Archbishop **Tait** and his
despicable and disastrous Public Worship Regula-

tion Act have rendered all ecclesiastical government in the Establishment simply impossible and out of the question—as events before our eyes too conclusively prove. To fondly imagine that by some future appeal to numbers—to Conferences or Lay-gatherings — to the Rabble, in fact — Spiritual Authority can anyhow be restored to the Anglican bishops or to a set of new "Church Courts," is to move blindly about in Utopia, and to allow a playful Imagination to develop into harmless *mania*. The Broad Church "Happy-Family" theory—to the comprehensive cage of which all parties seem willing to contribute specimen birds and beasts, with their claws trimmed and teeth drawn—seems alone possible and practicable. As an outcome of this, others than Canon King might testify that Religion is rapidly dying out. In the present generation its influence on all classes is at the lowest possible ebb; in the next generation—under the Atheistic School Board tutelage—it will be *nil*. I shudder at the thought of the new scientific breed, without religion and without morality, ungovernable and ungoverned, save by Brute Force—grimacing apes with undying souls.

Roman Catholic Englishmen, as well as all members of the Established Church who are Christians, must surely deplore these evils; and I hope and believe earnestly desire some efficient remedy—some bold and broad scheme of self-defence, by which such expanding dangers may be met and overcome. To show you, however, that a clear, sharp, undeviating policy is not always workable, without some relaxation or certain needful exceptions, permit me to call attention to a fact before our eyes. Because of our unhappy divisions in England, Christians are obliged " to put up with a system of national education which is at its root distinctly atheistic ; and," as some persons add (I am not myself amongst the number), " to make the best of it." Amongst these latter are all the Catholic, as well as all the Anglican, bishops. Now, in itself, atheistic education, like divisions amongst Christians, is at once odious and dangerous. If, however, the one can be tolerated in act for the sake of pounds, shillings, and pence, surely the other may be temporarily endured in mere theory—but only in theory. For actually all the baptized, though accidentally separated, are by grace very truly and really one. In fact here, for the sake of anticipated advantage " the end obviously justifies the means."

But to revert once again (now that the position has been broadly set forth) to your gravest charge. Sacrilege, in your judgment, it appears, is an act not inherently and essentially sacrilegious. It only sometimes becomes so when done apart from authority. Now to my mind true sacrilege in its essence is always true sacrilege; and no accidental circumstances can change its nature, though they may of course add to its guilt. For example, if one of the Rulers in the O.C.R. were to validly give the Sacrament of Confirmation to a baptized person, that act in itself would not only not be sacrilegious, but true and righteous. But the want of explicit authority in your opinion makes an otherwise true and righteous . act distinctly sacrilegious. This *may* be so, I admit. I cannot agree with you, however; for in any authoritative judgment on the point given in a church court, accidental circumstances (reasons, motives, aims, intentions) would come in for the Judge's consideration; while nothing which was not in itself inherently sacrilegious could be made so by any possible judgment or decree; and, if you decline to admit as much, I fear we must agree to differ.

In the argument under consideration everything turns on this practical point:—" Is an Anglican clergyman guilty of sacrilege in baptizing conditionally a person regarding the validity of whose baptism there exists a reasonable doubt?" For myself, I firmly believe that he is not only not in the remotest degree guilty of sacrilege, but that, on the contrary, he is doing a distinct and direct duty—both from an Anglican and Catholic standing-point—in so acting. This being so, I further maintain that, if such a conditionally-baptized person held, for example, the position of a Church-of-England clergyman, it would be right for him to receive conditional confirmation or conditional ordination as a consequence of such conditional baptism. For note this—the change from a state of nature (the state of the unbaptized) to a state of grace (the state of the baptized) is essentially and actually greater and more momentous than the change effected by any ordination. Ordination does but take an ordinary Christian and make him an office-bearer in the Church of God; whereas the grace of baptism makes one who by nature is an alien a fellow-citizen of the saints and of the household of God. Where then, I ask, is the sacrilege[1] of which you endeavour to make the rulers of the O.C.R. guilty? It has no existence whatsoever, save in the imagination of the misinformed and mistaken. Those rulers—who are no more sacrilegious than Greek or Armenian clergy are sacrilegious—might just as reasonably be charged with bigamy, burglary, or murder.

---

[1] Cardinal Newman freely admits that the "National Church has hitherto been a serviceable breakwater against doctrinal errors more fundamental than its own."—*Apologia pro Vitâ Suâ* (p. 342). The late Mr. A. W. Pugin, fifteen years previously, styled it "a great breakwater between the raging waves of Infidelity and Catholic Truth in this land."—*Church and State*, 4th ed. (p. 31). The great Bishop John Milner, writing of Anglicans, said, "I wish to prevent them from frittering away their Religion, and launching into Latitudinarianism. If they will not be good Catholics, I am desirous that they should remain good Church-of-England men."—*Letters to a Prebendary.* Can it be sacrilege,

No one, so far as I am aware, maintains that the O.C.R. is in itself perfect. No one belonging to it regards it as otherwise than a reasonable and legitimate means to an end. It is pro-temporary, tentative, and exceptional. Its members pray and labour for Corporate Reunion, a programme at once sensible, rational, and wise. Our nation, as a nation, and not at all realizing what was being done, was long ago and to its great loss, separated visibly in things spiritual from the rest of Christendom. Why should not the nation (or at least those of the Established Church who still believe in the fundamental doctrines of Christianity) return in a body to visible unity? In the Past large national bodies and communities have lapsed and been corporately restored. Why not in the Present?

In the Church of God, as everyone knows, various Societies and Orders have from time to time been set up to compass and complete certain specific works. Some of these Societies have been misunderstood, their purpose has been often misrepresented, and themselves sometimes disapproved. Some, again, have been let alone, neither disapproved nor approved, neither blessed and privileged by authority, nor condemned. The O.C.R., no

then, to repair and restore this breakwater from time to time, to enable it more effectively to resist the winds and waves of terrible storms?

doubt, can work quietly, disobeying no law, and infringing on no one's rights, and can well afford to wait. What is it to bear for a while jeers or misrepresentations, to be called by nick-names, or to be accused of being traitorous schemers, "guilty of sacrilegious excesses," if, by the favour of Heaven and the aid of the Saints, a hardened schism can be reversed, and past divisions healed ? Great works have always been condemned at their outset; witness, for example, your own illustrious Society. Prudence and patience are, after all, not vices; while the possession of a right Faith and valid sacraments are certainly no mean nor unimportant gifts. To God, who by human instrumentality so providentially bestowed them, be all praise and glory! They will, no doubt, be guarded by the Authorities as the apple of their eye, as a " pearl of great price;" while their discreet use and prudent exercise, full of the holiest consolations, will be accounted for at the Great Tribunal of all.

Of this I feel perfectly certain that should the time come when the motives, intentions, and line of action of the O.C.R. might, in the face of the Church, be prudently set forth and be prepared for consideration by competent Catholic Authority, no injustice will be done to any of its members. They will not be maligned and misrepresented, nor will they be snubbed or insulted; they will be sure to obtain fair-play and a full hearing in open court; they will be allowed to formulate their own pleas without prejudice, and to plead their own righteous cause unfettered. Their motives will be fairly and impartially judged; the complex difficulties of their unprecedented situation and unique position will be righteously taken into consideration. It will not be forgotten, moreover, that they are not the authors of the unhappy schism, secured and sealed under Elizabeth Boleyn, but the unfortunate and sorely-hampered heirs to it. And it will be seen that their intention —honest, pure, and sanctified—was neither to maintain an old schism—God forbid!—nor to make a new one. They will certainly never be condemned unheard.

For the Supreme Rulers of the Church of God, guided by the Holy Ghost, cannot possibly, in the long run, commit an act of intentional injustice nor maintain error. Truth of every kind belongs to God and His Church. This acknowledged dogmatic fact may well serve, therefore, as the foundation of a sure hope and certain conviction on this point; and enable members of the O.C.R., at the same time, to bear patiently the no doubt well-meant criticism under consideration, and all other of a like kind.

Call to mind, Sir, that it took half a century of legal savagery, conceived with Satanic art and applied with demoniacal fury,—torture, fines, imprisonments, and martyrdoms,—to visibly sever the Ancient Church of England from the rest of Christendom. Savagery under the form of "law," by the way, is its most detestable form. Those, therefore, longing for Corporate Reunion may well afford to exercise a little patience in labouring to remedy and reverse the evil. That evil is practically before us in this our beloved country, in the hundred and seventy discordant sects, all contradicting each other, and rendering Christian teaching more and more difficult of success. At all events, no good work can be completed and crowned until it has been commenced. Some, I know, maintain that though St. Peter of old used a net in fishing, and so took in multitudes by the operation, yet now fish should only be taken one by one, as it were with a fishing-rod. May there not just now be right and reason for both methods? The original commission was, "Go ye, therefore, and teach all nations." A national restoration by Corporate Reunion, as under Cardinal Pole, can alone, humanly speaking, preserve Christianity to the Nation we love; securing social order and good government, with all their attendant blessings, for those who may come after us.

All Saints', Lambeth, 1881.

III.—THE MOVEMENT FOR CORPORATE REUNION.[1]

PEAKING altogether in my private capacity, and not as a member of any order or organization—for we are met this evening as individuals, without present regard for any particular society, each one committing himself only by his spoken words—in the Name of the God of Peace, I respectfully and heartily welcome you one and all to this Conference.

The earnest longing for Reunion, a reasonable outcome of the great Oxford movement of 1835, has certainly spread and deepened in intensity during the past fifty-two years. Amongst Roman Catholics, Bishop Doyle, of Kildare; Bishop Moriarty, of Kerry; Cardinal Wiseman, Mr. Æneas Macdonell, Father Ignatius Spencer, Mr. de Lisle, Father Lockhart,[2] and Father Tondini have each advocated united Prayer for this object.

[1] An Address delivered by the Author, as President of a Public Conference held in Palace Road, Lambeth, July the 19th, 1887.

[2] Father Lockhart, one of the original Founders of the A.P.U.C. in 1857, wrote thus to the Author, July 10, 1887, in reference to the Conference at which this Address was delivered:

In 1857 an Association for Prayer — the A.P.U.C.—was set up in Westminster. Twenty years later a religious order of a still more divine character was formally established. No less than fifty thousand persons, in round numbers, during the past thirty years, are believed to have given their adhesion to one or the other of these. Both have been singularly blessed, while each has tended to keep before the minds of Englishmen the one most deep and pressing duty of labouring to restore such visible intercommunion between the national Church of England and the one world-wide unerring Church Universal.

Without presuming to judge the motives and actions of others, who have personally solved the difficulty of the situation for themselves, it surely cannot be wrong for baptized Englishmen, cor-porate members of the National Church, yet patently separated from so many of their brethren in Christ, both to pray and labour for such Re-union. This is all the more necessary when

—"I regret that I shall be engaged preaching a Mission and Retreat in Dublin, so I can be with you in spirit only. This I shall be every day, but especially in the Holy Mass. You know that I have never changed my views as to the soundness of the original basis of the A.P.U.C. What we meant was misunder-stood by those among us in authority. To their decision I was, however, bound to bow. Let us hope much, as I do, from this new departure. I honour your courage in boldly presenting the question before a public meeting which will, I suppose, consist of persons of various shades of religious opinion."

Liberty has so largely developed into licence, that the wildest and most senseless theories of life, as degrading in their consequences as they are offensive in themselves, are launched forth by writers—saying in their hearts "there is no God"—who proclaim, as the outcome of physical research, that man has no soul, and is like the beasts that perish.

England, as we all know, was violently separated from the rest of Christendom under the Tudors, whose policy, as we have discovered, has been very far-reaching. This separation was not the work of the people—poor souls! who did all in their power to ward off the evil. It was artfully effected by powerful Machiavellian statesmen and by cruel Sovereigns. Houses of God were pillaged, defiled, or razed to the ground. It has been calculated that no less than seven thousand churches and guild or chantry-chapels were then absolutely destroyed, and their various revenues appropriated. And that, between the years 1530 and 1603, not less than two hundred thousand Englishmen were slaughtered, starved, or otherwise cruelly punished by imprisonment, merely because they refused to participate in such changes. Thus the old Faith of England was persecuted and cast out, while a modified form of Catholic Christianity, set up and patronized by the State, was expected to occupy effectively the ancient strongholds of Truth.

In the course of three hundred and fifty years, however, we may note at length that the like principle of Reform being newly applied, no less than a hundred and seventy new sects have from time to time broken off from the same and set up on their own accounts. Such organizations, as we know, have been formed by self-pleasers and self-seekers, who, not satisfied with what existed, arranged these mere human organizations; always wild and extravagant in their conception, and often ludicrous and contemptible in their outcome. At the same time, be it uttered in sorrow, of practical religious authority scarcely a shred or shadow remains. As a consequence of this, as those who are not blind may see, the beneficent influence of Christianity is being disregarded; while, now that Religion is purposely ignored in Public Life, the difficulties of civil government, by any other principle than that of artful compromise and physical force, are steadily increasing. Thus temporal governors, owning great responsibility, find themselves unwilling and unable to govern; while actual power is occasionally seized by some darling of the people, a soldier of fortune, or a self-seeking adventurer without a shred of good principle—Brute force without Christian morals being the direct consequence.

During the last three hundred and fifty years, as History sets forth, various well-intended attempts at Reunion have failed, because as I myself distinctly note, both in plan and project, the See of St. Peter has been passed over by those who from time to time have made them. Archbishop Laud, our noblest post-Reformation prelate, attempted little more than mere Reunion at home; and this mainly to preserve the Crown and save the State. The learned divines of Charles the Second's time, faced by cantankerous agitators and lawless religionists, in their own home troubles too often forgot their proper relations to the chief See of Christendom. They failed to remember their true spiritual relationship with the whole family of God, and to regard dutifully the official position of the Father of the faithful. So it was later on with the Nonjurors. Many special statements and attempted improvements of these pious persons were in themselves respectively true and righteous enough; but in their elaborate proposals for intercommunion, they directly and exclusively turned to the petrified systems of the East. In due course this movement died of utter inanition. It soon appeared altogether dry and sapless, its lofty aims were utterly brought to naught, it altogether withered away.

The Oxford movement in its initiation did something towards promoting Reunion, and when Mr. Keble's " Prayers for Unity " were first issued, appeared to promise much more. For all that has been effected by that movement—its literature, dogmatic, ecclesiastical, and moral—we should thank God continually. At its outset its authors undertook a distinct work of restoration and construction. Defiled and desolate sanctuaries were restored and used. Slovenly services were improved; new churches of a true and beautiful type built. Baptism began to be administered with greater care and less chance of the Sacrament being invalid. Mean and unfurnished tables of communion, flanked by the lion and unicorn, or pictures of Elizabeth or James I., gave place to lighted altars adorned with the crucifix or cross; while the maimed Eucharistic rite, which, under foreign innovators, had been profanely degraded to a meal, has in a few cases of late years come to be celebrated with care and dignity. Our cathedrals where so many ministerial pedants vegetated, or preached the worthless negations of Geneva or Germany, are now again used as regards both nave and choir, baptistery, ambulatory, and sanctuary; while everywhere churches of the Church of England are beginning to appear as of old, and the senseless prejudice against the Faith of our forefathers is steadily diminishing. For the system of negation-mongering, as anyone may note—though its disquieting noises may occasionally be heard— is rotten and falling to pieces. The logical and direct development of such—Theism, Agnosticism, and Atheism, steadily advancing—are naturally taking its place. It is with a total denial of God's existence, not with Protestantism, that we shall soon have to deal. The justification-by-sentiment men and the Calvinistic fatalists of preceding periods have turned out to be the heralds of what Carlyle forcibly called "the pig-and-gutter philosophy"— a philosophy at once irrational and degrading. Another "school of thought," by its foul and dreary literature, explicitly declares that Christianity is false, that property is robbery, and that chastity is a crime. Such philosophy seems to myself worthy rather of the stye than of the schools.

Now our present state of confusion and disorder, the outcome of which is impotence, a policy of "drifting," and of placidly agreeing to differ, has arisen chiefly from the want of Authority. In the future, the line of demarcation between Truth and Error—Error as protean as ever—will become still more definite and marked. Those who accept the Catholic Faith in the fulness of its natural growth and due developments, must, of course, be found banded together, shoulder to shoulder, in its defence; those who deny and reject it, and laugh it to scorn, will gather steadily and in force for renewed attacks. And these attacks, as historical precedents all too plainly tell us, are likely to be neither mealy-mouthed, nor feeble, nor few. Not the men of words, but the men of deeds—and probably of dark deeds—may then make their sinister influence felt.

Humanly speaking, if Historical Christianity is to be preserved in England, in connection with the Established Church, such will only be done by Corporate Reunion—the union of one body with another. The national precedent for this—" lux in tenebris "—is the beneficent action of Cardinal Pole in 1553. That was effected under lawful Church Authority, by wisdom and prudence illumined from on high—the Nation by its representatives openly consenting, the perfect Faith of Christendom being ever had in view. As a precedent for this precedent, there had been the great Council of Florence, held in 1439. Other precedents in less remote periods may also be referred to. The Report of Father Leander, concerning the Church of England in 1634, both in its dogmatic and hierarchical features, was a consequence of the desire of Pope Urban VIII. for the restoration of our country to Catholic Unity. A little later Gregorio Panzani, the Holy Father's confidential agent, could write from England thus:—" If the affair of the Union should not succeed, I am content to grow grey in the drudgery towards accomplishing it;" while, on the Anglican side, Bishop Mountagu, of Chichester, declared in writing that, " He was satisfied both the Archbishops, with the Bishop of London and several others of the episcopal order, besides a great number of the learned inferior clergy, were prepared to fall in with the Church of Rome as to a supremacy purely spiritual; and that there was no other method of ending controversies than by having recourse to some centre of ecclesiastical Unity." A still more recent precedent for such Reunion is that of forty years ago, when in its corporate capacity the "Eutychian Church of Syria," as it was termed, with its Patriarch, prelates, and clergy, were formally restored to visible intercommunion with the Holy See.

What is wanted now, however, on all sides, is not an exact parallel for action, or a perfect historical precedent—on such, an adept in the art might split words for a month—but good faith, a loyal disposition, earnest zeal, glad self-sacrifice, and hearty charity. "Where there is a will there is a way."

On the part of Rome, it should not be forgotten that without the co-operation of the early Tudor prelates, validly ordained and clothed with authority, neither the initiatory nor subsequent courses of revolutionary action under Henry VIII., Edward VI., and Elizabeth, could have been taken with success. The work then done was not that of Protestants, be it remembered, but of bad and faithless Catholics, false to their divine trust.

Again. All official condemnations made during these eventful reigns directly concerned only those personally condemned, not persons of subsequent periods, and certainly not their nineteenth-century successors.

We, on our side of the wall of separation, are the heirs, not the authors of the evils now complained of. From these evils English Roman Catholics alike suffer with ourselves. The atheistic Board School system, legislation without God, public indifference to Christianity, and mixed marriages—all direct consequences of the old breach of unity—are playing sad and serious havoc with them. We deplore this.

Again: We none of us desire the extension or perpetuation of such evils, whether remote or proximate; but all earnestly wish for their removal. God be thanked, the Christian tradition has been broadly and constantly maintained amongst us; while, on the whole, we have good reason to believe that the English are a baptized race. During the last fifty years the work of restoration, both in the moral and religious life of the nation, as also in Christian education, has been mainly effected through the National Church. Even amongst Roman Catholics, some of the most active and able were once Anglicans.

No one, let it be furthermore noted, who is earnestly and continuously labouring to remove and banish divisions, can be rightly or righteously regarded as a schismatic.

At the same time, the work of restoring inter-communion should be made not as difficult, but as easy as possible. This obligation, be it remarked in all proper humility, lies under God upon the rulers of both sides. When such is frankly admitted, it will no doubt soon be acted upon.

Corporate Reunion, let it now be added, would give energy and secure a blessing to individuals, affording at once a common ground for their work, and a crown to their labours. Much demoniacal discord would soon cease. The everlasting wranglings of professional and often ill-conditioned controversialists would most happily terminate. Such at last might be obliged to promote Christian knowledge by a loftier method, or adopt some other calling. The force and value of Home and Foreign Missions, again, would be promptly doubled or quadrupled. The spectacle of Christian contending with Christian would cease. To unity of faith would, of course, follow unity of worship. The endless and perplexing varieties of service and observances in the National Church would give place to one sacred Liturgy—with corresponding subsidiary forms of devotion grouped round it—authorized by divine Authority, and because of unvarying rules of duty, universally performed. For the silly " Ultramarine theory," as it is called, of travellers and others, that the Catholic of Calais, for example, becomes a schismatic at Dover, and the itinerant Dover

Catholic a schismatic in France and Belgium, there would be no possible use. It might be deposited in any literary lumber-room, or as a piece of effeminate sentimentality wisely flung to the winds. But, to return: That deposit of Faith, which is everywhere and at all times part of the common heritage of the baptized, would thus become a portion of our every-day lot. The rank roots of the upas-tree of discord would be removed and destroyed; its bitter fruits would drop off. Instead of divisions, religious co-operation based on God's perfect revelation would be secured; instead of opinion, Faith; instead of dissensions, unity and peace.

In all our disappointments and vexations that the chariot-wheels of this divine scheme often labour heavily, and appear to make but slow progress, let us ever pray more earnestly, enlist more Saints as our patrons, and cast all our care upon God. We may, at the same time, most appropriately note that, even in human affairs, the few, and not the many, effect great works. In all such, as history declares, the man is known rather than the multitude.

But We ourselves must end and give place to the more worthy. It may be asked generally—what can be done? Or particularly and individually—what can I do?

In reply to such questions the true answer seems

to be—Prayer in conjunction with the Divine and most efficacious Sacrifice, persistent labour, the removal of rooted prejudices, and, finally, the maintenance of Truth, each in our different spheres. Such means are certainly open to us all. Union artfully arranged upon Latitudinarianism would only turn out to be the increasing discord of misbelief and the untimely recognition of "schools of thought;" as though the Church Universal were a human academy rather than a divine kingdom. Union based upon such dogmatic compromise, or upon ignoring the teaching office of the Church, would be only based upon shifting sand. Self-pleasers, as we all know, only co-operate temporarily, so long as all of them are pleased with themselves and with their temporary allies. When such cease to please, the temporary combination is certain to break up, and the well-intended work, as a matter of course, comes to an end. By and through another, a nobler and a more divine method, the power and influence of prayer—constant, systematic, hearty, devout, and earnest, a call to welcome and practise which is now upon each of us—may God, in His own time and way, bestow upon all the blessing of visible unity and a divine and enduring peace!

IV.—Scheme for Public Lectures on Reunion,

Submitted for approval and acceptance to the Committee of the A. P. U. C., at 32, Charing Cross, on March 8th, 1886.

1.

MANY of the present political, social, and religious disorders in England have their root and origin in the Ecclesiastical Tudor changes.

2. As the Church-of-England pastor of every parish acknowledges his bishop to be his superior, so the bishop himself (visible head of every diocese, representing our Divine Lord,) owns a direct ecclesiastical superior in the lawful Archbishop of his particular province.

3. No Archbishop of a province, however, can finally determine and define the Faith, nor settle controversies. Such can only be done by a General Council presided over by its divine mouthpiece. For a body without a head is either an abortion or a corpse.

4. Since the Tudor changes, the Archbishops of the National Church, whether *in camerâ* or in Convocation, have acknowledged no spiritual superior, except the British Monarch—from whom

they dutifully receive such jurisdiction as they
claim and possess.

5. The cure for ecclesiastical and other dis
orders is the corporate restoration of England
to Catholic Unity, and the efficient renewal o
spiritual Authority, upon the important principle
and beneficent action of Cardinal-Archbishop Pol
in 1553.

Sexagesima, 1886.

V.—Practical Suggestions for Corporate Reunion.

N unauthorized change there is no prin
ciple of finality.

1. One reform, under the Tudors
involved and implied others.　Thos
persons who admitted the need of the former, wer
often morally compelled to approve of the latter
`Many uncalled-for changes have followed.

E. *g.*, It has been asked, but not answered, " Why wer
valid forms of ordination (which all recognized as valid), mad
to give way to others, regarding which there have been an
are so many disputes as to their value and validity ?"

2. Authority comes from above, not from
below; from God, not from the People. Wher
ecclesiastical Authority is destroyed or enslaved

all social and political authority is weakened, and in danger of being rendered feeble, or lost.

3. The absence of Authority led and leads to the adoption of individualism—" Every one for himself, and God for us all."

A case was recently mentioned at a public meeting in London of a certain family, consisting of eleven persons, including parents, of whom seven different persons or portions attended seven different places of worship or meeting-houses.

Hence the existence of no less than 170 various Christian sects (independent of the Catholic Church) in England.

" The true force of Dissent lies in the abnormal separation of the National Church from the rest of Christendom. What the Church of England could do against Authority which she had previously admitted, her children could equally do against herself. Hence, no sooner had Elizabeth consummated the severance from the Holy See, and the rest of the Catholic Church, than her own subjects acted on the precedent, and the union of the National Church was broken by the secession of the Puritans."
—*Ambrose de Lisle.*

Consequences.

A. Want of legitimate authority.
   Ecclesiastical.
   Political.
   Social.

B. Absence of general co-operation.

C. Independent and not co-operative action.

D. Active contention and disputation, even on the fundamental principles of Christianity.

E. Organized strife and disputation, followed by legal persecution arranged and sustained by special societies (*i.e.*, barratry. See p. 227).

F. Loss of energy and power.

G. Waste of money and time.

H. Impotence of home and foreign missionary operations.

PROPOSALS.

1. Restoration of Supreme Ecclesiastical Authority.

> The acknowledged principle of Patriarchs, Archbishops, and Primates involves the unity of such Authority.

2. Such Authority vested, not in a Board, a Bench, a Committee, a Convention, or a group of persons, whether elected by others or self-chosen, but in a single individual.

What is wanting in all Christian communities as regards

1. The Faith.
2. Ecclesiastical Order.
3. Canon Law.
4. Ecclesiastical Discipline for Clergy and Laity.

To be restored and accepted by competent Authority.

The Reunion of all such Christian communities, in which Baptism is validly administered, upon the principle of Authority and Faith, should be made as easy and not as difficult as possible.

Examples of Corporate Reunion from Church History.

1. The Donatists.
2. East and West (Council of Florence).
3. England under Pole (A.D. 1553).
4. The Syrian Reunion under the Archbishop of Keriatim (A.D. 1846).
5. The Slavs (A.D. 1886).

Practical conclusion.

To apply the principle and policy of Cardinal Pole to the present needs of the age:—

<table>
<tr><td rowspan="6" style="vertical-align: middle">That is :</td><td>(1.) To the National Church of England.</td></tr>
<tr><td>(2.) To the " Episcopal Church of Scotland."</td></tr>
<tr><td>(3.) To the " Disestablished Church of Ireland."</td></tr>
<tr><td>(4.) To the " Protestant Episcopal Church in the United States of America."</td></tr>
<tr><td>(5.) To the various Colonial and Missionary Churches acknowledging the See of Canterbury.</td></tr>
<tr><td>(6.) To the various Dissenting communities of England, America, and the Colonies, in which the Sacrament of Baptism is validly administered.</td></tr>
</table>

By which means and method the Christian Religion throughout the world would be increased and strengthened, and missionary operations everywhere rendered more effective and successful.

GENERAL INDEX.

ACT of the **Six Articles, 190.**
Adrian, Pope, the First, 21.
Adrian **IV., Pope,** 138.
A'Lasco, 226.
Alcuin, 138.
Alison, Sir Archibald, quoted, 253.
Allington **Castle, 68.**
Altars to **be consecrated, 169.**
A. P. U. C., The, 262, 263, 286, **287.**
Arnold, Sir Nicholas, 68.
Arundell of Wardour, **Lord, 257,** 258.
Arundel, Archbishop, 177.
Arundel, Earl of, 134.
Augsburg, Cardinal of, 223.
Augustine, St., 145, 222.
Aumbries or Tabernacles, **168.**
Authority weakened, 26.
A'Wood, Anthony, 157.

Bale, John, 226.
Barlow, William, **75.**

Basilica of SS. Nereus and Achilleus, 20.
Bath, **Earl of, 49.**
Becatelli, 216.
Bedingfield, **Family of, 49.**
Bellay, **Bishop of Bayonne, 14.**
Bembo, **Cardinal, 10.**
Berengarius, **Errors of, 188.**
Berkeley, Sir **Maurice, 71.**
Bernard's **College, St., 157.**
Bird, **John, 74.**
Black Friars at Beverley, **155.**
Bloxam, Rev. Dr., 5.
Boleyn, **Anne, 16.**
—— Elizabeth, 58.
—— sent to the Tower, **84.**
Boleyn's, **Elizabeth, Protest, 86.**
Bonamico, **Lazarus, 10.**
Bonner, **Bishop, 88, 234.**
—— his benevolence, **176.**
Book of Common Prayer, **103,** 108.
Bourne, **Dr., 191.**
—— Sir John, **205.**
Brett, Captain, **69.**
Brooks, Bishop, 184.
Bruce, **Mr.** John, quoted, **176.**

Bucer, Martin, 159, 226.
Bullinger, Henry, 56, 158, 226.
Burleigh House, Portrait of Queen Mary at, 237.
Burnet, Bishop Gilbert, 235.
—— quoted, 94, 105.
Bushe, Paul, 74.
Byeleigh, Priory of, 155.

Calvin, John, 75, 226.
—— testimony as to religion of, 185.
Cambray, 30, 31.
Campian, Edmund, 157.
Canon Law restored, 98.
Canterbury, 27.
—— Cathedral, 43.
—— Cathedral, Pole's Visitation of, 206.
"Canterbury Cathedral," Dart's, 246, 253.
Care of Church fabrics, 167.
—— of Church ornaments, 168.
Carew, Sir Nicholas, beheaded, 33.
—— Sir Peter, 68.
Carthusian monastery at Sheen, 13.
Castille and Leon, Peter, King of, 4.
Cathedral of Winchester, 93.
"Centenary Studies," De Lisle's, 54, 75, 178, 192.
Charles I., King, 251.
—— the Great, 138.
—— V., Emperor, 64, 68, 82.
Christ Church, Oxford, 157.
Church of the Grey Friars, 43.
—— furniture restored, 169.
Churches filled with foreigners, 200.
Clarence, George, Duke of, 3.

Claymond, Dr. John, 6.
Cobham, Lord, 118.
Coinage, depreciation of the, 41.
Colet, Dean of St. Paul's, 14.
Collier, Bishop Jeremy, 184.
—— Bishop Jeremy, quoted, 189.
Commendone, Gianfrancisco, 66, 67.
Consolidation of Chaos, 225.
Contarini, Gaspar, 10.
Contention and disorder, 185.
Corbett, Sir Richard, 72.
Coronation pageants, 57.
Corporate Reunion, 81, 96, 100, 108, 113, 155, 160, 246, 250.
—— movement for, 286, 296.
—— scheme for Lectures regarding, 299.
Corpus Christi College, Oxford, 7, 210.
—— Register of, 6.
Country depopulated, The, 41.
Courtenay, Edward, 51.
—— Lord, 85.
Cox, Richard, Bishop of Winchester, 7.
Cranmer, Archbishop, 42, 60, 62, 72, 76, 103, 180, 226.
—— disastrous influence of, 179, 181.
—— policy of, on the divorce, 101.
—— and others committed to the Tower, 77.
—— confinement of, 186.
Croft Elizabeth, 192.
—— Sir James, 68, 72.
Croke, Richard, 39.
Cromwell, Thomas, 13, 18, 28, 39.
—— policy of, 19, 22, 29.
Current misrepresentations, 177.

Dacre, Lord, 234.

Dalkeith House, Portrait of Queen Mary at, 238.

Day, Bishop, 88.

Decay of old families, 23.

Degradation of clergy, 184.

De Lacy, Bishop, 93.

De Lisle, Mr., 286.

—— Mr. Edwin, quoted, 54, 75, 178, 192.

Del Piombo, Sebastian, Portrait of Pole by, 257, 258.

Dermond, 216.

Devotus, Bishop, 93.

Dionysius, St., 21.

Domitilla, St., 20.

Dormer, Jane, Countess of Feria, 236.

Doyle of Kildare, Bishop, 286.

Drury, Sir Robert, 49.

Dudley, Lord Guildford, Execution of, 71.

—— Sir Andrew, 63.

Duff House, Portrait of Queen Mary at, 238.

Dugdale, Sir William, 40.

Durham College, Oxford, 156.

Earle, John Charles, quoted, 260.

Edward VI., King, 23, 38, 40, 41.

—— will of, 45.

—— enactments of, 55.

Edward's, St., Shrine restored, 215.

Egmont, Count, 231.

Elizabeth, Princess, sent to the Tower, 84.

—— Queen, 60.

English Hospital at Rome, 21.

English laws strong and effective, 55.

Episcopal visitations, 104, 105.

Erasmus, 226.

—— portrait of, 124.

Essex, Thomas Howard, Earl of, 49.

"Eutychian Church of Syria," 294.

Exeter, Henry Courtenay, Marquis of, 32.

"Extracts from Convocation Registers," Heylin's, 154.

Feckenham's, Abbot, testimony, 208.

Ferrar, Robert, 74.

Fisher, Bishop, 13, 17, 25, 30, 157.

—— warning of, 25.

Florence, Council of, 162.

French king, policy of the, 83.

Foreign complications, 233.

Form of restitution of a married priest, 204.

Formby, Rev. Henry, 11.

Foxe, John, 53, 235.

—— misrepresentations of, 189.

Gardiner, Bishop, 51, 58, 64, 88, 97, 100.

—— ring of, 213.

—— death of, 213.

—— burial in Winchester Cathedral of, 214.

Gates, Sir Henry, 63, 72.

—— Sir John, 63.

Gatcombe *Secunda*, Prebend of, 6.

Gibbons, Bishop James, on the Inquisition, 194.

Goldwell, Thomas, 21.

Goodman's "The Superior Magistrate," 193.

Gregory the Great, St., 20, 145.

Grey Friars, church of, 202.

Grey, Lady Jane, 45, 47, 65, 180.
—— proclamation of, 48.
—— execution of, 71.
—— Lord, 68.
—— Sir Thomas, execution of, 72.
Guidi's description of Queen Mary, 238.

Haddon, James, 56.
Hall, the chronicler, 226.
Hampton Court, portrait of Queen Mary at, 237.
Harley, John, 74, 89.
Hastings, Lord, 111.
—— Sir Edward, 118.
Heath, Dr. Nicholas, 215.
Henry VIII., King, 14, 16, 18, 19, 22, 23, 194.
—— divorce of, 11, 101.
—— evil influence of, 25.
—— enactments of, 55.
—— irregularities of, 17.
—— sacrilege of, 240.
—— death of, 37.
Herbert of Cherbury, Lord, quoted, 37.
High treason, Acts concerning, 180.
"History of Canterbury Cathedral," Dart's, 246, 253.
Holbein, Hans, 231.
Holgate, Robert, 74.
Hooper, John, 89, 226.
Horne's, Bishop, reforming policy, 207, 208.
Hospital of the Savoy restored, 215.
Howard, Lord William, 70, 71, 85.

Innes House, portrait of Queen Mary at, 238.

Inquisition, The, 233.
Inverary Castle, portrait of Queen Mary at, 238.
Irreligion, suppression of, 226.

Jackson, Ralph, 215.
James I., King, 221.
Jerningham, family of, 49.
John's, St., College, Oxon., founded, 157.
Julius III., Pope, 65.

Katherine, Queen, 11, 16.
—— divorce of, 12.
Keble's "Prayers for Unity," Mr. 290.
Kerrich, Rev. Mr., 237.
Kerry, Bishop of, 269.
King, Bishop, on Unbelief at Oxford, 276.
Kitchen, Bishop, 88.
Knox, John, 193.
—— "Blaste against the Monstruous Regimen of Women," by, 193.

Lambeth Chapel, 123.
—— House, 124, 126, 127, 147.
—— Palace, portraits of Pole at, 258.
Laud, Archbishop, 251.
Latimer, Bishop, 76, 176, 182.
—— violence and treason of, 62.
—— degradation of, 184.
Laxity of the clergy, 165.
Leander, Father, 293.
Lectures on Reunion, Scheme for, 299.
Lee, Captain William, 49, 66.
Lee, Sir Anthony, 68.
Legatine privileges, 219, 221.
Liberty destroyed, 26.

"Life of Pole," by Becatelli, 220.
Local visitations under Pole, 207.
Lockart, Father, 286.
—— on the A. P. U. C., 287.
Lollards' Tower, The, 125, 128.
Lollardism, Statutes against, 192.
Longolius, Christopher, 10.
Loss of Calais, 233.
Lupsett, Thomas, 10.
Luther, 75, 226.

Macdonell, Mr. Æneas, 286.
Madden, Sir Frederick, quoted, 52, 234, 235, 240.
Magdalene College, Oxford, 5, 203, 210.
Maitland, Rev. Dr. S. R., 176.
Marche, Roger Mortimer, Earl of, 4.
Martin, Mr. Wenman, portrait of Mary belonging to, 237.
Mary, Queen, birth of, 43.
—— attacks on, 235.
—— proclamation of, 48.
—— marriage of, 92, 96.
—— relations to France, 216.
—— restores the Shrine of St. Edward the Confessor, 215.
—— closes all English ports against messengers from Rome, 219.
—— personal appearance of, 237.
—— restores tithes and first-fruits, 214.
—— difficult position of, 53.
—— no persecutor, 189.
—— death of, 234.
—— burial of, 241.
—— portraits of, 237.
Mary Queen of Scots, 90.
Mason, Sir John, 209.

Mazière Brady, Dr., quoted, 46.
Melancthon, 226.
Merchant Taylors' Company, 156.
Middle Ages, The defamed, 196.
Milner, Bishop John, on Church-of-England men, 281.
Montague, Katherine, 111.
Montague, Lord, 32, 112, 118.
"Month, The," Reply to, 267.
Moral gloom, influence of, 231.
More, Sir Antonio, Mary's portrait by, 237.
More, Sir Thomas, 17, 157.
Moriarty, Bishop, 269, 286.
Morison, Sir Richard, 158.
Mortimer, Lady Anne, 4.
Morton's Register at Lambeth, 124.

Nevill, Lady Cecilia, 4.
Nevill, Lady Isabella, 3, 4.
Nevill, Sir Edward, 32.
Neville, William, 178.
"New Men," policy of the, 224, 232.
Noailles, M., 58.
Northumberland, Duke of, 44, 56, 64.
Northumberland, Speech of Duke of, 179.
Northumberland, Duke of, trial of, 63.
Norfolk, Duchess of, 43.
Norfolk, Duke of, 51, 69.

Old rites and worship restored, 59, 106, 133.
Orange, Prince of, 231.
Order and Patriotism, 199.
Order of Corporate Reunion, 263, 267, 269, 270, 272, 273, 274, 280, 281, 282, 283, 284.

310   GENERAL INDEX.

Orders, controversies concerning, 228.
Oxford, Disputations at, 181.
Oxford Movement, 290.
Oxford University, 7, 210.

Padua, city of, 8, 39.
—— University of, 9.
Paget, Lord, 49, 85, 111, 118, 234.
Palazzo della Ragione, at Padua, 8.
Palmer, Katherine, 216.
—— Sir Thomas, 63.
Panzani, Gregorio, 293.
Paris, University of, 14, 17, 138.
Parker, Matthew, 159.
Parliamentary enactments, 101.
Parks of Hide and Maribone, 239.
Paston, Family of, 49.
Paul IV., Pope, 158.
Peckham, Sir Edward, 40.
Pembroke, Earl of, 50, 70.
Pendleton, Dr., 191.
Persecution, 55.
—— principle of, 56.
Pestilent publications, 162.
Peto or Peyto, William, Bishop of Salisbury, 21, 219, 221.
—— predictions fulfilled, 38.
—— created Cardinal and Legate, 219.
Petrarch, 8.
Philip of Spain, 67.
—— reception of, 91.
—— marriage of Mary and, 92, 96.
—— departure from England of, 218.
—— treatment of Mary by, 233.
—— general feeling against, 233.
Phillips, Family of, portrait of Mary belonging to, 237.

Phillips, Rev. Thomas, quoted, 246.
Pickering, Sir William, 63.
Plantagenet, Katherine, 43.
Pole, Reginald, birth of, 3.
—— at Oxford, 5, 6.
—— at Padua, 8, 10.
—— at Sheen, 4, 13, 14.
—— appointed Dean of Wimborne, 6.
—— at Paris University, 14.
—— created Cardinal Deacon, 20.
—— created Cardinal Priest, 21.
—— armorial bearings of, 203.
—— appointed Papal Legate, 65.
—— nominated Archbishop of Canterbury, 201.
—— his legatine commission recalled, 218.
—— his letter to the Pope, 221.
—— personal appearance of, 246, 247.
—— characteristics of, 109.
—— his register, 117, 205, 223, 243.
—— his register book at Lambeth, 202, 203, 204, 205, 223, 243.
—— Becatelli's life of, 220.
—— portraits of, 256.
—— portraits of, engraved, 257.
—— published works of, 255.
—— Sir Geoffrey, arrested, 32.
—— Sir Richard, 3.
Pollard, Sir Hugh, 53.
Pope, Sir Thomas, 155.
Poynet, John, 193.
Poynet's "Treatise on Politic Power," 193.
Priuli, Bishop Aloysius, 10, 216, 252.
Pugin, A. W., on the Church of England, 281.

Punishment, the question of, 175, 178, 194, 195.

Religion, influence of, 196, 197.
Religious Orders, The, 198.
Renard, the French Ambassador, 87.
Reply to " The Month," 267.
Reunion, 131, 134, 155, 171, 245.
Reynolds, Archbishop, 124.
Rhodes, Island of, 28.
Richard II., King, 180.
Ridley, Bishop Nicholas, 45, 46, 47, 76.
—— degradation of, 184.
—— farewell to London, 182.
—— execution of, 172.
Rocci, Family of, 257.
Rome, 20, 22.

Salisbury, Earl of, 3, 178.
Salisbury, Margaret Plantagenet, Countess of, 332.
Sander, Dr. Nicholas, quoted, 53.
Sarum Service Books, 211.
Scarborough Castle, 217.
School of Carmelites at Oxford, 5.
Scorey, Bishop John, 75.
See of Canterbury void, 180.
Sheen, Monastery at, 4, 13, 14.
Shrewsbury, Earl of, 116, 118.
Sion House, 38.
Sion House Monastery restored, 216.
Siricius, Bishop of Ramsbury, 21.
Smith, Rev Dr., 269.
Social corruption, 42, 66, 226, 227, 230.
Society at Oxford, 8.
Somerset, Duchess of, 51.
Somerset, Duke of, 45, 108.
Spencer, Earl, 257.

Spiritual Courts, The, 43.
Stafford's rebellion, Thomas, 217.
Stapleton, Dr. Thomas, 28.
State Papers, Record Office, British Museum, &c., 39, 41, 42, 45, 49, 51, 53, 54, 64, 72, 77, 84, 86, 113, 116, 119, 124, 149, 160, 182, 187, 190, 202, 203, 209, 215, 226, 236, 239, 240, 241, 242, 244, 252.
St. John's College, Oxford, 156.
St. Leger, Sir John, 54.
St. Quintin, Battle of, 218.
Storey, Dr. John, 134, 215.
Stour Castle, 3.
Suffolk, Duke of 68.
Suffolk, Duke of, Execution of, 72.
" Superintendents," 103.
Suppression of disorders and heresies, 226.
Sussex, Earl of, 49.
Swithun, Bishop, 93.

Taylor, John, 74-88, 89.
Tabernacles or Aumbreys, 168.
Thomas of Canterbury, Citation of, 39.
Thomas, St., Shrine of 27.
Thomas, William, 191.
Throckmorton, Sir Nicholas, 68, 72.
Thorndon, Richard, 207.
Titian, portrait of Pole by, 257.
Tower of London, 51.
Trent, Council of, 171.
Trinity College, Cambridge, portrait of Queen Mary at, 237.
Trinity College, Oxford, founded, 155.
Troughton's petition, 48.
Tunstall, Bishop, 51, 88.

Unordained persons, 165.

Vander Werff, portrait of Pole by Adrian, 257, 258.
Van Heere, Lucas, 237.
Virtues of ancient Churchmen, 199.
Visible unity, 137, 138, 139, 141, 143, 150, 153, 161, 250.
Visitation articles, 207.
Warham, Archbishop, 124.
Warton's " Life of Sir Thomas Pope," quoted, 210.
Warwick, Earl of, 63.
Wayneflete, Bishop, 93.
Westminster Abbey, 216.
Westmoreland, Richard Nevill, Earl of, 3, 4.
Weston, Dr., 70.
Whaddon Hall, 68.
Wharton, Bishop, 88.
Wharton MSS. quoted, 144, 206.
White, Bishop, 239.

White, Sir Thomas, 156, 157.
Whitehead, David, 193.
Wickliffe's heresies, 178, 188, 199.
Wilberforce, Archdeacon Robert, 268.
Williams, Sir John, 49.
Winchester Cathedral, 214.
Wiseman, Cardinal, 286.
Woburn Abbey, 237.
Wolsey, Cardinal, 22, 43.
Wootton, Nicholas, 207.
Wyat, Sir Thomas, 39.
Wyat, Sir Thomas, rising of, 68, 69, 70, 82.
Wyat, Sir Thomas, execution of, 72.

York, Archbishopric of, The, 15.
York, Nicholas Heath, Archbishop of, 202.

Zwingle, 226.

THE END.

Ad majorem Dei gloriam.

CHISWICK PRESS:—C. WHITTINGHAM AND CO., TOOKS COURT, CHANCERY LANE.

www.ingramcontent.com/pod-product-compliance
Lightning Source LLC
Chambersburg PA
CBHW021803110726
47902CB00006B/1631